Transforming Social Work

Practice Theory in Context

Change is rife in welfare organisations but expectations for sound and effective practice continue to rise. More than ever, professionals need to be able to remake ideas and principles for relevance in a range of different circumstances as well as transfer learning from one context to the next.

This new series focuses on approaches to practice that are common and prevalent in health and social care settings. Each book succinctly explains the theoretical principles of its approach and shows exactly how these ideas can be applied skilfully in the pressurised world of day-to-day practice.

Pitched at a level suitable for students on introductory courses, the books are holistic in ethos, also considering organisational and policy contexts, working with colleagues, ethics and values, self-care and professional development. As such, these texts are ideal too as theory refreshers for early and later career practitioners.

Published

Laura Béres
The Narrative Practitioner

Fiona Gardner
Being Critically Reflective

Laura Béres
Practising Spirituality

Stanley L. Witkin
Transforming Social Work

Transforming Social Work

Social Constructionist Reflections on Contemporary and Enduring Issues

Stanley L. Witkin

 macmillan education palgrave

First published 2017 by
PALGRAVE

Palgrave in the UK is an imprint of Macmillan Publishers Limited, registered in England, company number 785998, of 4 Crinan Street, London, N1 9XW.

Palgrave® and Macmillan® are registered trademarks in the United States, the United Kingdom, Europe and other countries.

ISBN 978–1–137–34642–1 paperback

This book is printed on paper suitable for recycling and made from fully managed and sustained forest sources. Logging, pulping and manufacturing processes are expected to conform to the environmental regulations of the country of origin.

A catalogue record for this book is available from the British Library.

A catalog record for this book is available from the Library of Congress.

To Frannie

Contents

Foreword

Ian Shaw

Co-founder and president of the Global Partnership for Transformative Social Work, and more widely known for his tenure as editor of the NASW journal *Social Work*, Stanley Witkin, in a visit to my university a few years back, anticipated his talk on 'Living a Constructionist Life: A Personal Narrative'. 'My idea,' so he said, 'is to reflect on the ways in which adopting a social constructionist mindset has influenced the way I understand and "do" my life (including my work). My approach (will) be in the form of a narrative in which I highlight the salient encounters and events that formed the road on which I now seem to travel'.[1]

The enduring countercultural editorial essays that marked his time at the helm of *Social Work* provide the seedbed for this, his latest book. He puts his cards on the table from the opening. 'This book is about transformative change and how such change might be approached within social work and related fields'. Acknowledging the dual meanings of 'transform', he says it is 'about a kind of social work and related professions whose work is transforming and/or about the transforming of these professions. This was intentional as I believe both are needed'. 'Transform' has the sense both of a process and an outcome – a new form. Though Marx does not make a personal appearance in this book, the author might concur with his oft-quoted remarks about permanent revolution, and also with Foucault's insistence 'I don't write a book so that it will be the final word; I write a book so that other books are possible not necessarily written by me' (a translation by O'Farrell, 2005: 9).

In his hands, much is transmuted. Risk, human rights, ethics, a strengths perspective (and by implication resilience), globalization, cultural competence – notions that in most cases carry positive associations in the social work community – all come under his spotlight. I wonder how some ideas less present in his writing – kinds of knowledge such as common sense or tacit knowledge – might fare at his hand. In so doing, unlike most mainstream American social work writing, he is well aware of social theory and philosophy that have their home east, west, and south of the United States.

Levinas, Gergen, and Bauman are among the most apparent influences on his thinking. Not only so, but a constantly refreshing quality of his writing is that he generally avoids the parochialism of much American social work scholarship.

'Often, when the topic of change is brought up in the context of social work it refers to individual or social change. Although these are important and relevant to this book, my focus is primarily on intellectual change'. In understanding this, Witkin's emphasis on the value of perspectives is central. Take, for example, his approach to the strengths perspective – associated with his friend and late colleague Dennis Saleebey. He suggests, 'readers might wonder why it has remained merely a perspective and not 'progressed' to a theory'. In response he says, 'Unlike theories which are about something, perspectives are locations of noticing' and invites us to ask 'How does the donning of strength-tinted lenses affect our notic- ing, understandings, and relationships'? Again, reflecting on globalism, he believes 'it may be useful to retain the notion of a global perspective. A perspective implies understanding from a particular vantage point; there can be other vantage points as well. No one is necessarily right but all may be assessed regarding their utility and congruence with cherished val- ues. Therefore, multiplicity is encouraged'. Hence he earlier remarked that 'social construction is not prescriptive. You will not find specific social constructionist methods or techniques for addressing certain problems or situations'. I was reminded of Marilynne Robinson's remark, in her essay on 'Freedom of Thought', that 'there is a tendency to fit a tight and awk- ward carapace of definition over humankind, and to try to trim the living creature to fit the dead shell. The advice I always give my students is the same advice I give myself – forget definitions, forget assumption, watch' (Robinson, 2012: 7).

Here we meet one among the most important terms in this book. The language and ideas of social construction have been around in social work for about a century. Ada Sheffield, that sadly forgotten figure in early social work, was perhaps the earliest to develop such a position (Sheffield, 1922; c.f. Shaw, 2015). I cannot resist a moment of Sheffield promotion. For her it was the 'situation', that is, the unit of attention, rather than the individual – 'a definite web of elements, current and past, that reveal and explain his present need in its wider bearings' (Sheffield, 1922: 78). She talked of how this makes social work 'less client-centered' and the 'unit of treatment has become a dynamic field of experience, a field in which the individual or the family figures within an aggregate of interactive and inter-dependent factors of personality and circumstances'.

Along with social construction Witkin's argument is shaped through ideas of discourse, postmodernism, and relational contexts for life and meaning. Once the reader gets into the book the central themes of the argument will be readily grasped. For example, when talking about a strengths perspective he reminds us of the realist grounding of much social work thinking and sets against it a relational, constructionist stance, and says, 'strengths are understood as individual attributes that can be mobilized to help clients achieve their goals. An alternative conceptualization ... considers strengths as relationally generated and variable across contexts'. Hence '[v]iewed relationally, strengths and deficits are not distinct, internal properties, but interdependent constructions, generated in interactions across varied contexts'. In this way he effectively counters the comforting assumption that 'the strengths perspective appear[s] to be simply the expression of fundamental, well-established qualities of good practice'.

A critical response to the conventional understanding of science in social work figures largely in this context. 'The postmodernist challenge has been most evident regarding the centrality of science to the profession' – 'dislodging the authority of science' as he expresses it. What repeatedly concerns him is how what counts as risk, culturally competent practice, and so on 'derives its authority from its association with science, and its claims to be objective'.

He anticipates a likely response that his position will be seen as embracing relativism, when he speaks of 'common misconceptions about the meaning of social construction and the critique that social construction is radically relativist and therefore impedes action'. He probably suspects the allegation will rise when he says his concern is with truths rather than Truth, realities rather than Reality. He counters in the terms of Staub-Bernasconi who 'suggests that it is not universalist and relativist positions per se that are irreconcilable, but their extreme versions which she terms hegemonial universalism and fundamentalist pluralism. Basically, both extreme versions are intransigent in their beliefs and nonresponsive to criticism or compromise'.

The argument that positions such as Witkin's impede or paralyse action is not new. An exchange with Michel Foucault is of interest. The question was put to him that 'if one talks to social workers in the prisons, one finds that the arrival of *Discipline and Punish* had an absolutely sterilizing, or rather anaesthetizing effect on them, because they felt your critique had an implacable logic which left them no possible room for initiative'. Foucault would have nothing to do with this!

Who has been paralyzed? Do you think what I wrote on the history of psychiatry paralyzed those people who had already been concerned for some time about what was happening in psychiatric institutions? ... I'm not so sure what's been said over the last fifteen years has been quite so – how shall I put it? – demobilizing ... If the social workers you are talking about don't know which way to turn, this just goes to show that they're looking, and hence are not anaesthetized or sterilized at all – on the contrary. And it's because of the need not to tie them down or immobilize them that there can be no question for me of trying to tell 'what is to be done'. If the questions posed by the social workers you spoke of are going to assume their full amplitude, the most important thing is not to bury them under the weight of prescriptive, prophetic discourse. (Foucault, 1991)

For readers who may think they know where Witkin stands, he has the capacity to surprise. On evidence-based practice, for example, he says, 'I am not advocating that we get rid of EBP but that we keep it from being the ultimate or automatic justification for what we do or a justification for eliminating alternative approaches'. There is a pragmatic strand running through his writing. It can be seen in his interest in seeing social work through the lenses of perspectives rather than theories or rules we infer from them. For example, alongside the words on evidence-based practice from near the close of the book, he sets out his stall early on when he says 'Although this book is about transformative change, this does not mean that other kinds of change are not worth pursuing. In fact, the everyday work of social workers and human service professionals is primarily directed toward incremental changes'. Then again, in talking about human rights he says, 'Instead of continuing to debate relatively intractable positions about the rational grounding or universality of human rights and why everyone should accept a particular position, we would be better off accepting human rights as a cultural expression and exploring respectful ways to communicate the merits of our positions'. In case we should think these are accidental asides he subsequently remarks, 'Despite these limitations and shortcomings, I am not arguing for the elimination of the concept of cultural competence. Rather, my task will be to show that there can be other ways of approaching the notion of difference and of thinking about these issues in the context of social work practice'. He is not a pessimistic naysayer. Hence 'the central issue is not whether social work should adopt a global perspective, but how'.

There are different ways one can navigate this book. If you are drawn into it by sympathy with the basic propositions, then it can be read as it stands, starting with the Introduction and first chapter. The enticing chapter on Difference, Noticing, and Cultural Competence would work well as your next move. But if you arrive with questions as to how his position 'works' then you could follow the Introduction with the chapter on human rights or that on the strengths perspective.

I much appreciated the invitation to write a Foreword for this book. In part as a European, and also because the author knows I have taken rather different positions on some of his more general arguments. But even if you demur, the comfort of the status quo will not be a safe port of call. It will open the reader to bad news, as Alvin Gouldner once described news springing from opposing positions, and thus to the potential for transformation that lies at the heart of this book.

Notes

1   From a lecture at the University of York, England, 2009.
2   Parton and Byrne (2000) perhaps would not follow him at this point.

References

Foucault, M. (1991). Questions of method. In G. Burchell, C. Gordon, & P. Miller (Eds.), *The Foucault effect* (pp. 73–86). Chicago: University of Chicago Press.
O'Farrell, C. (2005). *Michel Foucault*. London: Sage Publications.
Parton, N., & Byrne, P. (2000). *Constructive social work: Towards a new practice*. London: Palgrave Macmillan.
Robinson, M. (2012). *When I was a child I read books*. London: Virago Press.
Shaw, I. (2015). Sociological social workers: A history of the present? *Nordic Journal of Social Work Research, 5*(1), 7–24.
Sheffield, A. E. (1922). *Case-study possibilities, a forecast*. Boston, MA: Research Bureau on Social Case Work.

Acknowledgements

The inspiration for this book goes back to the period between 1998 and 2002 when I had the privilege of being editor-in-chief of the journal *Social Work*. During that time, I wrote 19 editorial essays on a range of topics that I thought were important for social workers to consider. Since then, I have heard from numerous colleagues and some students about the usefulness of many of these essays, particularly for their courses. Several also suggested that I consider publishing them as a book. These comments kindled the idea that I should 'do something' with these writings. Although the incubation period has been long, this book represents that 'doing'. Since the time has long passed where simply reprinting these essays would be viable, I have instead used some of them as a springboard for more extensive analyses based on my current thinking and for exploring new topics that are of current interest and influence. Still, I have tried to capture the character of those previous essays in their relevance, accessibility, and invitation to think differently.

My primary orientation for this book is postmodernism, particularly its expression in social construction. One of social construction's important contributions to my thinking has been to sensitize me to the significance of relationships in everything we do. Thus, I am very aware of how this book is a co-construction reflecting the ideas and insights of many. Simply put, this book would not have been possible without the relationships I have had over many years – relationships that inspired, supported, clarified, challenged, and nurtured my thinking and ability to sustain a project like this one.

There are many to whom I wish to express my gratitude. At the same time, I recognize that a brief acknowledgment will likely omit some who deserve mentioning. I hope those inadvertently omitted will understand such oversight was not intentional.

First and foremost, I want to thank my spouse, Frannie Joseph, whose many contributions include perceptive questioning, candid feedback, substantive suggestions, and not least, tolerance and support of the long hours and ups and downs that inevitably accompany such a project.

Another important source of support and inspiration has been the many colleagues associated with the Global Partnership for Transformative Social Work (GPTSW) (www.gptsw.org), an organization that I cofounded with Dennis Saleebey in 1999. Our annual 'Vermont Gatherings' are a continuing source of community connection, renewal, and exciting ideas. Particularly rewarding has been the relationships developed with GPTSW board members Allan Irving, who keeps me unknowingly wandering from the margins, Roberta Iversen, Dan Wulff, Sally St. George, Jan Fook, Nigel Parton, Mirja Satka, Adrienne Chambon, and Chris Hall, all of whom have contributed in important ways to my thinking and published works over the past 15 years.

I want to give special acknowledgment to my dear friends and colleagues Dennis Saleebey and Ann Weick, seminal scholars and inspirational human beings, who passed away in 2014. In significant ways, their ideas are infused in the pages of this book. As noted above, Dennis cofounded the GPTSW and his creativity and humor remain an indelible part of the group's identity.

I thank my current and former colleagues in the Department of Social Work at the University of Vermont, particularly J.B. Barna, Suzie Comerford, Kelly Melekis, Susan Roche, and Brenda Solomon, for their support of and belief in the value of a social-constructionist-informed social work. Their courage in maintaining this approach in the face of institutional opposition has been inspirational. Also, I want to acknowledge the students in the UVM MSW program, particularly those in my Integrative Applications course, which in many ways mirrors the structure of this book. Your questions, reactions, and interpretations have importantly influenced this text.

My long-term relationship with the University of Lapland in Rovaniemi, Finland, has been important in terms of providing a supportive work environment, collegial relationships, and friendships. I particularly wish to acknowledge Merja Laitenen, Liisa Hokkanen, Kyösti Urponen, and the late Juha Perttula.

My connection with the Taos Institute as an associate and doctoral faculty member is another important source of support for social constructionist ideas. Ken Gergen's visionary writings, intellectual courage, and personal support have contributed greatly to my thinking.

A 'shout out' goes to the University of Calgary, Faculty of Social Work where I was a visiting scholar for two months in 2016, for providing me with the setting and space to complete this manuscript.

Important contributions of many others are evidenced in the references and quotes that are prominent in the following pages. Although in many cases my relationship with these scholars is through the printed page, their writings have led me in directions that have been invaluable to my current thinking.

Finally, I want to express my appreciation to readers of my previous publications who have taken the time to share their impressions with me. Writers need readers and your feedback keeps my labors sustainable. I look forward to your comments on the present work.

Introduction

This book is about transformative change and how such change might be approached within social work and related fields. In my view, change of this magnitude is needed if we are to meaningfully address important issues facing humankind and to redirect the precarious course in which our species seems to be heading. These issues are complex and range from interpersonal to international relations and from local concerns to global ones. This assessment was responsible, in part, for my use of the double entendre 'transforming social work' in the title. As used here, this term can mean a social work whose aim is to transform and/or about the transforming of social work itself. This was intentional as I believe both are needed. Although social work is limited in its ability to effect change of the magnitude that is needed, its unique location between the dominant social order and those who are marginalized and disadvantaged by that order provides an important standpoint from which to reflect on social processes and to envision new ways of going forward.

From my perspective, there is a contradiction between social work's self-promotion as an advocate for progressive social change and its conservative intellectualism. The latter reflects the dominance of 'modernist' thinking and conventional science as models for social work research, practice, and education. For example, in contrast to the social change aspirations of social work, conventional research is inherently conservative, accepting the extant world as an independent reality whose truth can be discovered through the judicious application of reason and methods. This position has many implications for social work such as an emphasis on skills, the use of certain types of information (called evidence) as justifications for classifying people and how they are treated, and the silencing or marginalizing of diverse perspectives. Changes (often called improvements, advances, or progress) generated by this model are incremental and largely status quo maintaining.

A second source of this conservatism is the increasing neoliberal influence at national and international levels. Neoliberal doctrine, for example, the use of the market as a blueprint for social policy, constitutes part of the context within which social institutions and professions like social work function. Hence, they will tend to reflect its prevailing ideology. For example, academic institutions have become less the bastions of educational enrichment and incubators of marginal or unpopular ideas and more extensions of government and the market preparing 'knowledge workers' (students) to fill the employment needs of capitalist economies. The emergence of this 'knowledge economy' has led to a restructuring of knowledge to become 'alienable, privatizable, and commercializable' (Slaughter & Rhoades, 2004: 230, cited in Welch, 2015). Social work has been disturbingly compliant with this trend.

Often, when the topic of change is brought up in the context of social work, it refers to individual or social change. Although these are important and relevant to this book, my focus is primarily on intellectual change, exploring how the prevailing substructures of assumptions, beliefs, and practices (e.g., what Michel Foucault called discourses) influence what we come to view as real, important, and right. This focus stems from how our thinking and actions are bounded by dominant knowledge systems. Consequently, what I am calling transformative change will require new ways of thinking that do not draw predominately on the assumptions and beliefs associated with modernist discourses of science and individualism, but with more 'postmodern' perspectives, particularly social construction. This book is an exploration of applying these ideas to a range of topics germane to social work and the human services.

Social Construction as a Transformative Framework

Postmodernism and social construction may themselves be considered as transformative changes from the tenets of modernism. Although the complexity of these movements has generated a plethora of views about their meaning and the extent of their break with modernism (if at all), they have germinated certain ideas that seem to represent profound changes. Social construction, in particular, has inspired the translation of many of these ideas into practices – although not in a prescriptive manner – and therefore constitutes the primary intellectual resource of this book.

We might conceive of these ideas as transformative shifts in thinking about ontology, epistemology, and the processes of change. Some examples that I will simply identify here but appear throughout the book include (1) the shift from transcendent, universal Truth to truths that reflect historical, cultural, and social realities; (2) the shift from language as reflecting Reality to language as constituting realities; and (3) the shift from the individual to the social as the starting point for interpretation and analysis. It is important to emphasize that these shifts are not presented here as representing new truths, but alternative ways of understanding that have the potential to generate radically different ideas.

Our interpretations and beliefs influence our interactions and what we view as reasonable and attainable goals. Thus, despite this intellectual focus, the potential consequences of these shifts extend to areas such as values and morality and ways of living. This is illustrated in the discussion about cultural competence (Chapter 4) where it is argued that our hoped-for understandings of others may limit our acceptance of diversity. The implications of each of these shifts is potentially enormous and my hope is to give readers a sense of these implications in the chapters that follow.

Organization of Book and Chapter Summaries

Chapter 1 covers the topics of change, transformation, postmodernism, and social construction. I begin with a discussion of change, its inevitability and complexity. Change is described as relational rather than individual. As a social construct, the meaning of change is subject to social influences and the vicissitudes of social intercourse. Transformative change also can have various meanings evident, for instance, in its different grammatical forms. In relation to the current context, transformative change is characterized as foundational, systemic, and critically reflective. This view distinguishes it from more common incremental change that leaves foundational assumptions and beliefs largely intact.

As noted, postmodern and social constructionist thought are my primary frameworks for exploring transformative change. I use these frameworks to propose transformative possibilities. Since postmodernism is the forerunner of social construction, they share many ideas and perspectives. Social construction's distinctive contributions stem from its integration of various critiques of modernist assumptions and practices, its applications to contemporary social issues and practices, and its relative accessibility to practitioners. My introduction to social construction addresses the central ideas of truth, language, and discourse. I also respond to some common misconceptions about the meaning of social construction and the critique that social construction is radically relativist and therefore impedes action on important social issues.

The rest of the book applies these ideas to topics germane to social work and related fields. Some of these topics such as ethics have been around since the profession's early days, while others such as risk are contemporary but increasingly influential.

Chapter 2 addresses a topic that is closely aligned with social work's history and meaning. The chapter begins with a brief discussion of the relationship between values, ethics, and morality. This is followed by a succinct comparative overview of three major Western ethical theories: consequentialism, deontology, and virtues. I then discuss how social work has taken up these theories and the tensions between their modernist roots and contemporary realities, for example applying ethical principles in an environment characterized by ambiguity and uncertainty. This discussion segues into a postmodern critique with an emphasis on the limitations of professional codes of ethics. I then turn to a discussion of alternatives beginning with social construction. The aim of this perspective is not to assess the best ethical theory and eliminate others but to explore how to develop and maintain respectful relationships while accepting differences. I augment this perspective with a discussion of communicative ethics which is concerned with dialogic situations and the contextual factors that shape them. This focus helps reveal the performative aspects of ethical practices and the influence of power. Also highlighted is listening as 'ethical communicative action'. I conclude with some suggestions about how we might use these ideas to integrate ethics into practice, for example by adopting a more narrative approach.

An important expression of social work ethics is human rights (Chapter 3). I begin this chapter with a succinct overview of human rights and their relationship with social work. I then discuss the relationship between human rights and social justice and the arguments within social work for highlighting one over the other. Although support for human rights is widely endorsed, the concept is controversial. I review some of these controversies that are relevant to social work, in particular attempts to ground human rights in a way that justifies their universal application while respecting cultural diversity. I highlight some creative attempts to shift the focus from arguing for certain rights that all must accept to an emphasis on regulating how people with diverse views manage their differences. Whereas the former view tends to lessen diversity, the latter tends to support it. Drawing on ideas from social construction, the philosopher Richard Rorty, and the social theorist Zygmunt Bauman, I propose a view of human rights as a discourse. This view redirects focus from justifying a particular universally applicable definition in favor of how different conceptions of human rights function. For example, Bauman notes that the belief in transcendent truth generates a hierarchical relation between the truth-holder and the other. Such a relation may subvert the very values that human rights advocates favor. Rorty proposes that instead of trying to convince others of the rightness of our position, we would do better by relying on sentimental stories that generate a sense of empathy for people who are viewed as different. Despite the issues regarding the conceptualization of human rights and their expression, I conclude by making the case for retaining the concept of human rights albeit in a way that does not depend on its rational grounding and universal application.

Another topic with significant ethical dimensions is cultural competence (Chapter 4). Although initially developed as a way to help practitioners be more sensitive to people from other cultures, its conceptualization and impact has been controversial. Of particular concern is its potential to mask the perpetuation of the kinds of harm it was originally developed to prevent. I address some of these issues by discussing the broader topics of noticing and difference and by proposing an alternative approach to working with others.

Noticing is a cultural, social process that is necessarily selective. Although we may not know what we are not noticing, we can notice, as the psychiatrist R.D. Laing has stated, 'that we fail to notice'. It follows that differences among people that we notice or fail to notice are also shaped by cultural and social factors. Cultural competence identifies certain differences and attempts to provide practitioners with knowledge and skills that will make them 'competent' in addressing them. Besides its inevitable incompleteness, the very notion of being competent in another's culture or, more generally, knowing the other, can be questioned. I draw on the philosophy of Emmanuel Levinas to illustrate this position and to suggest an alternative. For Levinas, the Other is unknowable and the belief that we can know another through an approach like cultural competence is a denial of their 'singularity' and a form of violence. In contrast, Levinas directs our attention to relationships and our obligation to others. His position encourages a radical respect in which we embrace differences and view them as opportunities for expressing our responsibility to the Other and in doing so transcending the limits of our understanding. Additionally, Levinas's approach invites a relational humility and openness to the Other in a way that competence diminishes.

The notion of risk (Chapter 5) has become pervasive. Drawing on the pioneering work of Ulrich Beck and his idea of the risk society I explore this concept and how it functions in social life. I also discuss its implications for social work. In contrast to the proposed benefits of risk analyses, I explore how scientific approaches to risk as expressed in instrumental rationality, actuarialism, and statistics generate problems. For example, when risk is decontextualized by treating it as a statistical, probabilistic object it is stripped of moral and ethical concerns. This deflects attention from issues such as the increased surveillance of marginalized groups. Within the human services, risk thinking has contributed to a 'culture of blame' in which social workers also become objects of risk assessments and where they too are subject to increased surveillance. Such an environment supports a defensive proceduralism to lessen the risk of being accused of being derelict in the carrying out of their responsibilities. The chapter concludes with some thoughts about how a social constructionist perspective can generate understandings and actions that counter some of the deleterious impacts of a risk orientation.

Another significant topic in contemporary social work is the strengths perspective (Chapter 6). Although the strengths perspective represents an important change from a pathological model, it is not necessarily transformative. A primary reason for this is its interpretation as an individualistic approach, for example, strengths as attributes of persons. Therefore, in this chapter I argue for a shift in understanding the strengths perspective from an individual to a relational orientation. I apply ideas from social construction and positioning theory to reconceptualize the strength perspective as co-constructed in relationships. This reconceptualization shifts the role of social workers from focusing on identifying strengths to developing strength-based and strength-generating relationships. Rather than having the responsibility to identify strengths within clients, social workers become participants in the cocreation of meaning.

The term 'strengths perspective' may seem less scientific (and authoritative) than if it was called something like strengths theory. However, there are advantages to retaining its status as a perspective such as openness to diverse meanings and interpretations. In contrast, the related movement known as positive psychology actively promotes its 'scientific' foundation. While this may contribute to its widespread popularity, I argue that compared to the strengths perspective, positive psychology's scientific orientation contributes to its individualism and insensitivity to cultural differences making it less useful for social workers and human service practitioners.

Chapter 7 – 'Social Work from a Global Perspective' – addresses the increasingly global nature of social work. Social work services and educational programs now operate in many countries in which they previously were absent or suppressed. Also, there is now broad recognition of the global origins and implications of issues relevant to social work. Although this recognition has spurred increased attention in service and educational contexts, they are often addressed by extensions of traditional social work approaches rather than new conceptualizations.

Although I agree with the necessity of adopting a global perspective, I argue that this context requires new analytical frameworks that can potentially inspire innovative approaches to the complex social issues of a global environment. Toward this end I again propose using the concept of discourse as a framework for understanding and addressing global issues. I illustrate the use of this framework through an analysis of the concept of globalization. I discuss the various ways that globalization can be understood, for example, as global capitalism, or as a deterministic force, and their different implications. Rather than attempting to arbitrate among different positions, I propose that we think of globalization as a site in which various discourses compete for dominance. I illustrate how a discourse perspective can sensitize social workers to 'hidden colonialisms' such as the ideology of consumerism, the commodification of children and the 'benevolent colonialism' sometimes perpetuated by social workers. Given the daunting magnitude and complexity of global issues, I propose ways that social workers might 'enter the discourse' to affect change. These strategies include promoting globalization from below, problematizing and challenging the assumed and taken-for-granted, interrogating our own understandings of globalization and a global perspective, incorporating values related to inequality and oppression into globalization discourses, and engaging in and fostering dialogue. I conclude by emphasizing the importance of finding ways to respect differences rather than striving for uniformity or consensus.

In the final chapter (Chapter 8), I explore the concept of evidence as a justification for practice decisions, in particular how it is manifested in the movement known as evidence-based practice (EBP). I begin with a brief review of social work's historical relationship with science and how it has influenced views of practice. I then discuss EBP starting with its origins in evidence-based medicine and moving to its incorporation into social work. I address some salient issues raised about EBP such as whether its use in social work faithfully reflects its original conceptualization and whether those who practice from an EBP perspective are more effective practitioners. I discuss related issues concerning the impact of 'common factors' to treatment outcomes, the problem of generalizing from research studies to practice, and the various possible interpretations of research results.

In the next section I explore ethical arguments for EBP, in particular the responsibility of practitioners to be knowledgeable about empirically-supported treatments (ESTs) and their ethical obligation to fully inform their clients about the evidentiary status of potential treatments or interventions. I address various interpretations of what it means to be informed, for example the limitations of summary reviews of research that are now readily available and the issue of practitioner transparency regarding recommended treatments. I also explore the concept of evidence – how it is understood and generated within the EBP model and other possible perspectives. Relevant to this discussion is how the political context of EBP, for example its mandated use by government organizations, has influenced what counts as evidence. This leads me to question the belief that research generates knowledge rather than information that is assumed to be knowledge and to argue for practice as a primary site of knowledge generation. This argument is not based on integrating research methods into practice but on recognizing how practice approaches such as critical reflection produce knowledge. Potential benefits of this change include the generation of actionable knowledge and forms of knowledge (e.g., tacit knowledge) that are outside the purview of research. I conclude with some suggestions for dissolving the research–practice binary.

A Note to Readers

In my view, social construction represents a transformative alternative to mainstream understandings. Therefore, if you are relatively new to social construction, it may be helpful to keep a few things in mind when reading. First, social construction is not prescriptive. You will not find specific social constructionist methods or techniques for addressing certain problems or situations. Although some readers might desire this type of guidance, another way to consider this position is that there are no bounds on how you might express social constructionist ideas. You are free to respond to the particularities and exigencies of situations in new and creative ways.

Second, social constructionists tend not provide formal definitions of concepts. Rather, they are more likely to discuss the different meanings that people hold. One reason for this is that social constructionists believe (following Wittgenstein, 1953) that meaning is tied to use which can vary across contexts. Additionally, formal definitions tend to be static and silence other points-of-view.

Third, social constructionists support a plurality of ideas, values, and positions. Their focus is not on proving or demonstrating the rightness of their position (social construction too is socially constructed) but on creating space in which diverse perspectives can be expressed and considered. Social construction reminds us that we are always located somewhere – not only geographically, but socially, culturally, and historically. Thus we inevitably encounter others whose standpoint and understandings are different than our own. A challenge is how to coordinate our understandings and actions with others in ways that do not silence them or force them to adopt our own views. The latter sometimes happens when we believe that our particular standpoint is privileged, our values Right and our beliefs True (capitalizations intended).

In keeping with the above, although my analyses of the topics in this book are heavily influenced by postmodern and social constructionist ideas, I have not applied any litmus test to assess whether I have been 'true' to these frameworks. Although certain general themes are identi-fied with social construction (see, e.g., Gergen, 2015; Witkin, 2012), from my perspective, social construction also includes a plurality of ideas and perspectives. Furthermore, my concern is not so much about providing an extensive treatise on social construction but to illustrate through analyses of various topics how using social construction as an interpretive framework might lead to interesting, sometimes novel, and possibly transformative understandings.

As you go through the book, you will likely notice some repetition of concepts and ideas, for example, reification, individualism, and discourse. Besides their applicability to the topics being addressed, I wanted it to be possible to read each chapter alone. Second, based on several years of experience as a teacher, I believe that for many these will be unfamiliar concepts and repetition will be a useful reminder of what I mean by the concept in the context of the topic in which it is being applied.

Although this book is about transformative change, this does not mean that other kinds of change are not worth pursuing. In fact, the everyday work of social workers and human-service professionals is primarily directed toward incremental changes. This is a pragmatic necessity. People need support, advice, assistance, and resources. Whether the issue concerns helping someone find employment, developing a hospital discharge plan, supporting a mother or father with parenting issues, or advocating for a policy that would provide more resources to people who need them, social workers must respond to these needs. On the other hand, the demands of everyday practice need not be mutually exclusive with transformative change. There are at least three reasons for this. First, sometimes small changes can grow into transformative ones. This may not happen directly or in a cumulative fashion, but because such changes give people confidence or a sense of optimism that things *can* change (e.g., Weick, 1984) and creates a climate in which more profound change will be pursued. Second, becoming more aware of the dimensions of transformative change (as through reading this book) can become part of how we assess situations. In other words, we can have a clearer understanding of whether change will likely be transformative and whether such change is called for, for example assessing whether the proposed change is part of a larger issue that needs to be addressed. Third, knowledge of transformative change might provide ideas about how to approach such change should we believe it to be necessary. Thus, despite the challenges of taking on a change of this magnitude we might be more likely to at least contribute to such an effort.

The social theorist Zygmunt Bauman, who I cite liberally throughout this book, has written, 'Questioning the ostensibly unquestionable premises of our way of life is arguably the most urgent of the services we owe our fellow humans and ourselves' (1998: 5). This quotation aptly sums up my approach to this book. I strongly believe that we live in a time when such questions must be raised if we are to find our way through the current morass of incivilities, insensitivities, disparities, and atrocities that plague humankind. At the same time, I am aware that many of us try to live differently, swimming against a tide that pushes us toward a shoreline that promises to reward us for our conformity and obedience. Many of these people are (or will be) social workers and others in the human services. It is primarily for you that I write this book in the hope that it will provide some new ideas that can be shared and developed in ways that will fortify your resolve and ability to contribute to a more hopeful future.

References

Bauman, Z. (1998). *Globalisation: The human consequences*. Cambridge: Polity Press.

Gergen, K. J. (2015). *An invitation to social construction* (3rd ed.). Thousand Oaks, CA: Sage.

Slaughter, S., & Rhoades, G. (2004). *Academic capitalism and the new economy: Markets, state, and higher education*. Baltimore, MD: Johns Hopkins University Press.

Weick, K. E. (1984). Small wins: Redefining the scale of social problems. *American Psychologist, 39*(I), 40–49.

Welch, N. (2015). Educating for austerity: Social reproduction in the corporate university. *International Socialist Review, 98*. Retrieved from http://isreview.org/issue/98/educating-austerity

Witkin, S. L. (Ed.) (2012). *Social construction and social work practice: Interpretations and innovations*. New York, NY: Columbia University Press.

Wittgenstein, L. (1953). *Philosophical investigations*. Oxford: Blackwell.

1 Social Construction as a Transforming Framework

Change is inevitable. Even the dead change. Their bodies decay and eventually become organic matter. Nor is change limited to individuals. Families change. Organizations change. Societies change. Only a metaphysical being like God can be conceived of as unchanging.[1]

Change is complex. It can be unidimensional or multidimensional. It can occur in one or several areas. For example, we might change our appearance, but not our thinking, or we might change both. An organization can change its personnel policies but not its way of relating to those outside of the organization. Sometimes a change in one area produces changes in other areas. For example, an organization changes its mission statement which leads to changes in the services it offers. An individual might change jobs resulting in a change in their feelings of self-worth.

Change implies difference. It involves a process of going from something to something else. In part, this way of thinking is based on the rules of language. It does not make sense, for example, to say that something both changed and stayed the same. Therefore, when we use the word 'change' we are implying that something about the subject of our sentence is different from a previous state. Thus, the naming of something as a change cannot be disentangled from the 'actual' change.

Change occurs over time. Difference implies process which implies temporality. This process can be quick or slow. How we experience this temporality depends on factors such as at what point a change is considered to have occurred and its desirability. Consider, for example, comments like 'It's taking forever to get into shape' and 'I lost a pound in only one day!' Process can also vary in how it is perceived; for instance, it can be considered as the cumulative result of many small changes or as one cataclysmic event.

We can choose to change. Although change is inevitable and therefore ubiquitous, it is not necessarily involuntary. It might even be said that a characteristic of humans (and other sentient beings) is that we often seek or instigate change in ourselves and our environments (as well as trying to prevent it).

Because human life is social and relational, the process of change and its impact are not confined to individuals. A significant change by one person will generate pressure for others in relationship with that person also to change. For example, it is well known that success at weight loss is related to social support. When this support is from an intimate other, the attempted change will also affect aspects of the relationship such as the nature of the couple's social interaction. The pressure on the other to change will depend on, among other things, the degree to which the change affects relational stability. Thus, it is not surprising to find that in such situations others may try to resist or even undermine a change, even when it is considered to be positive.

Change can be understood in different ways. Conceptualizations of change and how it is experienced can vary across different dimensions such as scope (the number of dimensions affected), impact (the magnitude of its effects), duration (how long a change lasts), and significance (its importance in different contexts). If we think of these dimensions as being on a continuum from low to high, then I would describe the kind of change that is the focus of this book as approaching the high end. This kind of change might be thought of as profound or deep in contrast to what might be judged as superficial or incremental change. This 'deepness' is based on a change in the assumptive foundations of beliefs, values, or practices rather than simply the beliefs, values, and practices themselves. Such change will often be viewed as transformative because people (or other entities) who experience it will view themselves as profoundly different. For instance, people may not only have different beliefs about what is true, but question their understanding of truth itself. They may no longer accept what was previously taken for granted or they may regard their very selfhood in a radically new way that leads them to relate differently to themselves and others.

Although such changes will usually be observable to others, the degree to which this occurs may vary. One reason for this is that people hold multiple beliefs that sometimes counteract each other (see p.15 for other reasons related to language). For example, we know that people's actions may not be consistent with their professed beliefs. Usually this means that they are acting in accord with another, different belief. For example, I may not give money to charity although I believe that I should (i.e., it is consistent with my values), because I also believe that I need to conserve my funds for anticipated expenses. Sometimes people fear that expressing change will have negative consequences. For example, although I may have changed my assumptions about what it means to learn, I may feel constricted by organizational mandates or the reactions of colleagues to implement the new ways of teaching that would be an expression of my changed thinking. Thus, although significant change will usually result in observable changes, it is not inevitable.

You may have noted that some of my examples suggest that how we comprehend change can vary depending on social relationships and language. This is consistent with postmodern and social constructionist thought, my primary analytical frameworks for promoting transformative change.[2] In the rest of this chapter I will lay the groundwork for the other issue-focused chapters in the book by first elaborating on the concept of transformative change and then introducing relevant ideas of postmodernism and social construction.

Transformative Change

'Transformation' has become a popular term that is used rhetorically to suggest that a change will be out of the ordinary or of a noteworthy magnitude. Examples abound: an ad for an exercise program that guarantees to transform the way you look; a book that will transform how you feel about yourself or your relationships; a pill or even surgery that has been shown to dramatically change your physical appearance and outlook on life. In all of these cases, there is a promise of a substantial change, one that will be noticeable to you and others, a change that will make you a different person. Despite these promotional uses of transformation, I believe that the idea of transformative change can be useful for addressing long-standing and seemingly intransigent social issues and in envisioning new futures.

I have spent much of my adult life in the hallowed halls of the academy. Like many academics of my generation, I have seen gradual changes over the years in institutional ethos and practices. Not surprisingly, these changes reflect the neo-liberal trends characteristic of many Western nations: increased managerialism, proceduralism, marketization, and accountability in the form of quantified outcomes. Although social work strives to portray itself as a socially progressive field, it has generally acquiesced to these institutional changes, readily adapting to their pedagogical requirements and market strategies (e.g., Reisch, 2013). For those who find such changes onerous and troubling, there is incentive to consider possibilities for change that would counteract these developments. From my perspective, most of these changes are normative and only a relative few are potentially transformative.

One way of understanding this difference is through the categories of first, second, and third-order change (Witkin, 2014a). In general, first-order change sustains the status quo. It is usually seen as linear, additive, incremental, and/or evolutionary. For example, an organization changes its hiring practices from a sole reliance on interviews to one in which various aptitude tests also are used. Changes of this type are system maintaining.

In contrast, second-order change is systemic and challenges the status quo. Thus, it may be perceived as revolutionary.

The meanings of first- and second-order change will vary across disciplines.[3] For example, writing from an ICT perspective, Moursund (2002) describes first-order change as an amplification of what we already do; for example, changing from a typewriter to a word processer. He notes that the change is one of doing a familiar task better and faster. Second-order change, from his perspective, is 'disruptive' as, for example, the move to desktop publishing. In the field of family therapy, a second-order change may involve changing from an approach in which families are thought of as a collective of individuals to one in which the family is viewed as a system.

Second-order change is often described as transformative. It also may be used analogously with the term 'paradigm change' (e.g., Lyddon, 1990). Notwithstanding the vagaries around the word 'paradigm', the thrust of this expression is one of a conceptual shift in what constitutes reality and how to understand it (e.g., Loftis & Mortensen, 2015).

Depending on how second-order change is defined, the paradigm metaphor may also be used to describe third-order change (e.g., C.M. Hall, 2011). For example, Buchanan and Badham's (1999) definition of second-order change as 'new perspectives of organizational subsystems' (p. 615) leaves room for a more foundational (third-order) change. Writing in the policy field, Carstensen (2015) cites Peter Hall's (1993) view of a third-order change as a shift in the 'framework of ideas and standards that specifies not only the goals of policy and the kind of instruments that can be used to attain them [second- and first-order changes], but also the very nature of the problems they are meant to be addressing' (p. 279). This implies a change in the assumptions underlying how something becomes a social problem.

Failure to recognize these differences sometimes occurs when the 'map is confused with the territory'. This may result in what Watzlawick, Weakland, and Fisch (1974) called an error of 'logical typing', the attempt to instigate a change at one level when another level is needed. This is similar to the argument that social workers have made when they critique 'the use of individual change strategies when problems are a function of underlying social determinants' (Swerissen & Crisp, 2004: 126).

Another view of third-order change is the capacity of a system to transform itself (e.g., Bartunek & Moch, 1987). That is, to become aware of how change occurs and how to use these processes for doing so. This type of change is similar to that expressed in the concept of a learning organization (Senge, 1990) in which an organization seeks to gather and use information to create its own future.

Change and Transformation as Language[4]

Change and transformation are words, the former connoting the perception of difference, the latter identifying a quality of that difference. Whether or not a change will be perceived will depend on various cultural and social factors. These include:

1. How change is understood. We do not, for example, consider being a minute older or the loss of one hair as a change. They have no significance in our culture.
2. What is noticeable, both in the sense of what is perceptible; for example, we do not see molecules changing, and the kinds of things our culture lead us to notice or not notice; for example, we may notice a different hairstyle but not a change in the style of one's shoe laces.
3. What is sensible, both grammatically as discussed previously on page 11, and culturally as in the statement, 'the frog turned into a prince'. Such a statement would not be taken as an observation, but as a metaphor[5] or an imaginary.

This focus on language also reflects the social constructionist interest in how words function rather than trying to prove what 'change' really means. For instance, words like 'fact' or 'objective' may function to authoritatively establish that a change has actually occurred. It should also be noted that the use of the word 'change' (or its synonyms) is part of what constitutes a change. In other words, in a sense there is no change until something is named as such.

The word 'transformation' can function as an adjective, a noun, a verb, or an adverb.[6] Most common is its use as an adjective as in the phrase 'transformative practice'. This phrase might imply a kind of practice that aims to transform or the practice itself, for example, the use of certain techniques of change.

As a noun, 'transformation' may refer, implicitly or explicitly, to a changed state – for example, she underwent a transformation in her values – or the nature of the change – for example, 'to be an effective force for change, social work will require a transformation in its practices'. The specific meaning of transformation will be related to factors such as context, beliefs, the assessment of change, how transformation is conceptualized, and how the situation preceding a transformation is understood.

As a verb, 'transformation' refers to the process or action of change. Often there is a judgment that something is having a transformative effect – for example, 'the education program transformed the students' understanding of poverty' or 'the legalization of marijuana is transforming the way people think about psychotropic substances'.

Finally, the adverbial form of 'transformation' suggests the capability to be transformed, that is, to be transformable. This usage has received comparatively less attention, possibly because transformation is often associated with a kind of cataclysmic change as in a religious conversion experience or a traumatic event. This view implies that transformation is somewhat involuntary requiring an external jolt to one's belief system. Less common is the view of transformation as the culmination of a long-term sequence of contingent events and deliberate choices and actions (see, for example, Witkin, 2014b).

This adverbial usage also is relevant when considering the capacity of people, organizations, and institutions to transform themselves (third-order change) or, conversely, the degree to which they are resistant to foundational change. Additionally, to be transformable implies that transformation is not an end state (as long as the capacity to transform continues to exist) but a point at which a transformative change is identified and articulated.

Developing a Transformative Orientation

An aim of this book is to encourage the adoption of a transforming orientation – an interest in analyzing assumptions, taken-for-granted and dominant beliefs, ideas, and practices in the service of transformation. The development of this orientation can itself be considered transformative. For example, early in my academic career, the changes I made to my teaching were primarily first-order changes such as writing better syllabi. My assumptions and beliefs about learning or educating were not changed (see Witkin, 2007, for an extended example). Some years later, as a result of several factors, I dramatically changed my understanding of foundational concepts like knowledge, learning, truth, and facts. For instance, I went from assuming that knowledge is individualistic and internal – the possession of individual minds – to thinking of it as communal and constructed in social intercourse (Gergen, 2001a). I also changed my view of concepts as reflections of things in the world, to ideas that gained their intelligibility through social practices within different social contexts (Jha, 2012). These changes in assumptions and ways of knowing were not only examples of transformative changes in beliefs but enabled the possibility of a transformative orientation. I began to reconsider not only changes in *what* I thought but *how* I thought, that is, identifying the sense-making frameworks that I was using. In retrospect, an important contributor to this process was my study and practice of postmodern and social constructionist ideas.

Although change is often considered an individual achievement, it is inseparable from its social context (see p. 12).[7] Without any social acknowledgment of a change, its occurrence would be in doubt and its meaning difficult to discern. Consider the client who claims to have a radically different outlook on life, but no one acknowledging that they perceive any difference.

Changes that are socially recognized produce alterations in the web of one's relationships. The strands of these webs are loosely or tightly interconnected in number and strength.[8] The meaning of a potential change will vary in relation to the nature of this interconnectedness as well as factors such as the relationship history and the contexts within which relational activities are carried out. Thus, change or attempted change, if significant to a relationship, may be met with a complementary change or a response that impedes or undermines it. For example, the teacher who no longer prestructures a course with a syllabus but asks students to co-create the course with her is changing the relationship between teacher and students and, possibly, what it means to perform as a teacher and a student. For some students, this may seem like an exciting opportunity, while for others such a relationship change may be threatening (Witkin, 2007).

For social workers and those in related fields, it is important to consider the processes that will invite support or opposition to change efforts. Not surprisingly, attempts at transformative change that challenge foundational or taken-for-granted assumptions and beliefs upon which relationships have developed can generate a feeling of uncertainty, confusion, or upheaval. Moving from relative certainty to uncertainty is challenging and likely to be resisted. This is more likely to occur if the change is unilateral such as, in the case of the previous example, if the teacher imposed her desired change rather than discussing or negotiating it with the students. This is an exercise of the teacher's authority and inconsistent with the change that is proposed. In contrast, engaging students in authentic dialogue about the proposed change can lead to its co-creation and a perception of collective ownership that reduces potential threats and fosters relational conditions conducive to support.

To recapitulate, transformative change, as used here, whether individual, organizational, or societal, refers to change that goes beyond appearances, the embellishment of putative understandings, the enhancement of existing practices, or the maintenance of taken-for-granted beliefs. Rather, it connotes change that is perceived and experienced as foundational and systemic. It is not confined to substantive change, that is, the content of beliefs, but may include new ontological and epistemological understandings, for example, the nature of knowledge or what constitutes reality.[9] Finally, change, and particularly transformative change, is not an individual phenomenon but best understood as relational. The bases for this perspective in postmodern and social constructionist ideas will be my next topics.

Postmodernism: The Basics

Although the term postmodernism first appeared in the late 19th century in relation to art, my focus will be with the impact of postmodernism as a social and intellectual movement in the social sciences. Therefore, for my purposes, the term 'postmodernism' will refer to a period beginning around 1950 characterized by questioning, critiques, and alternatives to the assumptions, beliefs, and consequences of modernity and the modernist project, in particular its epistemic universalism and its grand narrative of inevitable progress through science.

Strictly speaking, postmodernism is the period after modernism; however, there is no consensus on when Modernism ended, or even if it has ended, and the postmodern period began. Modernism generally refers to a period beginning in the 17th and/or 18th century (depending on the source) in which reason, as exemplified in science, began to replace immutable religious and sovereign authority. The philosopher Immanuel Kant in his famous paper 'What is Enlightenment?' (1784), a typical name for this period, saw this change as the use of reason to discover truth, that is, as a way to be enlightened. Kant believed, as most still do, that reason would lead humanity to understand the world as it really is and therefore, to certain progress and enlightenment. Science was/is seen as the archetype for reason. Through scientific reasoning we will come to know Reality.

As a reaction to modernism, postmodernism, as commonly understood, has been shaped by its opposition to modernism's constituent principles. Some most relevant to this discussion include:

- the belief in reason through science to generate cumulative knowledge about the natural world (its patterns and laws) reducing uncertainty and progressing toward truth;
- foundationalism – that all knowledge rests upon an ultimate, non-inferential foundation;
- essentialism – 'a belief in the real, true essence of things, the invariable and fixed properties which define the 'whatness' of a given entity ...' (Fuss, 1989: xi). Essentialism is also related to reductionism, that complex, diverse forms of social life can be explained by essential causes;
- individualism – the proposal that 'within each human being ... lies a bounded and sacred sanctuary of the mind, a domain governed by autonomous capacities for careful, conscious observation and rational deliberation' (Gergen, 2001b: 804). This (scientific) observation is represented in language which functions as a neutral representation of the real.

In contrast to these positions, postmodernist perspectives accept, even embrace, a more diverse, particularistic, uncertain, and fluid world. Knowledge is not a reflection of reality but a historical, cultural product subject to the vicissitudes of social intercourse. Language does not function as a 'mirror of nature' (Rorty, 1979) but generates our realities.

Some of these views are expanded on below.[10]

1. *The myth of foundationalism.* The belief that there are 'context-transcending standards of epistemic validity' has no credibility given the world's socio-cultural diversity (Simon, 2015: 6). The postmodern view on this issue was summed up by the French philosopher Jean-Francois Lyotard (1984) as an 'incredulity toward metanarratives', the latter referring to grand theories or 'stories a culture tells itself about its practices and beliefs' (see Klages, n.d.), such as the belief in the inevitable progress of science. For postmodernists all so called foundational discourses are local and ethnocentric and 'all knowledge claims are relationally contingent in terms of both their formulation, by a particular actor, and their reception, by other actors' (Simon, 2015: 9).

2. *Anti-essentialism.* Essentialism (in the context of this book) is the view that entities – individuals or groups – have an underlying nature or essence that transcends experience. Experience within a social category such as race or gender is assumed to be 'a stable one, one with a clear meaning, a meaning constant through time, space, and different historical, social, political, and personal contexts' (Grillo, 1995: 19). For postmodernists, essences do not constitute persons or groups. Rather, our understandings are social constructions constituted by the language and the historical/cultural beliefs that such language reflects.

3. *Power.* Postmodernists consider all knowledge claims to be expressions of 'culturally specific practices performed by spatiotemporally embedded entities' (Simon, 2015: 9). This embeddedness suggests that such claims will function in ways that support certain understandings and the practices that sustain them and undermine others. According to Simon (2015), this leads postmodern social theory to be pluralist in its critical stance and involvement in struggles related to 'variables such as class, gender, ethnicity, age and ability' (p. 10). This position is also reflected in Michel Foucault's concept of power/knowledge. For Foucault, power was something that operated through discourses, historically based systems of knowledge that constrain and enable how we can think, speak, and represent the world (McHoul & Grace, 1993). Dominant discourses, for example, about medicine or gender, constitute what we consider natural and sensible. More than language, discourses are inscribed in our institutions and expressed through our practices. By bringing certain realities into

being and obfuscating others, discourses become exercises of power, justifying, for example, how certain categories of people, like those judged insane – themselves products of discourses – should be treated.

4. *Meaning as a language game.* The concept of a language game comes from the writings of the philosopher Ludwig Wittgenstein (e.g., 1969). Although Wittgenstein did not identify as a postmodernist (the term was barely in circulation during his lifetime), many of his views have been appropriated by postmodernist and social constructionist scholars. A language game highlights how meaning is related to use. Such use is bound by rules that determine what can be sensibly expressed in different contexts. Such rules go beyond grammatical use to include how we use words, for example that something cannot be two mutually exclusive things at the same time (see, for example, my previous example about changing and staying the same). Language games are congruent with the previous discussion of power in that one language game cannot be adjudicated as superior to another based on appeal to some universal epistemic criterion. Therefore, their rules will be arbitrary and changed depending on the power relations determining their use. Finally, language games are expressions of what Wittgenstein called 'forms of life', broad cultural contexts that form the background assumptions that enable participants of the culture to comprehend what is being expressed.

As a profession established in the late 19th and early 20th centuries, social work developed around and continues to hold many of the tenets of modernism identified above. In particular, the postmodernist challenge has been most evident regarding the centrality of science to the profession. The precursor to this challenge was the debate between social work as a science or art (e.g., Boehm, 1961). This debate took on another form in the 1980s with the challenges to the increasingly dominant positivist-oriented movement in the profession (Weick & Saleebey, 1998). Beginning with Heineman-Pieper's (1985) critique of empirical metatheory (also, see Martinez-Brawley, 1999) there developed a small but vociferous critical literature that often drew upon postmodern ideas to question the assumptions of empiricist practices and their relevance to actual social work (e.g., Witkin, 1991).

Although postmodernism remains somewhat marginal within academic social work, particularly within the United States, its mantle has been taken up in other forms, notably social construction. Virtually all of the assumptions and beliefs identified above are embraced by social construction and have been incorporated into its positions. In addition, social construction makes its own distinct contributions. These occur in at least three areas: its integration of different avenues of critique, its emphasis on the social, and its application to contemporary social issues.

The Social Construction of Social Construction

There is a lot of confusion around the concept of social construction. Quite often I hear students make a distinction between something that is 'only' a social construction and something that is not. The implication is usually that the former is 'less real' and thus somewhat arbitrary and potentially changeable whereas the latter is a feature of reality and therefore immutable. Another common misunderstanding is that social construction holds that we each create our own individual reality. Finally, there is the widespread belief (evident among academics) that social construction is radically relativist both morally and ontologically. Therefore, the narrative goes, there can be no moral preference for any act no matter how heinous nor is the existence of elephants any more real than the existence of unicorns. As a way of introducing social construction, I will try to address these views in the following general discussion and specifically at the end of the chapter.

As noted, social construction developed out of the social and intellectual changes associated with postmodernism particularly as expressed in philosophy, literary studies, and the social sciences. Briefly, these influences included changes in the philosophy of science as exemplified by the seminal work of Thomas Kuhn in his book *The Structure of Scientific Revolutions* (1962). Kuhn's study of the history of scientific knowledge change led him to propose a radical alternative to the dominant view that scientific knowledge progressed in a linear, cumulative fashion toward truth. In contrast, Kuhn's analysis showed that scientific knowledge change was dependent on cultural and social factors operating within communities of scientists in particular fields. The influence of Kuhn and others (e.g., Feyerabend, 1993; Hanson, 1965) was taken up in the social sciences leading to inquiry into the psychological, social, and ideological dimensions of research. Examples included debunking psychological myths about scientists (e.g., Mahoney, 1976), showing how research findings were socially negotiated (e.g., Knorr-Cetina, 2013), and how science as a white, male-dominated institution ignored, and thereby perpetuated, its own ideological privilege (e.g., Keller, 1985). Other theoretical work such as Berger and Luckmann's *The Social Construction of Reality* (1967) was laying the conceptual groundwork for a more socially interactive understanding of human behavior. Finally, theorizing in the fields of linguistics and literary studies also seeded the intellectual ground from which new ways of understanding would grow. These contributions, often categorized as poststructuralism, focused on how language constitutes reality and how social processes of power are instigated in the naming of these realities. A key figure here is Jacques Derrida (1974, 1978) whose pioneering work led to a rethinking of how linguistic binaries such as nature–nurture and male–female that 'appear to be the 'foundation' for a system of thought is but a hypothetical construct, one that reveals more about the society that produced it than the supposed character of the real world' (Dixon & Jones, 2004: 83). These analyses led to questions about how categorizations express 'social relations of power … [and] … which social groups have the discursive resources to construct categories; that is, who has the ability to name the world'? (p. 84). Also important here is the work of Michel Foucault, in particular his concept of discourse and how knowledge is related to power, a topic I will take up later in this chapter.

Rather than identifying with any one of these fields, social construction draws on all these strands of critique, integrating them into its framework and applying their ideas across diverse fields. These critiques problematize the authority of science and taken-for-granted beliefs and create 'space' and impetus for new understandings and practices.

Like postmodernism, social construction can seem like a slippery concept for those wishing a specific definition. In fact, there is resistance among social constructionists to defining it in a way that is taken as truth. One way of addressing this situation is by thinking of social construction as plural, that is, social constructions. This allows for multiple meanings without one being definitive. This does not, however, mean that social construction is devoid of meaning; rather, its different meanings might be thought of as what the philosopher Ludwig Wittgenstein called family resemblances. As the term suggests, these are similarities as you might find among family members. No two family members are identical yet they share a number of similar characteristics. These 'resemblances' can be enumerated as follows (Witkin, 2014c).

- A view of knowledge as historically, culturally, and socially contingent. There is no ultimate, transcendent foundation, such as sense experience, that arbitrates between what is true or false.
- A concern with the social generation and maintenance of meanings, particularly through language use. For social constructionists, language is 'world constituting' (Gergen, 2001b: 805), not a transparent vehicle that reflects reality.
- A critical stance toward taken-for-granted knowledge, for example, the common dichotomous categories such as male–female, heterosexual–homosexual, that shape our understanding of reality.
- A view of knowledge as a form of power and social action. Different constructions invite and justify different kinds of actions. These knowledges are sustained by social processes. What we know becomes instantiated in the way society is organized and inscribed in our social institutions.

Gubrium and Holstein (2008) succinctly state the basic premise of social construction:

> The leading idea always has been that the world we live in and our place in it are not simply and evidently 'there' for participants. Rather, participants actively construct the world of everyday life and its constituent elements. (p. 3)

Social constructionists apply these ideas in different ways to a range of topics. Some focus on social construction as a process, that is, how 'people actively generate, maintain, and transform reality' (Harris, 2008: 231). This might involve, for example, exploring how people produce the meaning of family, including the language they use and the ways they establish particular meanings. Others focus more on the product, asking questions such as: what are the dominant and alternative meanings of 'childhood' in Western society, how are they maintained, and what are the implications of these meanings for how children are treated?

Another focus (not independent from the above) is on micro- or macro-level processes or phenomena. The primary interest for these social constructionists is on interpersonal interaction as might be expressed in dialogue or on larger-scale social entities such as social institutions or societal discourses.

These variations sample some of the range of social constructionist analyses. In this context, there are three interrelated topics that are integral to social construction as I will be using it in this book that I will highlight and briefly discuss: truth, language, and discourse.

Truth

The idea of truth is both a taken-for-granted belief and a complex, contested concept. What do people mean when they say something is true? My guess is that they generally mean that the words express a correspondence with reality (where, in somewhat circular fashion, reality is the true, existing state of affairs)[11] as in statements such as there is a mountain to the west or John is a boy. In both cases, we take it for granted that the statement can be judged as true or false. For social constructionists this view expresses the modernist perspective that there is a reality independent of our beliefs or perceptions that can be known and reflected in language. The implications of this view are far-reaching and significant.

One way it is significant is that it considers language as a transparent vehicle that conveys truth. That is, language is assumed to reflect a preexisting reality. It is also assumed that the meaning of a word is its referent; for example, the word 'mountain' means a particular material object. In contrast, for social constructionists there is no necessary relationship between an object and what it is called. The words we use are matters of community practices and cultural traditions. Also, language is viewed as constituting rather than reflecting reality. You might say how we 'language' the world becomes what is real. Whatever may or may not exist, once we communicate about it, even to ourselves, we are engaging in an interpretive process. As philosophers like Derrida have pointed out, referents too have meaning and that meaning is found in yet other words. Therefore, we can get no closer to 'the real' than our interpretive schemes.

Second, claims of truth tend to silence or suppress other competing claims. The authority of such claims will depend on factors such as the status of the claimant and the reasons given to support the claim. A psychiatrist who uses the DSM to diagnose his adolescent client has the credentials (an MD degree) and the reasons (the authority of the DSM) to give his claim the aura of an authoritative truth. As Bauman (1993) points out, this understanding of truth generates a relation of superiority between the holders of truth and those who hold contrary (i.e., untrue) beliefs (see Chapter 3 for additional discussion of this point).

A third issue relates to what I call taken-for-granted truths. These are assumptions and beliefs that are part of common cultural knowledge that are perceived, if perceived at all, as 'the way things are', for example that a person under twelve is a child. But where do these 'obvious' truths come from? One answer is that they are products of our history and culture expressed through societal discourses (e.g., the meanings of 'child', how these meanings function in society). Their obviousness makes them powerful regulators of our lives (I discuss the concept of discourse later in the chapter).

For social constructionists debating the issue of what is really true is less useful than exploring the meanings of truth and how these meanings function in social life. 'Truth' is a word, a concept; it is not viewed as reflecting a reality that transcends time and context. As Richard Rorty argues, truth is a way of justifying a belief (e.g., Thompson, 2001). Saying or implying that something is true functions rhetorically as an authoritative justification. If we assume or accept this status about a statement it gains considerable authority. This is a primary reason why science when seen as an objective, factual and truth producing activity is such an influential force in society.

Social constructionists do not deny reality, but consider it unknowable. Whatever reality is, it is. There can be no 'God's eye' perspective unmediated by history, culture, and language, no 'immaculate conception'. Nevertheless, consensus on treating certain beliefs as true is inevitable and necessary for a well-functioning social order. At issue is not the idea of beliefs functioning as truths, but the notion of Truth as transcendent and unassailable. In contrast to this latter position, social constructionists tend to view truth as plural, contextual, and communal. Different truths will exist within different knowledge communities such as science and religion. There is no way to adjudicate differences between communities because they operate within different world views and use different criteria for assessing beliefs. Of concern is not the differences, but that the attempt to impose Truth to enlighten the other 'is to privilege a particular under-standing or way of knowing and to diminish others' (Witkin, 2012: 25). Instead, we might ask '*whose* truth is being asserted and how does it func-tion in this community? Such an orientation aligns social construction with social workers' professed belief in legitimizing marginalized voices' (Witkin, 2012: 25).

Discourse

The social constructionist position is further enriched by Michel Fou-cault's concept of discourse. Foucault developed his concept of discourse as a way of understanding why certain beliefs and ways of understanding become dominant in different historical periods and how these characteris-tic ways of thinking (what he called episteme) are maintained. Discourses, in this context, are systems of representation that shape beliefs, meanings, and their expression. As Stuart Hall (1993) explains, they provide 'a way of representing the knowledge about – a particular topic at a particular his-torical moment ...' (p. 291). Discourses may be expressed in various forms such as written documents, verbal reports, and spoken words, or in non-linguistic forms such as in the practices and foundational assumptions of institutions and organizations. Foucault also speaks of discourse as 'a group of *rules* that are immanent in a practice, and define it in its specificity' (2002: 51). Medicine, for example, can be thought of as constituted by 'the group of rules, which, simultaneously or in turn, have made possible purely perceptual descriptions, together with observations mediated through instruments, the procedures used in laboratory experiments, statistical cal-culations, epidemiological or demographic observations, institutional regu-lations, and therapeutic practice' (p. 34).

Discourses do not simply reflect a state of affairs but do things. Foucault states that discourses 'systematically form the objects about which they speak' (Foucault, 2002: 54). As Leslie Miller (2008) illustrates, medical discourses bring doctors, nurses, and patients into being (and, I would add, the hierarchical structure of medical facilities like hospitals) and 'ascribes to them certain interests (health matters), and positions them in specific relationships …' Similarly, educational discourse forms teachers, student, and administrators, prescribes their relationship, their practices, and organizational structure. In doing so, it blurs the boundaries between saying and doing (Hall, 2001).

As noted in the above quote by Miller, by positioning people relationally, discourses generate relations of power. This positioning is based on a particular version of reality that is taken as natural or commonsensical. Thus, doctors and nurses, teachers and students, social workers and clients are all relationally positioned in a way that gives them different levels of rights and obligations (Langenhove & Harré, 1999).

Dominant discourses generate preferred versions of reality. As Vivian Burr (2015) writes, 'the power to act in particular ways, to claim resources, to control or be controlled depends upon the knowledge currently prevailing in a society. We can exercise power by drawing upon discourses, which allow our actions to be represented in an acceptable light' (p. 80). Foucault (1998) coined the term 'power/knowledge' to underscore the inseparableness of the two: 'It is in discourse that power and knowledge are joined together' (pp. 100–102). An important insight of Foucault was that power when effective operated invisibly. By encouraging the questioning of taken-for-granted, 'natural', and self-evident truths, social construction helps to reveal their historical and cultural origins and the forces that maintain them as truths and their social implications. Perhaps most important is that it helps us to realize that meanings can always be otherwise.

For social workers, focusing on how words like 'truth' function in relation to beliefs and the implications for understandings of social life seem more useful than debating the correspondence of words with 'reality'. Within the context of practice, it is more relevant to interrogate how ideas taken as truths, such as diagnostic categories, lead to and justify how we make sense of people's difficulties and our response to them.

So to conclude, let's go back to the three common notions about social construction with which I began this section.

1. Distinguishing between social constructions and nonsocial constructions. From my perspective, such a contrast is not tenable. Things are both social constructions *and* real (in the small r sense). We are born into a world of socially constructed beliefs and objects that are part of our lived experience. Thus, we experience things as real; however, we can also understand them as socially constructed in the sense of being aware that they might have been constructed differently. This is where different cultural beliefs can be illuminating. For example, when my father died, I certainly experienced this as a real event. Nevertheless, I am also aware that my experience of his death and the meaning it had

for me were culturally conditioned. If I were raised in certain Asian countries, I might have experienced it quite differently although just as real. There is also the issue of what criteria we would use to decide what is a social construction and what is not. Would these criteria not also be social constructions?

2. We each create our own individual reality. This belief confuses some versions of constructivism with constructionism. Although they have much in common, the constructivist position tends to be more individualistic in its assumption of the reality of separate minds. As Gergen (2015) puts it, 'where constructivism places the origin of knowledge in the head of the individual, social construction places the origin in social process' (p. 30). Thus, although the constructionist may concede that we cannot know another's experience, how that experience is understood and experienced will be a product of acculturation and social intercourse.

3. Social construction is radically relativist both ontologically (what is real) and morally (what is good). The first sense of relativism overlaps somewhat with the first misconception in that it tries to distinguish the real from the less real. In a well-known article entitled 'Death and Furniture', Edwards, Ashmore, and Potter (1995) show how even material objects – such as a table – can be understood as socially constructed. They discuss how a seemingly irrefutable demonstration – the thumping of a fist on a table – of an external reality can be questioned in various ways, for example, the solidity of the table, the warrant for generalizing from hitting part of the table to the whole or to tables in general or to anyone beyond the thumper. The authors note that while such issues may seem like nitpicking to the realist,[12] they reveal background assumptions that are necessary for this position to hold. They comment, 'What we have, on closer examination, is not so much a demonstration of out-there reality [i.e., the thumping], but of the workings of consensual commonsense. For relativists, consensual commonsense is an interesting topic. It can be examined for its workings, rather than wielded as a bludgeon against inquiry' (p. 30).

The moral argument that social constructionists have no basis for preferring one action, policy, or system over another is often coupled with the view that this leads to inaction and therefore contributes to the very evil that should be condemned. This argument is particularly relevant for social workers who tend to hold strong values about social issues. Despite its evocativeness, Edwards, Ashmore, and Potter (1995) point out that rather than being a refusal to have values, the social constructionist position amounts to not accepting what *realists* see as real. Also, the authors note that realist notions often encourage inaction (consider well-known imperatives such as 'accept reality'). Finally they point out that despite the dominance of realism, many bad things have and continue to happen, therefore, blaming relativism may be 'unrealistic'.

This argument also touches on the previous discussion about truth; that is, who knows definitively what is true? Such a position leads to the 'I am right; you are wrong' kind of arguments which, as previously observed, lead to a silencing of alternative views. Importantly, the authors dispute the belief that relativism means not having positions. They state:

> There is no contradiction between being a relativist and being *somebody*, a member of a particular culture, having commitments, beliefs, and a commonsense notion of reality. These are the very things to be argued for, questioned, defended, decided, without the comfort of just being, already and before thought, real and true. (pp. 35–36)

The ideas discussed in this chapter appear throughout the rest of the book. My hope is that despite the rather brief treatment I have given to somewhat dense and complex topics, it is sufficient to provide you with an overall framework for what is to follow and has piqued your curiosity about what these other chapters have to offer.

Notes

1 This is not always the case. Some religions, for example, might depict deities as angry or jealous. These characterizations imply the existence of a non-angry or non-jealous state, which would suggest a change.

2 These frameworks are not distinct as social construction is usually considered an expression of postmodernism.

3 Although I try to present a representative overview of transformative change, readers should note that there is a diversity of definitions regarding these changes within and across different fields such as therapy, organizational and policy studies. Also, even when there is general agreement on the meanings of these different types of changes, it does not necessarily mean high reliability on specific examples (e.g., Davey, Duncan, Kissil, & Davey, 2011).

4 This section is adapted from my article, 'Change and Deeper Change: Transforming Social Work Education' (2014a).

5 Also see the discussion of noticing in Chapter 4.

6 Adapted from Witkin (2014b).

7 The remainder of this subsection is adapted from Witkin (2007).

8 This notion is somewhat related to the concept of 'loose coupling' in which an organization is viewed as contain[ing] interdependent elements that vary in the number and strength of their interdependencies (Orton & Weick, 1990: 204).

9 I am not trying to define transformative change as much as giving readers a sense of how I understand this concept. I recommend considering this discussion as a potential resource for action rather than definitive pronouncements of the real.

10 Taken from Witkin and Irving (2014).

11 Of course, there are many other meanings of truth, for example truth as coherence and religious truth, and philosophical complexities that would require a much longer exposition than is possible here.

12 Basically, realists believe that things in the world exist and have certain properties that can be known and that these things and properties exist independently of our beliefs.

References

Bartunek, J. M., & Moch, M. K. (1987). First-order, second-order, and third-order change and organization development interventions: A cognitive approach. *The Journal of Applied Behavioral Science, 23*(4), 483–500.

Bauman, Z. (1993). Postmodernity, or living with ambivalence. In J. Natoli & L. Hutcheon (Eds.), *A postmodern reader* (pp. 9–24). Albany, NY: State University of New York Press.

Berger, P. L., & Luckmann, T. (1967). *The social construction of reality: A treatise in the sociology of knowledge.* Garden City, NY: Anchor Books.

Boehm, W. W. (1961). Social work: Science and art. *The Social Service Review, 35*(2), 144–152.

Buchanan, D., & Badham, R. (1999). Politics and organizational change: The lived experience. *Human Relations, 52*(5), 609–629.

Burr, V. (2015). *Social constructionism* (3rd ed.). NY: Routledge.

Carstensen, M. B. (2015). Conceptualising ideational novelty: A relational approach. *The British Journal of Politics and International Relations, 17*(2), 284–297.

Davey, M., Duncan, T., Kissil, K., & Davey, A. (2011). Second-order change in marriage and family therapy: A web-based modified Delphi study. *The American Journal of Family Therapy, 39*, 100–111.

Derrida, J. (1974). *Of grammatology.* Baltimore, MD: Johns Hopkins University Press.

Derrida, J. (1978). *Writing and difference.* Chicago, IL: University of Chicago Press.

Dixon, D. P., & Jones III, J. P. (2004). Poststructuralism. In J. S. Duncan, N. C. Johnson, & R. H. Schein (Eds.), *A companion to cultural geography* (pp. 79–107). Malden, MA: Blackwell Publishers.

Edwards, D., Ashmore, M. and Potter, J. (1995). Death and furniture: The rhetoric, politics and theology of bottom line arguments against relativism. *History of the Human Sciences, 8*, 25–49.

Feyerabend, P. (1993). *Against method.* London: Verso.

Foucault, M. (1998). *The will to knowledge: The history of sexuality* (Vol. 1). London: Penguin Books.

Foucault, M. (2002). *The archaeology of knowledge* (A. M. Sheridan Smith, trans.). London: Routledge Classics.

Fuss, D. (1989). *Essentially speaking.* London and New York: Routledge.

Gergen, K. J. (2001a). Social construction and pedagogical practice. In K. J. Gergen (Eds.), *Social construction in context* (pp. 115–136). Thousand Oaks, CA: Sage.

Gergen, K. J. (2001b). Psychological science in a postmodern context. *American Psychologist, 56*(10), 803–813.

Gergen, K. J. (2015). *An invitation to social construction* (3rd ed.). Thousand Oaks, CA: Sage.

Grillo, T. (1995). Anti-essentialism and intersectionality: Tools to dismantle the master's house. *Berkeley Women's Law Journal, 10*(1), 16–30.

Gubrium, J. F., & Holstein, J. A. (Eds.) (2008). *Handbook of constructionist research.* New York, NY: Guilford Press.

Hall, C. M. (2011). Policy learning and policy failure in sustainable tourism governance: From first- and second-order to third-order change? *Journal of Sustainable Tourism, 19*(4–5), 649–671.

Hall, P. (1993) Policy paradigms, social learning, and the state: The case of economic policymaking in Britain. *Comparative Politics, 25*(3), 275–296.

Hall, S. (2001). Foucault: Power, knowledge, and discourse. In M. Wetherell, S. Taylor, & S. J. Yates (Eds.), *Discourse theory and practice: A reader* (pp. 72–81). London: Sage.

Hanson, N. R. (1965). *Patterns of discovery: An inquiry into the conceptual foundations of science.* CUP Archive.

Harris, S. R. (2008). Constructionism in sociology. In J.A. Holstein & J.F. Gubrium (Eds.), *Handbook of constructionist research* (pp. 231–247). New York, NY: The Guilford Press.

Heineman-Pieper, M. (1985). The future of social work research. *Social Work Research and Abstracts, 21*(4), 3–11.

Jha, A. K. (2012). Epistemological and pedagogical concerns of constructionism: Relating to the educational practices. *Creative Education, 3*(2), 171–178.

Kant, I. (1784). *An answer to the question: What is enlightenment?* Konigsberg, Prussia, September 30. Retrieved from https://web.cn.edu/kwheeler/documents/What_is_Enlightenment.pdf

Keller, E. F. (1985). *Reflections on gender and science.* New Haven, CT; London: Yale University Press.

Klages, M. (n.d.). Postmodernism. Retrieved from http://evans-experientialism.free-webspace.com/klages.htm

Knorr-Cetina, K. D. (2013). *The manufacture of knowledge: An essay on the constructivist and contextual nature of science.* Amsterdam: Elsevier.

Kuhn, T. S. (1962). *The structure of scientific revolutions.* Chicago, IL: University of Chicago Press.

Van Langenhove, L., & Harré, R. (1999). Introducing positioning theory. In R. Harré & L. Van Langenhove (Eds.), *Positioning theory* (pp. 14–31). Oxford: Blackwell.

Loftis, M. W. and Mortensen, P. B. (2015). Transformative policy change. Working paper, Aarhus University. Retrieved from www.comparativeagendas.info/wordpress/wp-content/uploads/2015/06/Transformative-policy-change.pdf

Lyddon, W. J. (1990). First- and second-order change: Implications for rationalist and constructivist cognitive therapies. *Journal of Counseling and Development, 69*(2), 122–127.

Lyotard, J. F. (1984). *The postmodern condition: a report on knowledge.* Minneapolis, MN: University of Minnesota Press.

Mahoney, M. J. (1976). *Scientist as subject: The psychological imperative.* Oxford: Ballinger.

Martinez-Brawley, E. E. (1999). Social work, postmodernism and higher education. *International Social Work, 42*(3), 333–346.

McHoul, A. & Grace, W. (1993). *A Foucault primer: Discourse, power, and the subject.* New York, NY: New York University Press.

Miller, L. (2008). Foucauldian constructionism. In J. A. Holstein & J. F. Gubrium (Eds.), *Handbook of constructionist research* (pp. 251–274). New York, NY: The Guilford Press.

Moursund, D.G. (2002). Getting to the second order: Moving beyond amplification uses of information and communications technology in education. *Learning and Leading with Technology, 30*(1), 6. Retrieved from http://uoregon.edu/~moursund/dave/Article&Presentations/second_order.htm

Orton, J. D., & Weick, K. E. (1990). Loosely coupled systems: A reconceptualization. *The Academy of Management Review, 15*(2), 203–223.

Reisch, M. (2013). Social work education and the neo-liberal challenge: 'The US response to increasing global inequality'. *Social Work Education, 32*(6), 715–733.

Rorty, R. (1979). *Philosophy and the mirror of nature.* Princeton, NJ: Princeton University Press.

Senge, P. (1990). *The fifth discipline: The art and practice of the learning organization.* New York, NY: Doubleday.

Susen, S. (2015). *The 'postmodern turn' in the social sciences.* London: Palgrave Macmillan.

Swerissen, H., & Crisp, B. R. (2004). The sustainability of health promotion interventions for different levels of social organization. *Health Promotion International, 19*(1), 123–130.

Thompson, S. (2001). Richard Rorty on truth, justification and justice. In M. Festenstein & S. Thompson (Eds.), *Richard Rorty: Critical dialogues* (pp. 33–50). Cambridge: Polity Press.

Watzlawick, P., Weakland, J., & Fish, R. (1974). *Change: Principles of problem resolution and problem formation.* New York, NY: Norton.

Weick, A., & Saleebey, D. (1998). Postmodern perspectives for social work. *Journal of Religion & Spirituality in Social Work, 18*(3), 21–40.

Wells, C. (2008). What is enlightenment? Richard Rorty and enlightenment after certainty. *The Dialectic, 8,* 1–15.

Witkin, S. L. (1991). Empirical clinical practice: A critical analysis. *Social Work,* 36(2), 158–163.

Witkin, S. L. (2007). Toward a transformative social work. In S. L. Witkin & D. Saleebey (Eds.), *Social work dialogues: Transforming the canon in inquiry, practice and education.* Alexandria, VA: Council on Social Work Education.

Witkin, S. L. (2012). An introduction to social constructions. In S. L. Witkin (ed.), *Social construction and social work practice: Interpretations and innovations.* New York, NY: Columbia University Press.

Witkin, S. L. (2014a). Change and deeper change: Transforming social work education. *Journal of Social Work Education, 50*(4), 587–598.

Witkin, S. L (2014b). Autoethnography: The opening act. In S. L. Witkin (Ed.), *Narrating social work through autoethnography* (pp. 1–24). New York, NY: Columbia University Press.

Witkin, S. L. (2014c). Reality isn't what it used to be: An inquiry of transformative change. In S. L. Witkin (Ed.), *Narrating social work through autoethnography* (pp. 284–315). New York, NY: Columbia University Press.

Witkin, S. L., & Irving, A. (2014). Postmodern perspectives on social justice. In M. Resich (Ed.), *Routledge international handbook of social justice.* New York, NY: Routledge.

Wittgenstein, L. (1969). *On certainty.* G. E. M. Anscombe and G. H. von Wright (Eds.). D. Paul and G. M. Anscombe (trans.), Oxford: Basil Blackwell.

2 Revisioning Social Work Ethics[1]

Values, Ethics, and Morality

Values, ethics, and morals lie at the very heart of social work. From its early embrace of the value of charity to more contemporary, individualistic values like self-determination, values and the moral imperatives they imply have been an important dimension of social work's identity (Goldstein, 1987). Changes in these values over time have tended to reflect corresponding changes in the social and intellectual landscape (Barnard, 2008; Leiby, 1985). These changes have generated differences about the most appropriate values for social work and their proper expression in practice (Reamer, 2006).

In everyday discourse, values may express what people think is important or hold in high regard, qualities to which they aspire, and principles that function as guides for behavior, judgments, and decisions. Judgments about the expression of certain values are called ethics. For example, although we may value kindness toward others, its expression such as giving money to a beggar may be judged as good or bad (ethical or unethical). Thus, although there is a connection between values and ethics, the nature of this connection is not straightforward. Further complicating this relationship is that values can apply to specific domains (e.g., family, economics, religion), each of which provides a different interpretative context.

A third leg of this discussion is morality. Although often used interchangeably with ethics, I favor the position articulated by the social theorist Zygmunt Bauman. For Bauman (2000a), ethics is the existential condition of humans. As interdependent, social beings, we cannot avoid situations involving relations with others. We become moral beings, according to Bauman, when we take responsibility for our ethical existence, specifically for the Other.

Ethics and morality are complex topics encompassing many theories, subfields, and applications. It is not possible to provide a comprehensive review in this chapter. Rather, my focus will be on alternatives to mainstream views and their expression in social work. These alternatives fall under the general rubric of 'postmodern ethics', particularly positons informed by social constructionist perspectives. Also, I will focus primarily on practice rather than research ethics. Although there is considerable overlap, each context generates its own kind of ethical issues.

I begin with a succinct overview of the major Western ethical theories pointing out their fundamental characteristics and some potential shortcomings (also, see Wulfekuehler, 2008). This is followed by some postmodern alternatives and proposals for rethinking our understanding of ethics within the context of social work.

Mainstream Perspectives on Ethics

To do social work is to express views about how people ought to be treated, how they ought to act toward one another, and the responsibilities of society toward its members: in short, to embrace a particular moral stance. Most treatises on social work ethics are based on classical theories of moral conduct. These theories generally are classified into three perspectives: consequentialism, deontology, and virtues. Briefly put, consequentialism emphasizes the role of consequences of one's action. For example, the philosopher Jeremy Bentham believed that action should be guided by the assessment of its pleasurable or painful consequences (called utilitarianism). In contrast, deontological theories focus on rules or duties that one ought to follow or carry out in any situation. Immanuel Kant's categorical imperative – that one should be guided by principles that can be adopted by everyone – is considered an exemplar. In contrast to rules or principles, virtue theories stress the role of personal attributes or dispositions in ethical conduct. For example, Aristotle, the founder of this approach, was concerned with the kind of people we ought to be in order to live 'the good life' (Benn, 1998; Witkin & Iversen, 2012).

Hursthouse (2013) summarizes these differences: 'Suppose it is obvious that someone in need should be helped. A utilitarian will point to the fact that the consequences of doing so will maximize well-being, a deontologist to the fact that, in doing so the agent will be acting in accordance with a moral rule such as 'Do unto others as you would be done by' and a virtue ethicist to the fact that helping the person would be charitable or benevolent'. While this example suggests that in certain situations persons guided by these different perspectives might all render help, what they do may be influenced by their ethical reasoning.

Critiques of Mainstream Perspectives

While each of these perspectives provides useful analytical frames for assessing the rightness or wrongness of various actions, they also are limited in important ways. Although consequences are commonly considered when determining appropriate conduct, evaluating whether benefits outweigh harms can be difficult, particularly in situations involving nonmaterial goods (for example, well-being). Also, how particular outcomes are evaluated may vary depending on who is doing the evaluating and their social position. This is a familiar situation for social workers whose clients may hold quite disparate views about the benefits or harms of the 'consequences' of their actions, for example the removal of a child from their home (Witkin & Iversen, 2012). Another complexity is determining the connection between actions and their consequences. Often there are myriad factors that can be attributed causal properties including the understanding of the 'consequence' (e.g., Witkin, 2001).

Instead of determining moral actions based on their consequences (the good), deontological ethics looks to conformity with moral norms (the right). While following moral rules can be useful, it may sometimes lead to undesirable consequences based on how a rule is interpreted or the context in which it is expressed. Rules like Kant's universal ideals may be difficult to justify or apply in today's pluralistic world. Also, there can be situations in which different rules conflict. Reamer (2006), for example, drawing on the work of the philosopher Allan Gewirth (e.g., 1987), proposes a hierarchy of ethical rules in cases of such conflict; however, such 'metarules', like the rules themselves, do not account for the contexts in which actions take place.

Whereas consequentialism and deontological ethics can be differentiated by their respective emphases on the Good and Right, virtue ethics takes proper virtues rather than proper actions or consequences as antecedent to morality (Trianosky, 1990).

Virtues are historical, cultural constructs. For instance, Aristotle's virtues described what he believed to be the ideal Athenian male of the 4th century, probably not the archetype for contemporary global society. Also, virtues, like all concepts, may be interpreted differently in different contexts. I am reminded of an anecdote by Bertrand Russell (1933) about seeing an exhausted fox running into the forest. Shortly after, fox hunters ride up and ask him which direction the fox was running. For Russell, this is a situation in which lying is ethically justifiable. Is lying in this case a virtue or a vice? In large part, this is a question of perspective and judgment (the hunters and the fox would undoubtedly differ). A related issue concerns the notion of virtue as a kind of deep disposition. Can a person having such a disposition be virtuous in one area such as honesty, but not in another? Again, responses can vary.

Social Work Ethics

Like many professions, social work finds itself experiencing the tensions associated with the rapid social, technological, and intellectual changes that characterize the last sixty years. The political, cultural, and economic

ramifications of these changes such as globalized labor markets, the movement of large groups of displaced persons, environmental degradation,
epidemiological crises, and widespread violence present social workers with
unprecedented challenges. Addressing these issues has strained the credu-
lity of an objective or value-neutral stance associated with research and cast
a more critical gaze on the ethical positions of practice. Despite attempts to
refashion social work as a science, there is a continuing concern with the
moral and ethical approaches that inform understanding and professional
conduct. Such a focus seems critical to a profession that emerged from,
and continues to be viewed as representative of, moral discourse. In an era
of change and uncertainty, these concerns are ever more essential if social
work is to be a force for the vision of humanity to which it aspires. As Zygmunt Bauman noted in a speech at the Amsterdam School of Social Work:
'The uncertainty which haunts social work is nothing more nor nothing less
than the uncertainty endemic to moral responsibility' (Bauman 2000b: 10).
It is through the carrying out of this moral responsibility that the turn to
postmodern conceptions of ethics may provide new understandings.

The Postmodern Critique

The ethical theories previously discussed constitute what is broadly termed
as the modernist approach to ethics. They are modernist in the sense that
they seek to establish general laws developed through the exercise of reason
that can be universally applied. Further, these laws are seen as reflecting
a common or natural essence of humans (e.g., goodness or the pursuit of
pleasure). This approach leads to the establishment of standards which provide the right and wrong answers to moral questions that rational persons
are obligated to accept (Simpson & Williams, 1999).

    From a postmodern perspective, assumptions of universality, essen-
tialism, and individualism generate an illusion of certainty and objectivity. As such they are easily appropriated and used to impose judgments,
self-serving restrictions, and sanctions on others (practices that are typically viewed as unethical). Concerning the quest for universal standards,
Bauman (1993) writes that 'the moral thought and practice of modernity
was animated by the belief in the possibility of a *non-ambivalent, non-
aporetic ethical code*. Perhaps such a code had not been found yet. But it
surely waits round the next corner. Or the corner after next' (p. 9). This aporetic space is located in between rules. It is contradictory and undecidable
as even attempts at moral outcomes might generate immoral consequences
(Holtzhausen, 2015: 3; Loacker & Muhr, 2009; Swartz, 2007). In Bauman's
view, the endless quest for certainty reveals that 'an ethics that is universal and
'objectively founded', is a practical impossibility; perhaps even an *oxymoron*, a

contradiction in terms' (p. 10). It is the disbelief in this possibility, according to Bauman, that defines postmodern thought about ethics.

Clegg and Slife (2009) in a paper on research ethics identify four areas of contrast between modern and postmodern perspectives: interest in the particular versus the abstract, context, values (interpretive, perspectival), and other-focus. As noted, the modernist interest in the establishment of generalized laws leads to a lessened interest in the particular case. The particular is valued primarily as an instantiation of a more abstract law or theory. Within postmodernism this view is reversed with the concrete and particular being given priority. The discovery and application of general laws that apply to all people is extended in modernist discourse to contexts. Ethical principles apply everywhere. In contrast, for postmodernists context is inseparable from meaning. Therefore, ethical understanding is necessarily contextual and its conscious inclusion is vital to its meaningful application. For modernists, the objective nature of ethical principles is essential to their validity. Rational thought should be unbiased and not influenced by particular values or agendas. This position creates a separation between the objective and subjective in which the former is superior. For postmodernists, this separation is a historical artifact whose existence depends on the assumptions and beliefs of modernist thought. In contrast, values for the postmodernist are infused within all processes (practices) including divisions between objectivity and subjectivity. Rather than pursue the unattainable goal of eliminating bias, a better goal is to be transparent about the values that influence an analysis or position. Ironically, the masking of values under the cloak of objectivity can itself be viewed as an unethical practice. The so-called objective nature of modernist analyses diminishes the issue of power (an implication of Clegg and Slife's 'other focus') including, I would add, the power to determine what is ethical. Power in this context also is concerned with how relationships are fashioned by general ethical principles and their implications for the conduct of social life. It raises questions about who is privileged and who is disadvantaged by such principles. These issues arise in relation to a common modernist expression of ethics in professional organizations: codes of ethics.

Codes of Ethics

The development of ethical standards is a feature of professionalization. Such standards are embodied in a 'code of ethics', an enumeration and description of values, principles, and guidelines for professional practice endorsed by various professional societies. In social work, codes of ethics have been promulgated by professional associations of various countries as well as international organizations like the International Federation of

Social Workers (IFSW). Besides being a symbol of professional status, codes of ethics are considered necessary for the protection of clients and the regulation of professional conduct.

As noted, codes of ethics reflect modernist notions that ethics can be reduced to right and wrong standards and that through rational thought such right decisions can be made. In their analysis of the NASW (United States) code of ethics Freud and Krug (2002) write that 'The *Code of Ethics* purports to reach back to the philosophical, ethical roots of our Western culture, embracing the rationalist tradition which posits an autonomous moral agent who, through purely abstract reasoning, will discover and apply relevant principles to the ethical problem at hand' (p. 481). Similarly, in a study of codes of ethics in various countries, Briskman and Noble (1999) found that codes tended toward universalism, individualism, and in some cases a lack of definitions for key concepts such as social justice. They argued for a postmodern ethics that challenges broad categorizations of people, is responsive to diversity and otherness, open to negotiation, and therefore provisional. In particular, social workers would actively seek the perspectives of those toward whom social work services are directed and find ways to take account of their views on ethical practice, deprivileging any one position (Witkin & Iversen, 2012).

Similar concerns have been raised by feminist scholars who argue that ethics is gender-based and unresponsive to the realities of women's lives (for example, Jaggar, 1992).[2] Some of these analyses have focused on power, pointing out how acceptance of a male-centered ethic based on individuality, rationality, and males' experience in the world keeps women in a subordinate position. For these scholars, an ethic that does not focus on eliminating relationships of domination and oppression is morally vacuous. Other feminist scholars, while supportive of this position, have cautioned against reproducing a universalist orientation even for the purpose of redressing wrongs. Women are a highly heterogeneous group inclusive of diverse classes, cultures, and ethnicities among other group identities. From their perspective, any story that claims to be *the story* (of women) is suspect and reproduces the patriarchal view of a single and timeless 'truth' (see Tong, 2000; Witkin & Iversen, 2012).

I have also discussed the consequences of universalism and regulation in social work ethical codes (Witkin, 2000) noting that, 'without alternative perspectives the limits of our own belief systems become more difficult to assess' (p. 199). Such limits, in my view, are expressed in

> ethics that are more reactive than proactive, more about acts of commission than omission, more about individual conduct than collective responsibility, more about right or wrong than issues of

power (see, for example, Brown, 1994, chapter 8), more about sexual improprieties than draconian economic policies, more about the poor than the rich, and more about those who suffer from physical and emotional pain than those who restrict and profit from their care. (p. 199)

In other words, without alternative perspectives, we can easily lose sight of how our ethical positions may serve differential interests, unintentionally supporting existing institutional arrangements. The concern with regulation of professional conduct is particularly worrisome. Holtzhausen (2015) argues that codes of ethics are expressions of power. She asks, 'What can be more powerful than regulating the behavior of others?'

From a postmodern perspective, ethics and moral conduct can never be encompassed by a statement of codes, rather it entails a continuous and sometimes agonizing deliberation about what is the right thing to do in different situations (Bauman, 1998b). Some possibilities for alternative approaches that attempt to be responsive to this more fluid, contextual position are discussed below.

Social Constructionist Perspectives

As an expression of postmodern thought, social constructionist views on ethics tend to be congruent with those expressed by Bauman and Clegg and Slife. For instance, Gergen (1994) questions whether the search for 'universal standards of the good' is the best way to 'enhance the quality of cultural life' (p. 106). One problem he notes is that in declaring universals, alternative perspectives are dismissed or suppressed. Positions of ultimate superiority can be used to justify disruptions or eliminations of cultural traditions which function in important ways in the host culture. For example, various cultural and spiritual practices of indigenous peoples of North America were outlawed by their European-American conquerors in the name of a superior morality. More heinous is the use of moralizing principles to brutalize or even kill others. Such egregious acts become comprehensible when one's moral language renders the victims as nonhuman.

Gergen (2009) postulates two moral orders; the first (which he calls first-order morality) reflects broad societal consensus about social life. This is illustrated by our knowledge of how to act in various social settings. For example, when in a restaurant, patrons would not throw their food on to the floor and eat it with their hands nor would wait staff create a bonfire out of the chairs. Such acts do not occur (according to Gergen) because people are following moral rules, but because they are inconceivable; that is, they are nonsensical to what it means to be in a restaurant, or more broadly, a participant in the social order. Without such understandings, a functioning social order would not be possible. Nevertheless, while necessary, first-order moralities generate the conditions for moral judgment, the determination of good and evil. This occurs because implicit in each form of life is a 'good', a particular way of doing things that comes to embody the values of a particular group (large or small). But in determining the good we also create the not-good, for example ways of life that conflict with or threaten a particular tradition. (Gergen identifies, for example, different traditions in religion, government, and education.) Given the diversity of interests within and across cultures such differences are inevitable. Managing these differences moves us into the realm of second-order morality.

Here the challenge is how to choose among competing goods without eliminating the other. For Bauman (1998b) the key issue is whether to do away with or control pluralism, or to embrace it as virtuous. The first two positions invite monologue or universalism, while the third invites dialogue in which the good of the other is of primary concern.

Embracing pluralism does not necessitate regarding all positions as equal (moral relativism). The choice is not between absolute or universal rights and wrongs, but among different goods (Rorty, 1999), which encourages tolerance and compassion. However, as Gergen (2009) points out, these qualities are difficult to maintain in the face of what are considered significant evils. The key to countering this tendency is to keep a relational focus, that is, to adopt a relationally based 'moral pluralism' that recognizes how different goods derive their meanings and functions from the relational contexts in which they exist. For Gergen, this relational perspective seeks a 'non-foundational foundation' in which people work together from a position of relational responsibility where the primary focus is 'care for the relationship' (p. 365). He points to practices that bring different groups into dialogic relations that 'restore the possibilities of collaboration and the genesis of the good' (p. 370).[3]

Broadening the Conversation: Communicative Ethics[4]

The above revisioning of ethics represents an important step toward a potential broadening of social work's position in these areas. It is neither definitive nor prescriptive but an invitation to further exploration and dialogue about the interplay between moral discourse in social work and its practices. Gergen's argument about the inevitability of multiple views of goods sets the stage for a dialogal or communicative view of ethics.

The traditional approaches to moral conduct described previously – deontological, consequentialist, and virtue – provide the philosophical underpinnings of social work ethics. According to Arnett (2002), the distinction between communicative and philosophical ethics is that the former is concerned with the communicators, the historical moment, and the topic at hand. We move from viewing the standard as an ideal to the standard's being a rhetorical construct – composed of an ideal, form of communication, historical moment, and topic. Communication ethics evaluates the connection between all these communicative ingredients. (p. 498)

He also asserts that 'what is philosophically ethical is different from what is ethically appropriate in a communicative setting' (p. 498). These differences stem from philosophical ethics' focus on abstract principles, whereas communicative ethics is interested in the interplay of history, culture, and language. In addition, communicative ethics is concerned with performance – how we *do* ethics in our dialogic encounters.

A focus on communicative ethics can reveal the workings of power in our ethical practices and encourage interrogation of practices not typically broached by traditional codes of ethics. For instance, although social workers are aware of the totalizing effects of domination and oppression on conceptions of self, our ethics tend to be silent about such situations, focusing more on transgressions of appropriate conduct by social workers in relation to philosophically derived principles. In contrast, a social worker operating from the position of communicative ethics might ask, following bell hooks (1995): what is our ethical responsibility toward people whose domination has led them to form self-identities in terms of the dominant culture's depiction of them? Further, we may consider how ethical social work practice might look with clients considered discursively constructed and located within institutional structures (for example, the welfare system or the medical–mental health industry in the United States) that further their own oppression and domination. Is it unethical to encourage individuals to conform to oppressive social systems rather than oppose them? In such situations, do we have an affirmative obligation to provide, following Freire (1970), the skills and resources necessary 'to question institutional power'(Arnett, 2002: 493)? And how do we carry out such conscienticization without being patronizing or imposing our own vision on others while, at the same time, recognizing how our self and professional identities also are shaped in similar ways (see, for example, Weinberg, 2010)? These are not easy questions to answer. These difficulties are exacerbated by assumptions about communication, for instance, that interlocutors are operating from the same reality and that communication is the conveyance of meaning. Strong (2005) comments,

Ethically, interpretation and reflexivity point to considerations about how we attend to the meanings of others and ourselves play out in professional interaction. The presumption that humans operate from the same ontology that language can accurately represent, obviates a need to coordinate such meanings and interactions in more sensitive person-specific ways. (p. 98)

Communication is not only about speaking but listening. Bauman (2000b) believes that people often do not understand how their personal narratives express the public rhetorics of the media. Sensitivity to such rhetorics requires us to consider how we listen. Are we open to hearing many different narratives? Can we listen in a way that hears 'other plots, other constructions of heroes and villains, different crisis points, and alternative moral structures to the [received] narrative ...?' (Bracci, 2002: 481). Does our listening encourage self-reflexivity?

A view of listening as 'ethical communicative action', according to Bracci (2002), 'may require, for example, a form of humility with respect to narrative morals, an intellectual modesty with respect to knowledge produced from interested and imperfect claims' (p. 481). In a similar vein, Arnett, Bell, and Fritz (2010) interpret the work of philosophers/theorists Martin Buber, Hans-Georg Gadamer, Paulo Freire, and Hannah Arendt as suggesting that

> the power of listening [is its response] to the demands of a given moment rather than following a technique or a sense of personal demand. Listening begins the act of learning. Listening allows for awareness of the time, place, and content of a given conversation. Listening moves dialogic learning *to attentiveness to that which is before us, rather than that which we might prefer.* (p. 123, emphasis in original)

This position resonates with the Levinasian view of unconditional responsibility to the Other and the violence perpetrated by defining the Other within our own frames of reference (see also Chapter 4). Thus, a communicative approach encourages us to reconsider how we participate with others, through speaking and listening, in the construction of dialogic realities.

The performance emphasis of communicative ethics is consistent with social constructionist accounts of moral discourse. According to Gergen (1994), 'Rather than seek a specific moral solution to the relativistic ethos – a higher value around which we all might coalesce, an abstract universal to which we all might agree – constructionism invites a more pragmatic or practice-centered orientation to reconciling contrasting modes of life' (p. 109). Gergen proposes three implications of this shift:

1. The replacement of absolutist claims with 'a collaborative search for meaning, and disquisitions on transcendental goods with communal considerations of consequence' (p. 109). For example, we might inquire how we can engage in dialogue on ethical issues with our clients and others that will encourage expression of and respect for diverse perspectives.

2. The relocation of moral action from individuals to language. For example, rather than view morality as property of persons, we may ask how moral language functions in the lives of clients and in the practices of social workers.
3. A shift from theories or principles of the good to morality as a social achievement. For example, we might pay increased attention to issues such as identifying the conditions under which people are accepting of differences, or how alternative linguistic resources might facilitate collaborative practices.

Taking seriously these implications would require that social workers reanalyze existing ethical codes from the perspective of the people they serve. It would invite their participation in a mutual effort at defining 'the good' in particular situations. Finally, it would encourage ongoing examination of how language shapes the parameters of moral discourse. Less emphasis might be placed on codes as regulators of conduct, and more on the meaning of ethics – how it is constituted in language and functions in social life and professional practice. We might strive to understand and accommodate different ethical systems and how to fashion a moral language that is reflexive and contextual. Such considerations, I believe, can strengthen social workers' standing with the people they serve while making their practices sensitive and responsive to local realities and global concerns.

Toward a Transforming Ethics?

Much of what I have written presumes the necessity of a moral language or vocabulary: concepts and words that express judgments about what should or ought to be done. However, despite (or perhaps because of) the seeming obviousness of these linguistic resources, we might benefit from questioning how they function as part of social life. Gergen (1994), for instance, acknowledges the important role of moral languages and the language of individual morality to social life; however, he questions whether such precepts and their linguistic referents, such as 'should' and 'ought', are indispensable to an agreeable social order. He identifies relationships such as those of parents and children that are quite civil without relying on, or resorting to, moral principles. Rather than promoting morality, such languages, in Gergen's view, function as regulatory devices keeping potential transgressors in check. They do this by giving rhetorical authority to ways of acting that already are part of traditional social interchange[5] (Witkin & Iversen, 2012).

Although I think awareness of such processes can help us to recognize other options, I am uncertain whether it is possible to eliminate moral discourse that will function, at least in part, as regulatory mechanisms over oneself and others. Even without general terms like 'ought' and 'should', people will (and do) make moral comparisons between themselves and others through descriptive terms such as a person of integrity, a ruthless capitalist, a waffler (Rorty, 1991: 154). Still, consideration of our moral languages and moral vocabularies can enable a critical stance toward their taken-for-grantedness and draw attention to alternatives. For instance, we can consider the different ways in which people might speak about moral concerns and notice how identifying particular statements as moral principles or tenets express historical and cultural traditions. We can also locate such language within certain 'styles of moral reasoning' (Rorty, 1991), 'a set of rules of execution and operation, norms, standards, and so on – conventional arrangements that determine what counts as a good argument' (Simpson & Williams, 1999: 129). In other words, those criteria and processes of argumentation that are valued within particular knowledge communities. Additionally, these styles will depend on certain philosophical assumptions; for example, the presumption of 'right answers to moral questions which all reasonable people are obliged to accept' (Simpson & Williams, 1999: 123) or the prioritization of individual rights.

The above orientation shifts the focus from general moral principles to how moral languages function. For example, we can ask what kind of person do we become when we adopt a particular moral language, what realities are generated, and what can we do to increase awareness of alternatives. Also, as Gergen's example of parent–child relations suggests, we can look to various practices as illustrating relationships that express what we take to be moral actions. Critique itself can be viewed as a form of ethical practice. Such critique is not used as a form of judgment, but for exploring the possibilities of the discourse and generating new ways of thinking (Cooper & Blair, 2002). This shift from general principles to practices helps us to view morality as relational and contextual.

Practicing a relational, dialogical ethics will not be easy. In the current, evidence-based environment, generating the discursive spaces necessary for such practices presents a formidable challenge. As Bauman (2000b) observes, 'This [neo-liberal] discourse has no place, is even hostile to, the current human services system in which proceduralism dominates. The latter functions, in part, as a way of silencing, or perhaps avoiding, the issue of our moral responsibility to the other' (p. 10).

What can we do in such an environment? In addition to the modest suggestions above, we might seek and develop approaches that integrate ethics into practice in an active, contextual way and provide new ways of thinking about and doing ethical practice. For example, Hugman (2003) uses Husband's (1995) concept of 'the morally active practitioner' to suggest elements of a discursively ethical practice. Such practitioners would, among other things, highlight values without being prescriptive, approach contradictions as opportunities for enrichment, respect diversity, support moral reflection and deliberation over rule following, and be responsive to context. Such an approach is congruent with a 'participatory consciousness' that includes 'freeing ourselves from the categories imposed by the notions of objectivity and subjectivity ...' and 'an attitude of profound openness and receptivity' (Heshusius, 1994: 15, cited in Kotzé, 2002: 5). Participatory consciousness also supports what Kotzé (2002) terms participatory ethics, a position that goes beyond the consideration of differences and disadvantages of the other, but locates ethics 'in discourse and praxis *with* the disempowered and marginalized' (p. 18). Within this discourse, practitioners must always be sensitive to such questions as who is allowed to speak, what can be said (by whom), and how must things be said.

Becoming morally active and practicing participatory ethics begins with our relationship with the Other. It is here where Levinas's and Bauman's philosophies are particularly important in emphasizing our unlimited responsibility to the Other and in countering the dominant approach that seeks to understand or know the Other via our categorical frames (see Chapter 4 for a fuller discussion of Levinas's philosophy).

Narrative Ethics

Recently, narrative ethics has gained popularity as an alternative to more principled approaches to ethics. From a 'strong' narrative perspective, all personal stories are moral stories,[6] there are inevitable judgments of right and wrong, good and bad, choices of words, omissions, emphases, and so on. Additionally, part of narrative's appeal is its relational, dialogical, and contextual potential. Stories are socially constituted, temporal, and rich in detail. Narratives also are relational in the sense of being told to someone (including oneself). The telling constitutes a new version of the narrative.

In keeping with his participatory ethics, Kotzé (2002) views narrative ethics as a way of communicating the complexities of ethical issues and choices. Rather than the means for justifying prescriptive ways of acting, stories are ways of 'ethicizing', of doing ethics together with others. This process is inclusive and collaborative, in which 'the good life' is negotiated from multiple perspectives.

Storytelling as a dialogical process will depend on the relationship between interlocutors (in their various roles such as practitioner–client). This relationship will influence what story is told, how that story is represented to others, and how it is told. In an important sense the identity(ies) of the interlocutor is configured in the story. This process is articulated by the Russian literary theorist Mikhail Bakhtin (1929/1984) who notes that the person 'becomes for the first time that which [she or] he is … not only for others but for himself [or herself] as well' (p. 252; quoted in Frank, 2002: 15). Identity is co-constructed through the act of telling the story.

Of course, not all narratives will be dialogues. Sometimes they can be monologues and used to further a particular ethical imperative. Wilks (2005), for example, discusses how narrative approaches can favor particular types of narrative or retain a principalist approach. In contrast, he describes a third approach which is primarily relational, focusing on the client's story in the local context. Thus, our views about ethics and relationship will have important implications for *how* we engage in narrative and its dialogical expression.

It is important to underscore that adopting a postmodern or social constructionist ethical orientation does not mean a relativism that is insensitive to conditions of oppression. In contrast, I believe they can further sensitize us to issues of power and the unseen violence that is perpetrated against others through the imposition of Truth in our interactions. Rather than getting caught up in futile arguments about which ethical approach is the true or right one (see, for example, Lantos, 2014), we are invited to adapt a pragmatic approach.[7] For instance, we might ask, what are the implications of particular ethical orientations for social life?

Individual and Social Morality

Much of what I have written about relates to what might be termed individual morality, how individuals come to decide what is good or bad, right or wrong. In doing so, I have focused on the interpersonal context, our encounters with others and our obligations toward them. I have also discussed, albeit briefly, social morality, 'the effects of social practices and institutions on others' (Rorty cited in Simpson & Williams, 1999: 121); for example, the impact of professional codes of ethics. As social workers sensitive to context, these broader social forces are of concern and are further addressed in Chapter 3 on human rights. As Weinberg (2010) emphasizes, the structural context and resource issues characteristic of social work create a context in which moral issues are generated and ethical decisions made. Social morality also raises issues and questions about our responsibility not just to the Other but to the systems that generate and maintain inequality and oppression. Do we have an ethical obligation to speak out and oppose social arrangements and institutions that result in unnecessary suffering? Does silence make us complicit in an unjust system? Responses to such questions will vary as they do with other ethical issues; nevertheless, they need to be kept in the forefront of our deliberations.

All social work is an exercise in ethics. Our understandings, practices, and the social contexts in which our work is carried out express moral judgments that have ethical implications. While treating ethics as a discrete area may allow for focused study, such separation constructs practice as something to which ethics is applied rather than an ethical expression. This has the effect of reducing the scope of ethics and focusing on discrete topics such as ethical dilemmas. At the same time, broader moral issues that impact practice such as neoliberalism are rendered invisible. Therefore, an important message of this chapter is to keep morality and ethics infused with practice, recognizing it as an integral constituent of social work.

The integrality of ethics to social work provides moral justification and accountability for social work as a profession and supports its commitment to serving marginalized and oppressed groups. Yet we must be cautious of the universalist, objectivist, and essentialist dimensions of traditional ethical theories, particularly in the context of a globalized world. Ethnocentrism and exclusivity lurk in the claims of superordinate, neutral principles of ethical conduct. The imposition of such principles on others tend to be exercises in power rather than respect or collaboration.

If social work is to take seriously its responsibility to alterity, respect for heterogeneity in its many forms, and work with others to develop and support communal notions of 'the good', then it needs conceptions of ethics that are dynamic, contextually sensitive, and relational. Such conceptions and their application must be generated collaboratively through dialogues in contexts of openness, safety, and respect. I have already noted the challenges we face in instituting such changes. And because my focus is on process rather than outcomes, there is the additional challenge of working with the current process to get to a new process. There is no blueprint to follow. Nevertheless, such change can be transformative and its reverberations felt widely.

Notes

1   This is a revised and updated version of a book chapter published in Finnish (English title 'Doing good: Ethics and human rights in social work') that originally appeared in M. Laitinen and A. Pohjola (eds.) (2003) *Sosiaalisen Vaihtuvat Vastuut*.

2   It should be noted that what might be called feminist ethics is not a unitary perspective, but can be considered to include several different approaches. For example, existential feminists and Marxist feminists would differ in their emphases on the importance of internal versus external changes for women. Despite these and other differences, the various feminist and women-centered approaches to ethics share an interest in making ethics more relevant to the lived experience of women and to bring about gender equity.

3   Gergen seems to differentiate his position from that of Levinas based on his prior-
    itizing responsibility to the relationship rather than to the (individual) Other. In
    my view, Levinas's position is strongly relational although with a greater emphasis
    on the singularity of the Other. Whether this difference translates into practice
    differences is not clear.

4   Parts of this section have been adapted from Witkin and Iversen (2012).

5   Similarly, Rorty (1989) notes that moral principles function as reminders or
    abbreviations for moral practices rather than justifications.

6   Baldwin and Estey-Burtt (2012) contrast weak and strong narrative positions. The
    weak position regards narrative as a useful supplement to understanding human
    behavior; the strong position sees narrative as a constituent of social reality.

7   Lantos (2014) writes that 'Moral systems offer internal consistency, but they are
    useless as a way of adjudicating disputes between two different, equally self-
    contained moral systems. Rival conceptions of the good cannot engage one
    another's first premises. Kantian arguments will never convince a utilitarian'
    (p. S14).

References

Arnett, R. C. (2002). Pablo Freire's revolutionary pedagogy: From a story-
    centered to a narrative-centered communication ethic. *Qualitative Inquiry*,
    8(4), 489–510.

Arnett, R. C., Bell, L. M., & Fritz, J. M. H. (2010). Dialogic learning as first principle in
    communication ethics. *Atlantic Journal of Communication, 18*(3), 111–126.

Bakhtin, M. (1984). *Problems of Dostoevsky's poetics* (C. Emerson, Ed. and Trans.).
    Minneapolis, MN: University of Minnesota Press (original work published 1929,
    revised 1963).

Baldwin, C., & Estey-Burtt, B. (2012). Narrative and the reconfiguration of
    social work ethics. *Narrative Works* [S.l.], August. ISSN 1925-0622. Retrieved
    December 29, 2015 from https://journals.lib.unb.ca/index.php/NW/article/
    view/20169/23262

Barnard, A. (2008). Values ethics and professionalization A social work history. In A.
    Barnard, N. Horner, & J. Wild (Eds.), *The value base of social work and social care:
    An active learning handbook* (pp. 5–24). McGraw-Hill Education.

Bauman, Z. (1993). *Postmodern ethics*. Oxford: Blackwell.

Bauman, Z. (1998a). What prospects of morality in times of uncertainty? *Theory,
    Culture & Society, 15*(1), 11–22.

Bauman, Z. (1998b). On universal morality and the morality of universalism. *The
    European Journal of Development Research, 10*(2), 7–18.

Bauman, Z. (2000a). Ethics of individuals. *Canadian Journal of Sociology, 25*(1),
    83–96.

Bauman, Z. (2000b). Am I my brother's keeper? *European Journal of Social Work,
    3*(1), 5–11.

Benn, P. (1998). *Ethics*. Montreal: McGill-Queen's University Press.

Bracci, S. L. (2002). Seyla Benhabib's interactive universalism: Fragile hope for a radically democratic conversation model. *Qualitative Inquiry, 8,* 463–488.

Briskman, L., & Noble, C. (1999). Social work ethics: Embracing diversity? In J. Fook & B. Pease (Eds.), *Transforming social work practice: Postmodern critical perspectives* (pp. 57–69). London: Routledge.

Burbules, N. C., & Smeyers, P. (2002). Wittgenstein, the practice of ethics, and moral education. *Philosophy of Education Archive,* 248–257. Retrieved July 4, 2015, from http://faculty.ed.uiuc.edu/burbules/papers/wittethics.html

Brown, L. S. (1994). *Subversive dialogues: Theory in feminist therapy.* New York, NY: Basic Books.

Clegg, J., & Slife, B. D. (2009). Research ethics in the postmodern context. In D. M. Mertens & P. E. Ginsberg (eds.) *The handbook of social research ethics* (pp. 23–38). Thousand Oaks, CA: Sage.

Cooper, M., & Blair, C. (2002). Foucault's ethics. *Qualitative Inquiry, 8*(4), 511–531.

Frank, A. W. (2002). Why study people's stories? The dialogical ethics of narrative analysis. *International Journal of Qualitative Methods, 1*(1), Article 6. Retrieved December 31, 2015 from www.ualberta.ca/~ijqm/

Freire, P. (1970). *Pedagogy of the oppressed,* trans. Myra Bergman Ramos. New York: Continuum.

Freud, S., & Krug, S. (2002). Beyond the code of ethics, part I: Complexities of ethical decision making in social work practice. *Families in Society: The Journal of Contemporary Human Services, 83*(5/6), 474–482.

Gewirth, A. (1987). *Reason and morality.* Chicago: University of Chicago Press.

Gergen, K. J. (1994). *Realities and relationships: Soundings in social construction.* Cambridge, MA: Harvard University Press.

Gergen, K. J. (2009). *Relational being: Beyond self and community.* Oxford University Press.

Goldstein, H. (1987). The neglected moral link in social work practice. *Social Work, 32*(3), 181–186.

Heshusius, L. (1994). Freeing ourselves from objectivity: Managing subjectivity or turning toward a participatory mode of consciousness? *Educational Researcher, 23*(3), 15–22.

Holtzhausen, D. R. (2015). The unethical consequences of professional communication codes of ethics: A postmodern analysis of ethical decision-making in communication practice. *Public Relations Review.* Retrieved from http://dx.doi.org/10.1016/j.pubrev.2015.06.008.

hooks, b. (1995). *Killing rage: Ending racism.* New York, NY: Penguin.

Hugman, R. (2003). Professional values and ethics in social work: Reconsidering postmodernism? *British Journal of Social Work, 33*(8), 1025–1041.

Hursthouse, R. (2013). Virtue ethics. In E. N. Zalta (Ed.), *The Stanford Encyclopedia of Philosophy.* Retrieved from http://plato.stanford.edu/archives/fall2013/entries/ethics-virtue/

Husband, C. (1995). The morally active practitioner and the ethics of anti-racist social work. In R. Hugman & D. Smith (Eds.), *Ethical issues in social work* (pp. 83–103). London: Routledge.

Jaggar, A. M. (1992). Feminist ethics. In L. Becker & C. Becker (Eds.), *Encyclopedia of ethics* (pp. 363–364). New York, NY: Garland Press.

Kotzé, D. (2002). Doing participatory ethics. In D. Kotzé, J. Myburg, J. Roux, & Associates (Eds.), *Ethical ways of being* (pp. 1–34). Pretoria, South Africa: Ethics Alive.

Lantos, J. D. (2014). What we talk about when we talk about ethics. *Narrative Ethics: The Role of Stories in Bioethics*, special report, *Hastings Center Report* 44, no. 1, S40–S44. doi: 10.1002/hast.269

Leiby, J. (1985). Moral foundations of social welfare and social work: A historical view. *Social Work, 30*(4), 323–330.

Loacker, B., & Muhr, S. L. (2009). How can I become a responsible subject? Towards a practice-based ethics of responsiveness. *Journal of Business Ethics , 90*(2), 265–277.

Reamer, F. G. (2006) *Social work values and ethics* (2nd ed.). New York, NY: Columbia University Press.

Rorty, R. (1989). *Contingency, irony, and solidarity*. Cambridge: Cambridge University Press.

Rorty, R. (1991). *Essays on Heidegger and others: Philosophical papers*. Cambridge: Cambridge University Press

Rorty, R. (1999). *Philosophy and social hope*. London: Penguin Books.

Russell, B. (1933). *The conquest of happiness*. Garden City: Garden City Pub. Co.

Simpson, E., & Williams, M. (1999). Restructuring Rorty's ethics: Styles, languages, and vocabularies of moral reflection. In G. B. Madison & M. Fairbairn (Eds.), *The ethics of postmodernity: Current trends in continental thought* (pp. 120–137). Evanston, IL: Northwestern University Press.

Strong, T. (2005). Constructivist ethics? Let's talk about them: An introduction to the special issue on ethics and constructivist psychology. *Journal of Constructivist Psychology, 18*, 89–102.

Swartz, R. (2007). Social work values in an age of complexity. *Journal of Social Work Values & Ethics, 4*(3), 1–14.

Tong, R. (2000). Feminist ethics. In E. N. Zalta (Ed.), *The Stanford Encyclopedia of Philosophy*. Retrieved from http://plato.stanford.edu/

Trianosky, G. (1990). What is virtue ethics all about? *American Philosophical Quarterly, 27*(4), 335–344.

Weinberg, M. (2010). The social construction of social work ethics: Politicizing and broadening the lens. *Journal of Progressive Human Services, 21*, 32–44.

Wilks, T. (2005). Social work and narrative ethics. *British Journal of Social Work, 35*, 1249–1264.

Witkin, S. L. (2000). Editorial: Ethics-R-Us. *Social Work, 45*(3), 197–200.

Witkin, S. L. (2001). Complicating causes. *Social Work, 46*(3), 197–201.

Witkin, S. L. (2003). Doing good: Ethics and human rights in social work. In M. Laitinen & A. Pohjola (Eds.), *Sosiaalisen vaihtuvat vastuut*. Jyväskylä Finland: PS-Kustannus.

Witkin, S. L., & Iversen, R. R. (2012). Contemporary issues in social work. In C. N. Dulmus & K. M. Sowers (Eds.), *The profession of social work: Guided by history, led by evidence* (Chapter 10). Hoboken, NJ: John Wiley & Sons.

Wulfekuehler, H. (2008). Ethical theories and social work. *Journal of Social Work Theory and Practice, 17*(1).

3 Human Rights: A Critical Analysis

The concept of human rights is central to the social work profession, arguably its most important ethical expression. However, despite its significance and taken-for-granted status, the meanings and expressions of human rights turn out to be quite complex and controversial. In this chapter, I will attempt to sort out some of these issues and propose some ways forward.

As a context for the chapter, I will begin by briefly discussing social work's involvement with human rights, both historically and in the present day. Next, I will discuss the relationship between human rights and social justice, terms that frequently appear together. I then will go a bit deeper into some conceptions of human rights; in particular, I will focus on the pivotal issue of universalism versus cultural relativity. I will also introduce postmodern and social constructionist perspectives on human rights highlighting the views of two influential scholars: Richard Rorty and Zygmunt Bauman. Finally, I will propose some ideas for how we might take up a human rights (or a congruent) perspective in social work practice.

Social Work and Human Rights

Although the modern concept of human rights can be traced back to the doctrine of Just War during the Augustine period and the Enlightenment conception of rights (Gordon, 1998; Ife, 2012), its contemporary institutionalization as a global ethical principle was developed in the aftermath of the Second World War, the subsequent Nuremberg trials, the establishment of the United Nations in 1945, and the passage of the Universal Declaration of Human Rights (UDHR) in 1948. More recently, the ending of the Cold War and the collapse of the Soviet Union gave further impetus to a human rights approach as central to social work (Reisch, Ife, & Weil, 2013).

According to Healy (2008), social work's involvement in human rights dates to the early days of the profession.[1] She notes three different types of involvement (past and current): (1) the congruence of social work's mission and values with official doctrines such as the UN declaration and the official statements of social work organizations (e.g., the International Federation of Social Workers – IFSW); (2) the involvement in human rights activities of early social work leaders such as Jane Addams and Bertha Reynolds in the United States and Eglantyne Jebb in the United Kingdom; and (3) the past and recent involvement of social work in human rights movements such as anti-war and anti-apartheid movements. On the other hand, she also notes that social work's academic and institutional focus on human rights is relatively recent with the publication of books (e.g., Ife, 2001; Reichert, 2003; Wronka, 1998) and the IFSW policy statement in 1988. Of particular significance was a report by the United Nations Center for Human Rights (1992) which stated that 'Human rights are inseparable from social work theory, values and ethics, and practice. Rights corresponding to human needs have to be upheld and fostered, and they embody the justification and motivation for social work action. Advocacy of such rights must therefore be an integral part of social work …' (p. 10). Thus, 'human rights' is now a central and influential concept and moral position of social work worldwide.

The Relationship Between Human Rights and Social Justice[2]

Social workers tend to view social justice in terms of social equality, which, like human rights, presumes an equal intrinsic worth of all people (Bonnycastle, 2011). Succinctly stated, rights refer to entitlements; social justice is concerned with how societies promote, protect, ignore, or abuse these entitlements. Social justice also refers to the ways societies distribute needed and desired goods. It is concerned with fairness and equity. Human rights identify those goods considered essential for human well-being. Thus, the discourse about human rights is directly relevant for understanding social justice.

Calling something an entitlement (e.g., a livable wage, freedom from government interference) implies that the group to whom it applies (e.g., poor people, humanity) has an indisputable claim on that 'good'.[3] Identifying an entitlement as a human right gives it a status that supersedes all other entitlements. Consequently, human rights have become an important rallying cry for those who believe that such entitlements are being withheld, infringed, or not protected. The authority for their claims rests on its moral force: how people should be treated and its (quasi)legal status as codified in various human rights declarations and covenants.

In general, the more a society is judged to uphold human rights, the more it is considered socially just. In particular, the focus is on those who are disadvantaged. In this regard, Carl Bankston (2010) writes that 'social justice is viewed primarily as a matter of redistributing goods and resources to improve the situations of the disadvantaged' and that 'this redistribution is not presented as a matter of compassion or national interest, *but as a matter of the rights of the relatively disadvantaged to make claims on the rest of the society'* (p. 165, emphasis added). The recognition of such rights and the enforcement of their correlative duties become indispensable features of a just society (Witkin & Irving, 2014).

Within social work, some have argued that human rights rather than social justice should be the primary organizing ethic of social work (e.g., Reichert, 2001; Rozas & Garrin, 2015). Ife (2012), although a social justice advocate, identifies two potential problems with using social justice as a central organizing principle for social work: (1) its use as a rationale for revenge against groups alleged to have acted unjustly or who threaten social justice and (2) the possibility that although laws might be administered evenly, the laws themselves may be unjust.

Others fear that the increased focus on human rights in social work has been at the expense of social justice. For instance, Reisch et al. (2013) argue that 'Ironically, in order to remain acceptable in mainstream discourse, proponents of human rights often fail to raise structural issues or challenge the distribution of power and wealth in a given society or on a global scale' (p. 79). This is particularly troubling since groups that experience the greatest social disadvantages are also the most likely to be unable to exercise their rights, for example having the right to work but being unable to get a job or having the right to shelter but not be able to afford decent housing.

Similarly, when rights are considered properties of persons, individuals are viewed as responsible for exercising the rights they are assumed to have. Not exercising these assumed rights may be viewed as evidence of moral failing. Overlooked, however, as social justice advocates are wont to point out, is the oppression or debilitating sense of powerlessness that may have undermined the ability to think or act in these affirmative ways.

Writing outside of the social work context, Miller (2012) argues that 'the purpose of a doctrine of human rights is to specify a global minimum that people everywhere, regardless of societal membership or cultural affiliation, are owed as a matter of justice' (p. 9). Whatever the degree of centrality assigned to human rights or social justice, linking the two is critical for justifying 'humanitarian intervention' into states that violate human rights.

Meanings and Controversies About Human Rights

Despite the prominence and importance of the concepts of social justice and human rights across a range of disciplines including social work, their meaning and justification has been subject to considerable debate. For instance, social justice has been understood as fairness (most notably in Rawls' theory of distributive justice, 1999), as the promotion of well-being (as in the capabilities approach of Sen, e.g., 1999, and Nussbaum, e.g., 2002), and as an expression of deliberative democracy (emphasizing collective discussion and participation, e.g., as in Habermas's theory of communicative action, e.g., 1994) to name a few. This plurality of meanings of social justice led Bonnycastle (2011) to propose that different views of social justice be understood as a continuum anchored on one end by social oppression and the other by social equality.

A similar situation exists in relation to human rights. In particular, two interrelated issues have been central to its meanings: ontology, that is, whether rights exist and if so in what form, and the issue of universalism (and absolutism) versus cultural relativity. I will briefly discuss these before proposing possible alternatives.

Do rights exist independent of whether or not we are aware of them? What do we mean when we say that someone *has* rights? In a review of the contemporary history of human rights, Langlois (2004) discusses how the philosophy of liberalism developed during the Enlightenment furnished the rationale for the idea of human rights as residing within a person and which transcended culture. Liberalism exalted the individual who, it was claimed, embodied a common, transcendent essence of humanity. Rights were viewed as an expression of 'the essence of what it means to be human' (p. 254). Particularly influential was the philosopher John Locke whose belief in the natural rights of individuals to life, liberty, and property formed the basis for the US Declaration of Independence.

The idea of natural rights and subsequently human rights derived from the notion of natural law, which asserted a law above the imperfect laws of humans. Langlois (2004) writes, 'Natural law is acclaimed as the law behind the law, the law which gives the ultimate sanction for, or the ultimate judgment upon, the positive laws of the day as enacted by individual sovereign states. The rights of man, revamped and modernised as human rights, similarly sought to provide a universal standard against which the behaviour of states towards citizens could be evaluated' (p. 248). From a natural rights perspective, certain rights are considered to be self-evident and therefore immune to critique. One problem, however, is that not everyone always agrees on which rights are natural or, if they do, how they are expressed.

Natural rights served as a foundation for universalism – that human rights are inherent in all persons and that they exist independently of culture, place, or time – and the related concept of moral absolutism – that certain acts are right or wrong regardless of circumstances or perspective.[4] This historical and philosophical legacy continues into the present day, most commonly in the belief that all people have human rights simply by virtue of their humanity. This has led to various attempts to provide a rational grounding for this position. Often this grounding is based on another characteristic or value, for example dignity, that is claimed to have universal justification and applicability (Fields, 2010).

Various sophisticated analyses have been developed in the pursuit of this aim. The philosopher Alan Gewirth (1987), for example, argued that all humans have fundamental rights to freedom and well-being. He based his argument on what he termed three core 'goods' that humans must value: basic goods – those that are necessary for purposeful activity, for example food; nonsubtractive goods – those whose loss would diminish the ability to pursue goals, for example being lied to; and additive goods – those that enhance one's ability to pursue goals, for example knowledge, wealth, and self-esteem. Frederick Reamer (1999) has used Gewirth's position as the basis for his approach to social work ethics and as a guide for resolving ethical dilemmas.

Another philosopher, James Griffin (2008), proposed grounding human rights on the basis of personhood. For Griffin, this criterion leads to three high-level human rights (each subsuming lower-level rights): autonomy, liberty, and minimum provision. Within the context of his argument, autonomy concerns deciding on and choosing a worthwhile life, liberty is the freedom to pursue this vision, and minimum provision are the goods needed to enjoy the first two.

Yet another position is to base human rights on needs (e.g., Miller, 2012). Although it is hard to argue against the need for goods like food without which a person could not survive, achieving consensus is more elusive when positing other needs. For example, Miller identifies the need for education (also typically identified as a human right). While this may seem straight-forward, the fulfillment of this need (or right) has sometimes been used in a way that subverts such a right, for example to socialize indigenous children into the dominant culture of a colonial invader while eliminating their own native cultural heritage (e.g., Skegg, 2005). In this regard, Miller acknowl-edges that although there should be consensus on the need for education, there can be legitimate disagreement on the type of education (e.g., religious education, p. 416). Such practices reveal another problem with these argu-ments: the potential discrepancy between the naming of human rights and their meaning in use, in this case as a cover for cultural genocide.

While an analysis of these and other philosophies could easily be chap-ters in themselves – each position has its supporters and critics – my pur-pose in sharing them (however superficially) is to provide examples of the kinds of effort that have gone into trying to ground human rights in a way that would justify their universal application.

The idea of *human* rights implies universality. But if rights are inherent to all humans solely by virtue of their humanity, how do we accommodate or even celebrate (a value closer to a social work position) the obvious diversity that characterizes humankind? From the perspective of cultural relativism, it is the uniqueness of traditions, values, and ways of life in diverse societies, not sameness, that must be acknowledged and respected (e.g., Klein, 2001). The attempt to reconcile these two seemingly incompatible positions has led to other creative human rights doctrines, two of which I will briefly describe.

Writing from a social work perspective, Staub-Bernasconi (2010) suggests that it is not universalist and relativist positions per se that are irreconcilable, but their extreme versions, which she terms hegemonial universalism and fundamentalist pluralism. Basically, both extreme versions are intransigent in their beliefs and nonresponsive to criticism or compromise. Thus, Staub-Bernasconi proposes a more moderate version of both positions. Essential to her moderate positions is that they are open to questioning and critique, that they share the goals of mutual understanding, cooperation, and compromise, allow an 'exit option' if resolution of disputes is not possible,[5] and a tolerance (with limits) for differences.

While Staub-Bernasconi's attempt to develop a workable solution to this long-standing dilemma has merit, it relies on a willingness of disputants to accept a particular framing that neither may be inclined to do. That is, why would they be inclined to abandon their position (which they likely would not identify as extreme) for her alternative? For example, Staub-Bernasconi bases her moderate universalism position on needs, specifically a list of 'universal' biological, psychic, and social needs. It is not clear why such a list would be accepted as universal or as the justification for human rights. Additionally, Staub-Bernasconi seems to assume that 'empirical evidence' is the ultimate arbiter of differences and that moral and empirical truths are equivalent, thereby overlooking a considerable critical literature on these topics.

Staub-Bernasconi's proposal still has disputants vying for the supremacy of their position, albeit in a civil manner. An alternative, proposed by Jones (2000), recommends a two-level framework in which human rights function as a way of mediating disagreements about specific rights. Most attempts to address diversity[6] through human rights employ what Jones calls a continuous strategy which tries 'to establish a continuity between the theory of human rights and the various doctrines to which people are committed. If it is successful, people will be able to recognize that human beings have rights, and to find reason for that recognition, from within their own systems of belief' (p. 34). Unfortunately, this is not the case – at least not universally. In contrast, he proposes a discontinuous strategy that does not attempt to establish a theory of human rights that we hope or demand others to accept, but rather employs human rights as a way of mediating differences about rights or moral doctrines.

Although Jones gives several reasons for rejecting the continuous approach, I will mention only one because of its particular relevance to the previously identified theories which are representative of a continuous strategy and because of its centrality to the value position of social work. Jones illustrates his position by asking us to assume that among all the diverse value positions in the world, we could identify a core of beliefs on which there would be consensus, for example 'that our basic biological needs should be met and that we should neither inflict upon others, nor ourselves have to endure, unnecessary physical pain' (p. 37). While this may seem uncontroversial, Jones points out that this discovery would have marginal value in 'try[ing] to work out how we should organize a world in which people have different and conflicting beliefs about how they all should live' (p. 37). He adds that searching for an overlapping consensus (or, I would add, a single unifying rationale) is a search for uniformity rather than a way to address diversity, that is, it avoids diversity.

Jones' discontinuous strategy avoids adding another point of view to the doctrinal mix. Instead, human rights would be independent of judging which position is better or more moral. Rather, its function would be 'how people ought to relate to one another as people with different beliefs' (p. 37). Doing this successfully would require, according to Jones, 'doctrinal neutrality' (as I have just discussed) and 'moral supremacy', that human rights, as understood in the context of his argument, would occupy a superior position relative to doctrinal disagreements. His regulating transcendent rule would be that everyone has equal status as persons, which, in my view, is similar to saying that everyone has a right to freedom (see Steiner, 2012).

Positioning human rights as a way of regulating disagreements about entitlements rather than trying to justify the universal acceptance of particular entitlements as human rights is a creative and potentially useful approach. Nevertheless, I have some reservations about this position; for example, is it a back-door way of slipping in a universal criterion – equal status of persons – without naming it as such? More troubling is the issue of who counts as a person. Throughout history and including present times, certain classes of beings (e.g., people with disabilities, indigenous peoples, enemies of the state, women, children) have been denied human rights or more accurately, they have been considered outside the purview of human rights, because they were/are not considered to be fully human. Jones concedes that the issue is not resolved by his framework: '[the] approach provides for differences of belief among the members of the moral community about how they should conduct their lives; it does not provide for disputes about who should count as a member of the moral community' (p. 48). Despite these possible shortcomings, there are aspects of Jones' approach, for example, the attempt to avoid justifying universal human rights, that resonate with social constructionist/postmodern, non-foundational views.

A particularly contentious issue in the universalism–relativism debate is whether human rights, as they are predominantly conceived and instantiated in various covenants and doctrines, are primarily a Western invention, reflecting Western beliefs and values, that are irrelevant, or even destructive, to the non-Western world. Some have even extended this argument to the concept of human rights itself. For example, Staub-Bernasconi (2010) quotes Makau Mutua, the chairman of the Nairobi-based Kenya Human Rights Commission: 'I have always found human suffering unacceptable. But I did not name my struggle against deprivation, dehumanization, and oppression a fight for human rights' (2002: ix). She notes Mutua's belief 'that human rights enterprise mistakenly presents itself as a final truth, as a glimpse of utopia without which human advancement is not possible' and its 'Eurocentric formula ... that aims to transplant the Holy Trinity of liberalism, democracy, and human rights' (p. 10).

Once again, what may seem like a clear violation of cultural sovereignty can, from other perspectives, look less straightforward. In particular, some human rights scholars have resisted the either/or view of this issue as it is positioned within the universalism–relativism debate and have argued for a position that recognizes Western bias without assuming this bias renders all conceptualizations and documents as having no value to the rest of the world. While it is not surprising, given the history of human rights, that the dominant discourse reflects the views of those in power, this does not *necessarily* mean that (all) the values expressed contradict those that might be valued in non-Western cultures. Fields (2010), for instance, argues that the either/or view assumes culture to be static and sealed off from the rest of the world. Although cognizant of the problems engendered by particular conceptions of human rights, he contends that 'There is no reason to accept the argument made by those in power in a given country that people who challenge the dominant customs or practices, such as women's rights activists in the South, are an illegitimate contaminant because they have been influenced by or in contact with rights advocates and activists elsewhere' (p. 72).

Additionally, Jones (2012) argues that critics have sometimes caricatured Western rights activists:

> For some Western critics, it would seem that nonwestern populations, in embracing human rights, are merely running headlong to their chains. Protests about the alien influence of human rights and liberalism are rarely accompanied by similar protests against the influence of ideologies such as nationalism and Marxism, which are every bit as 'Western' in origin and which often play a significant role in 'non-Western' violations of human rights. (p. 499)

He also notes that most human rights documents are written in ways that do not impose particular forms of life but provide people with the freedom to make choices about the lives they wish to live. On the other hand, this does not mean that constructing human rights from a different starting point would not lead to somewhat different doctrines.

Like these other authors, Jim Ife (2012) recognizes the potential deleterious impact of Western views of human rights but pushes back against the notion that because human rights are a Western expression they are colonialist and should be abandoned. Ife argues that there are many words such as freedom and democracy that are associated with the Western Enlightenment but that it would not be useful to abandon. Additionally, he notes that 'notions of human rights' although expressed in different terms are found in 'all major religious traditions and ... many different cultural forms and therefore are not exclusively Western' (p. 8).

While these discussions are important and helpful, they are not transformative in the sense that they remain somewhat tied to conventional views of human rights. That is, the counterarguments accept, to different degrees, the conceptualizations of human rights that are embedded within the so-called Western perspective. In contrast, postmodern and social constructionist views propose more radical changes to how we understand the idea of human rights. It is to these perspectives that I now turn.

Human Rights as Discourse

Central to many of the debates about human rights is the oft-posed question 'What are human rights?' Although perfectly sensible, the question already presumes that human rights exist as some sort of entity. This reification invites inquiries and theorizing that focus on the properties of human rights (Brinkmann, 2010), rather than problematizing their existence. Ironically, although such inquiry and theorizing contribute to the generation of human rights – as in the previous examples – they are often viewed as discovering them.

An alternative is to focus on how different conceptions of human rights *function* rather than debating what they are. As Harré (2005) expresses it: 'The question one must ask is: What are these words being used for? What discursive tasks are they intended to accomplish or to facilitate?' (p. 237). Viewing rights as constituted in discourse generates different understandings. For instance, they can be seen as rhetorical moves designed to put forth a convincing argument 'when one needs to obtain a concession from someone or to ensure that someone does what one believes to be required in some concrete circumstance' (Harré, 2005: 237).

This perspective enables us to see how human rights rhetoric can also be destructive. For example, as noted earlier, when human rights are viewed as absolute they can stifle alternative views or even justify acts of cruelty. Gordon (1998) gives the example of how human rights can justify economic sanctions against another country despite opposition from its citizens and the hardships it might cause those who are most vulnerable. Thus, because of its rhetorical authority, human rights need to be judged by how they are taken up and used in different contexts.

Human rights claims presume a moral status that supersedes other claims; however, this does not ensure acceptance. Such claims can be contested or dismissed depending on various factors. For example, in order for some act to be taken as the legitimate expression of a human right, one must have the authority to make such an assertion (or cite a legitimating authority) and others must concur. A problem is that such interactions are based on winners and losers. If the stakes are high, participants become combatants seeking to silence or even destroy their opponent. Such scenarios lead to questions about whether we can achieve the ideals of human rights without a transformation in the way we think. For example, Kenneth Gergen (2009) argues that any attempt to establish the good will inevitably generate the 'not good', thereby creating a destructive relational dynamic in which those in possession of the good are positioned in opposition to other less enlightened beings. This in turn can lead to the justification of destructive acts.[7] Therefore, what is needed, according to Gergen, is a change in the way that we relate to one another. This change, which he calls a second-order morality (see Chapter 2 on ethics), would make relationships, rather than individuals, primary: 'individual responsibility is replaced by *relational responsibility*, a collective responsibility for sustaining the potentials of coordinated action' (p. 364, emphasis in original). To the extent that second-order morality functions as a way of regulating how we relate to one another, it has some overlap with Jones' discontinuous strategy. Although Jones is not explicit about relationships in the way that Gergen is, they both seek to avoid furthering the disputatious interactions that result from judging the better of different 'goods'.

In a similar vein, the writings of the philosopher Richard Rorty and the social theorist Zygmunt Bauman provide generative analyses of human rights that invite the envisioning of new alternatives. What follows is a highlighting of some of their ideas relevant to this discussion.[8]

Richard Rorty[9]

Richard Rorty was highly critical of the notion, which he attributed to professional philosophy, that there could be a universally applicable, neutral epistemology by which knowledge or morality claims could be judged.

He rejected foundationalist or essentialist justifications for human rights, viewing the search for such justifications as superfluous to the realization of such rights: '... the question of whether human beings really *have* the rights enumerated in the Helsinki Declaration[10] is not worth raising' (Rorty, 1993: 170).

In an oft-cited article entitled 'Human Rights, Rationality, and Sentimentality' (1993), he argued against a universalist conception of human rights and its grounding in an Enlightenment (e.g., Kantian) view of rationalism. For Rorty, arguing for a transcendental common essence – rationality – has not been (nor could it be) effective in eliminating the atrocities and indignities that humans afflict upon one another. As an alternative to intellectual arguments for human rights, he emphasized the notion of sentimentality, 'hearing sad and sentimental stories' that help people imagine the suffering of others considered 'not like us'.[11]

Although critical of modernist conceptions of human rights, Rorty supports the idea of a 'human rights culture', seeing it, however, as an historically contingent development rather than the expression of an ahistorical truth: 'If one says that later societies made progress in recognizing the existence of human rights ... one should only mean that they conformed more closely to the way we wealthy, secure, educated inhabitants of the First World think people should be treated by one another. We are quite justified in thinking as we do, but we cannot check our view of the matter against the intrinsic nature of moral reality' (Rorty, 1998: 7).[12]

Barreto (2011) separates Rorty's anti-foundationalist position into two interrelated forms: epistemic and ontological. Epistemic anti-foundationalism is associated with Rorty's ideas about truth, in this case that human rights are an expression of our true human nature. In the Western canon, truth is an ahistorical, transcendent idea that expresses some aspect of 'the real'. In contrast, Rorty argues that there is no vantage point outside of our web of historically and culturally based attitudes and beliefs; that is, there is no access to such a reality that can be used as the basis for comparison to our beliefs (Kumar, 2005). The criteria for deciding among differences about what we should or should not do or the superiority of one claim relative to another is based on historical and cultural traditions and preferences. Rather than a reading of the real, truth for Rorty functions as a form of justification. He argues that we would be better off acknowledging this rather than trying to prove our superior knowledge.

Barreto (2011) describes ontological anti-foundationalism as a critique of the search for the transcendental grounds for humans; in this context, a basis for human rights that goes beyond history and culture. This search is related to essentialism in that human rights are considered an attribute of the human condition. For Rorty, to be human is itself a historical/cultural expression and there is no way for anyone to stand outside of history and culture. Since there is no 'god's eye' perspective, arguments about our true human nature will always privilege certain conceptions of being human over others which can undermine dialogue about possible futures: 'What is necessary is to abandon the question regarding 'human nature' and to answer the question as to what sort of human beings do we want to become' (Rorty, 1991: 13, cited in Beratto, 2011: 99). In other words, it would be more useful to focus on becoming the kind of beings to which we aspire than on debates about our true nature. Although it could be argued that the latter would inform the former, from Rorty's perspective the question is unanswerable in any ultimate sense, but instead functions as a site where various ideologies and interests compete for dominance.[13]

Rather than reason being the arbiter of competing claims, we need to promote new ways of understanding and 'languaging' the world, new ways to challenge discourses that underlie objectionable practices and policies and different vocabularies that move us closer to our social utopian ideals (Rorty, 1989). Human rights from this perspective are not 'a question of looking for transcendental grounds but of directly engaging with suffering – *of facing the situation of those in pain*' and 'the degree of our openness to others and the range of our encounters, as well as about our capacity to listen to outsiders who suffer' (Barreto, 2011: 99, emphasis in original).

To achieve these ends, Rorty advocates for an approach to human rights based on emotion rather than intellect. He sees the telling of stories, the use of poetry and literature as having a greater potential to generate a sense of empathy than philosophical arguments about rights and justice. Williams (2003) comments that

> for Rorty, the important instruments of moral change are not moral–political treatises, but novels (or perhaps journalistic exposés) that bring home to us the cruelty of our institutions: novels that make us feel the sufferings of the oppressed. In undermining the legitimacy of slavery, *Uncle Tom's Cabin* does more than *The Groundwork of the Metaphysic of Morals*. (p. 74)

Rorty's analyses imply that a philosophical approach to human rights based on Enlightenment tenets will lead nowhere and may even be harmful. Zygmunt Bauman holds a similar position although extending it in a somewhat different direction.

Zygmunt Bauman[14]

Bauman does not see postmodernity as a break with modernity, but another phase that he calls 'liquid modernity', a metaphor for representing the continuous change that characterizes contemporary social life. This state of affairs undermines the authority of previously held tenets and beliefs and creates a situation in which various sources of authority compete for hegemony (Bauman, 2000). Modernity addresses liquidity through ordering and production. A consequence of the latter is the generation of enormous waste, in the human as well as material sense. Modernist narratives emphasize production while rendering waste invisible, for example by confining it to 'dumping sites' like ghettos (Lemert & Goodman, 2007). Bauman (2004) writes, 'The story we grow in and with has no interest in waste. According to the story it is the product that matters, not the waste ... we do not stroll through rough districts, mean streets, urban ghettos, asylum-seekers' camps and other no-go areas. We carefully avoid them (or are directed away from them) in our compulsive tourist escapades. We dispose of leftovers in the most radical and effective way: we make them invisible by not looking and unthinkable by not thinking' (p. 27, cited in Lemert and Goodman: 198–199).[15] Paradoxically, modernity's attempts to deflect attention from such waste by increasing production and consumption results in increasing waste.

Like Rorty, Bauman rejects the idea of ahistorical, universal truth that will lead humanity to some utopian state of human dignity and justice through reason. Going further, he argues that the assumption of such truth *requires* others whose beliefs are false. This creates a relation that justifies telling these others to change their erroneous belief further 'confirming the superiority (read: right to command) of the holder of truth (read: the giver of command)' (Bauman, 1993: 10). Thus, truth as a social relation constitutes a hierarchy in which those who hold the truth (through, for instance, their membership in an authorizing institution like science) can claim hegemony over the beliefs of others. The modern project, according to Bauman, becomes an attempt to install a regime based on rationality, universality, certainty, and the elimination of difference. This situation is directly contrary to Bauman's belief that 'the idea of human rights means, first and foremost, the right to be different and to have this difference respected' (Bauman & Tester, 2001: 142).

Instead of certainty and universality, Bauman argues for an acceptance of contingency which necessitates the possibility that others might have different but equally justified views of what is just. This changes the relationship with others from one of enmity to one of tolerance. Bauman notes the overlap with Rorty's belief that 'the language of contingency creates a chance 'of being kind, by avoiding the humiliation of others'' (Rorty, 1989: 91). However, Bauman believes that tolerance is not enough; we must respect the other 'and respect them precisely for their otherness' (p. 14). This creates a condition that shifts contingency-as-fate to contingency-as-destiny, which promotes solidarity. However, Bauman is quick to point out that getting to solidarity is also contingent.

Bauman's ideas about truth as a relation suggest that a universally foundationalist human rights may subvert its own ideal by creating the subaltern, the ignorant other in need of illumination from the superior holders of true knowledge, a position that sounds very much like the justification for colonialism. As Bauman points out, from this position, difference 'could not but be treated as a temporary nuisance; as an error, sooner or later bound to be supplanted by truth' (p. 11). As noted previously, when human rights are located within modernist assumptions of universality, truth, and rationality, they can become a justification for oppression, adding to the hierarchy of truth a hierarchy of morality (the good and the bad).

Although Rorty's and Bauman's analyses may seem to dislodge the unassailability of human rights as commonly understood, their eschewal of the dichotomous option of acceptance or rejection, and of seeing human rights as one among many possible cultural narratives may offer a way forward. It does so by opening human rights to a kind of interrogation that might lead to new forms of understanding, for example by questioning the themes of our human rights narrative, its plot, heroes, villains, antagonists, protagonists, victims, and possible endings.

A Way Forward?

I have suggested that the critique of foundational, universal, and essentialist positions may be a catalyst for new ways of approaching human rights. I now turn to some affirmative themes gleaned from the previous discussion.

Irony, Literature, and Language[16]

Both Rorty and Bauman make use of irony in their work.[17] In *Contingency, Irony, and Solidarity* (1989), Rorty describes the 'liberal ironist', someone who abhors cruelty (the liberal) and holds to the belief that all beliefs (including this one) are perspectival (the irony); that is, there is no ultimate truth because there are always multiple points of view. Similarly, Bauman begins his book *Wasted Lives* (2004) with the sentence, 'There is more than one way in which the story of modernity ... can be told. This book is one of such stories' (p. 1; cited in Tester, 2007: 84). For both men, irony serves to unsettle and, in doing so, to open a space for questioning, to 'show to men and women that what they have taken for granted is not really necessary and inevitable at all ...' (Tester, 2007: 88). Such questioning can lead to new forms of thought and understandings.

Irony has an important connection to literature and to language. Rorty's advocatory position regarding 'sentimental stories' is based on literature that appeals, for example, 'to sentiment, or vivid descriptions of what it is like to suffer as one of the oppressed' (p. 179). Bauman's writings frequently draw on a diverse (non-scientific) literature which he uses to illuminate and support his positions. This influence is also evident in their use of language. For example, Jacobsen and Poder (2012) note 'Bauman's frequent recourse to metaphors as a fertile way of describing and analysing the human world – metaphors such as 'tourist' and 'vagabond' which have captured the sociological imagination of many scholars around the world' (p. 8). Literature can also help people expand their linguistic repertoire so that new understandings can be formulated. Rather than discover Truth, one employs a different vocabulary to construct a new truth. As Rorty (1998) explains,

> To become fully persons [and therefore human] women, blacks, gays need to invent rather than discover themselves. They do so by creating a vocabulary in which they are persons, in the same way that those already considered fully persons (e.g., Caucasian males) have done '… by getting semantic authority over themselves' [and] 'succeed[ing] in having the language they had developed become part of the language that everybody spoke. (p. 225)

This idea of gaining 'semantic authority' is reminiscent of some of the writings on gender-neutral and person-first language. Extrapolated to the area of human rights it suggests an interesting possible direction for development. This seems particularly poignant at a time when the English language grows increasingly dominant to the point where it fills the global linguistic terrain and marginalizes indigenous languages.

In addition to irony, literature, and language, the postmodern/social constructionist perspectives discussed are an inducement to creative thinking. Hassan (1993) writes,

> as an artistic, philosophical, and social phenomenon, postmodernism veers toward open, playful, optative, provisional (open in time as well as in structure and space), disjunctive, or indeterminate forms, a discourse of ironies and fragments, a 'white ideology' of absences and fractures, a desire of diffractions, an invocation of complex, articulate silences. (p. 283)

Freed from the straightjacket of modernist rationality, concepts such as human rights can be considered in atypical ways as illustrated in the narrative approach. In the current climate of global politics such creative efforts seem worthy of exploration.

Concluding Thoughts: The Case for Retaining Human Rights

As I hope this chapter has shown, human rights are a controversial issue with proponents and detractors making erudite and sometimes impassioned arguments for a range of positions. In some cases, these arguments are made on philosophical grounds as in arguments for the foundational grounding of human rights; sometimes they are made on political grounds as in the rejection of liberalism; sometimes they are made on pragmatic grounds, based on an assessment of the current state of world affairs and how human rights have helped or hindered this situation. For example, some would argue that contemporary human rights doctrines as exemplified by the UDHR have been a failure, while others see human rights as responsible for important gains in the quality of life for people. These assessments will depend on how the primary purpose of human rights is viewed, for example as a restraint on the abuse of political power, as a way to reduce human suffering, or as a way to improve the quality of life worldwide. These positions lead to recommendations regarding how to extend or constrain the reach and scope of human rights. As discussed, some argue that our best action is the rational demonstration of particular rights, others that we should use sentimental stories. Some argue for universal rights, others that we should always acknowledge that we are operating from a particular cultural perspective. Some argue that we should adjudicate conflicts about rights by convincing others of the superiority of one position; others believe that rights should function as a way of regulating the process of decision making.

As is often the case, most positions contain, to varying degrees, elements of all of these considerations. In this chapter, I have expressed doubt about the attempts to philosophically ground human rights; however, part of my reservations stems from a pragmatic concern about whether a universal position could ever be implemented for anything other than the most basic necessities of life such as food and shelter. And even these seemingly 'obvious' rights cannot hope to be achieved without substantial changes the in global political and economic environment. This complexity, and the ability to cite 'evidence' in favor of a particular position, makes resolution of differences hard to achieve.

Despite such reservations, I would not want to see the abandonment of the idea of human rights. Simply put, human rights are too well established to advocate for their elimination. Pragmatically, such an effort would not be successful and would likely do great harm, especially for people for whom human rights are their only resource for identifying abuses or advocating for better living conditions. As Fields (2010) argues (drawing on the work of Andrew Levine, 1981), human rights are a 'strategic necessity' because 'at the present ideological and institutional moment there is no other device that can serve as such an effective reference point for criticism of the political and economic effects of contemporary dominant institutions' (p. 68). Similarly, Gasper (2007) makes the important point that 'Ordinary people can and do grasp and use the human rights concept ... and the fact that people hold such values makes rights systems an effective policy instrument and driving force' (p. 12; see also Elliot (2007)).

In addition to their political currency, human rights can provide an alternative to explanations of human behavior that lessen personhood. For example, psychological or medical explanations tend to justify restrictions or surveillance over others. They also tend to hold people individually responsible for their problems and life circumstances while diverting attention away from broader social conditions in which such explanations are legitimized and supported. Reframing these situations as human rights issues destigmatizes the problem and directs attention toward environmental and structural contexts. A powerful example has been the global effort to define violence against women as a human rights issue (e.g., Chapman, 1990; Fitzpatrick, 1993; Kelly, 2005).

While it is also true that human rights have been used to perpetuate or conceal abuses, this in itself is not a compelling reason for their elimination, although it remains a concern. We can never know how a particular idea will be taken up and used. There is no guarantee that *any* position will not be appropriated in a way that benefits the powerful in a society. As Foucault observed, any position, even if it is right, can be dangerous. If anything, such use is a reflection of the idea's authority rather than its incorrectness.

What we can do, and what I have tried to suggest, is retain the idea of human rights but take it up in a different way, for example by exploring new vocabularies for its expression, by changing our basic understandings of social life, and revisiting its foundation in modernist notions of truth. Instead of continuing to debate relatively intractable positions about the rational grounding or universality of human rights and why everyone should accept a particular position, we would be better off accepting human rights as a cultural expression and exploring respectful ways to communicate the merits of our positions such as the sentimental stories advocated by Rorty.

The struggle to make the world a better place is ongoing and daunting in its immensity and complexity. Yet, it is a worthwhile struggle and therefore one that we need to approach with humility and openness. Addressing this enormous challenge requires that we work on all levels, from the local to the global, and that we utilize all the resources that we can muster. This chapter is an attempt to add to the analytical frameworks and other resources that can be used to enhance the effectiveness of that struggle.

Notes

1 Although the word or the concept of human rights might not have been used, social workers were involved in work that we now would identify as human rights work.

2 Parts of this section are adapted from Witkin and Irving (2014).

3 I am not using entitlement to mean a government program as is common in the United States. Although such programs can represent the expression of entitlement, I am using the word to suggest a more general concept as a special kind of claim. Also, it should be noted that claiming something as an entitlement does not insure its acceptance as such.

4 Gordon (1998) points out that human rights express a kind of 'moral trump card' which ironically because of its extremism may actually suppress moral discourse. She traces this issue to the Nuremberg trials following the Second World War. Although the trials were a setting for the moral condemnation of Nazi atrocities, they turned a blind eye to atrocities of allied forces. 'The Nuremberg accusations, in the end, functioned not as an occasion for moral discourse, but as a moral diatribe which effectively excluded the possibility of moral discourse' (p. 391).

5 Katiuzhinsky and Okech (2014) discuss a similar position that they term (following Brems, 1997) an 'opt out' approach based on the belief that individuals 'have the right to participate in their [community's] decision-making processes that determine and develop the community's cultural life, [and also] the right to leave the community if they believe their cultural rights are threatened ...' (p. 85). There are at least two concerns I have with this position as presented. First, it is not clear how individuals who believed that their rights were threatened (they give the example of an arranged marriage) would make their case and to whom and how it would be adjudicated. Second, and most important, not everyone has the option of leaving the community thereby rendering this option an alternative primarily for the privileged and making it somewhat irrelevant as a supportive rights position.

6 Jones notes that diversity per se is not necessarily an issue as most differences among cultures will not matter in relation to human rights. Rather, he identifies differences in values as most important within and across cultures.

7 Gergen doubts that even accepting the pluralistic nature of beliefs would keep people from condemning and acting against beliefs they found egregious.

8 The sections on Richard Rorty and Zygmunt Bauman are modest revisions of text that originally appeared in Witkin and Irving (2014). Readers seeking more in-depth information should consult the references cited at the end of the chapter.

9 Parts of this section have been adapted from Witkin and Irving (2014).

10 The Helsinki Declaration (also known as the Helsinki Accords) was established in 1975 by the Conference on Security and Co-operation in Europe in an attempt to reduce Cold War tensions between the West and the Soviet Union. Among its ten articles are the 'respect for human rights and fundamental freedoms,

including the freedom of thought, conscience, religion or belief' and 'equal rights and self-determination of peoples'.

11 Of course, what is heard as a sad and sentimental story will be culturally determined.

12 In social work, Wronka (2007) also proposes a human rights culture although it seems based more on the idea of universal human rights as an entitlement of one's humanity.

13 Rorty takes a similar anti-foundationalist position on social justice. He opposes the idea of justice as being a universal moral obligation based on what is considered an ahistorical conception of rationality. Rather, he argues that what we call social justice can be viewed as loyalty to groups that are 'people like ourselves' – 'the group or groups to which one cannot be disloyal and still like oneself' (1993: 141). These groups can range in size from the very small, such as one's family, to the very large, such as humanity as a whole.

14 Parts of this section have been adapted from Witkin and Irving (2014).

15 One can see in this passage how both Bauman and Rorty are influenced by literature and have integrated a literary style of writing into their analyses.

16 Typically, irony refers to incongruity, either in reference to an event (what is expected and what actually happens), or in the use of language, conveying a meaning opposite to the literal one, that often is associated with humor.

17 Parts of this section have been adapted from Witkin and Irving (2014).

References

Bankston III, C. L. (2010). Social justice: Cultural origins of a perspective and a theory. *The Independent Review, 15*(2), 165–178.

Barreto, J.-M. (2011). Rorty and human rights: Contingency, emotions and how to defend human rights telling stories. *Utrecht Law Review, 7*(2), 93–112.

Bauman, Z. (1993). Postmodernity, or living with ambivalence. In J. Natoli & L. Hutcheon (Eds.), *A postmodern reader* (pp. 9–24). Albany, NY: State University of New York Press.

Bauman, Z. (2000). *Liquid modernity*. Cambridge: Polity Press.

Bauman, Z. (2004). *Wasted lives*. Cambridge: Polity Press.

Bauman, Z., & Tester, K. (2001). *Conversations with Zygmunt Bauman*. Cambridge: Polity Press.

Bonnycastle, C. R. (2011). Social justice along a continuum: A relational illustrative model. *Social Service Review, 85*(2), 267–295.

Brems, E. (1997). Enemies or allies? Feminism and cultural relativism as dissident voices in human rights discourse. *Human Rights Quarterly, 19*(1), 136–164.

Brinkmann, S. (2010). Human vulnerabilities: Toward a theory of rights for qualitative researchers. In K. D. Norman & M. D. Giardina (Eds.), *Qualitative inquiry and human rights* (pp. 82–99). Walnut Creek, CA: Left Coast Press.

Chapman, J. R. (1990). Violence against women as a violation of human rights. *Social Justice*, 17(2), 54–70.

Elliot, M. A. (2007). Human rights and the triumph of the individual in world culture. *Cultural Sociology*, 1(3), 343–363.

Fields, A. B. (2010). Human rights theory: Criteria, boundaries, and complexities. In K. D. Norman & M. D. Giardina (Eds.), *Qualitative inquiry and human rights* (pp. 66–81). Walnut Creek, CA: Left Coast Press.

Fitzpatrick, J. (1993). The use of international human rights norms to combat violence against women. In R. J. Cook (Ed.), *Human rights of women: national and international perspectives* (pp. 532–571). Philadelphia, PA: University of Pennsylvania Press.

Gasper, D. (2007). Human rights, human needs, human development, human security: Relationship between four international 'human' discourses. *Forum for Development Studies*, 34(1), 9–43.

Gergen, K. J. (2009). *Relational being: Beyond self and community*. Oxford University Press.

Gewirth, A. (1987). *Reason and morality*. Chicago: University of Chicago Press.

Gordon, J. (1998). The concept of human rights: The history and meaning of its politicization. *Brooklyn Journal of International Law*, 23, 689.

Griffin, J. (2008). *On human rights*. Oxford: Oxford University Press.

Habermas, J. (1994). Three normative models of democracy. *Constellations*, 1(1), 1–10.

Harré, R. (2005). An ontology for duties and rights. In N. J. Finkel & F. M. Moghaddam (Eds.), *The psychology of rights and duties: Empirical contributions and normative commentaries* (pp. 223–242). Washington, DC: American Psychological Association.

Hassan, I. (1993). Toward a concept of postmodernism. In J. P. Natoli & L. Hutcheon (Eds.), *A postmodern reader*. Albany, NY: State University of New York Press.

Healy, L. M. (2008). Exploring the history of social work as a human rights profession. *International Social Work*, 51, 735–748.

Ife, J. (2001). *Human rights and social work: Towards rights-based practice* (1st ed.). New York, NY: Cambridge University Press.

Ife, J. (2012). *Human rights and social work: Towards rights-based practice* (3rd ed.). New York, NY: Cambridge University Press.

Jacobsen, M. H., & Poder, P. (Eds.). (2012). *The sociology of Zygmunt Bauman: Challenges and critique*. Aldershot: Ashgate Publishing.

Jones, P. (2000). Human rights and diverse cultures: Continuity or discontinuity? *Critical Review of International Social and Political Philosophy*, 3(1), 27–50.

Jones, P. (2012). The value and limits of rights: A reply. *Critical Review of International Social and Political Philosophy*, 15(4), 495–516.

Katiuzhinsky, A., & Okech, D. (2014). Human rights, cultural practices, and state policies: Implications for global social work practice and policy. *International Journal of Social Welfare*, 23, 80–88.

Kelly, L. (2005). Inside outsiders: Mainstreaming violence against women into human rights discourse and practice. *International Feminist Journal of Politics*, 7(4), 471–495.

Klein, R. (2001). Cultural relativism, economic development and international human rights in the Asian context. *Touro International Law Journal, 9*, 1–70.

Kumar, C. (2005). Foucault and Rorty on truth and ideology: A pragmatist view from the left. *Contemporary Pragmatism, 2*(1), 35–93.

Langlois, A. J. (2004). The elusive ontology of human rights. *Global Society, 18*(3), 243–261.

Lemert, C., & Goodman, M. (2007). Liquid waste, being human, and bodily death. In A. Elloitt (Ed.), *The contemporary Bauman* (pp. 198–216). London: Routledge.

Levine, A. (1981). *Liberal democracy: A critique of its theory.* New York, NY: Columbia University Press.

Miller, D. (2012). Grounding human rights. *Critical Review of International Social and Political Philosophy, 15*(4), 407–427.

Nussbaum, M. (2002). Capabilities and social justice. *International Studies Review, 4*(2), 123–135.

Rawls, J. (1999). *A theory of justice* (rev. ed.). Cambridge, MA: Belknap.

Reamer, F. G. (1999). *Social work values and ethics* (2nd ed.). New York, NY: Columbia University Press.

Reichert, E. (2001). Move from social justice to human rights provides new perspective. *Professional Development: The International Journal of Continuing, 4*(1), 5–13.

Reichert, E. (2003). *Social work and human rights: A foundation for policy and practice.* New York, NY: Columbia University Press.

Reisch, M., Ife, J., & Weil, M. A. (2013). Social justice, human rights, values, and community practice. In M. Weil, M. Reisch & M. Ohmer (Eds.), *Handbook of community practice* (2nd ed.). (pp. 73–103). Thousand Oaks, CA: Sage Publications.

Rorty, R. (1989). *Contingency, irony, and solidarity.* Cambridge: Cambridge University Press.

Rorty, R. (1991). *Objectivity, relativism, and truth. Philosophical papers vol. 3.* Cambridge: Cambridge University Press.

Rorty, R. (1993). Human rights, rationality, and sentimentality. In *Truth and progress: Philosophical papers vol. 3.* (pp. 167–185). New York, NY: Cambridge University Press, 1998.

Rorty, R. (1998). *Truth and progress: Philosophical papers vol. 3.* Cambridge: Cambridge University Press.

Rozas, L. W., & Garran, A. M. (2015). Towards a human rights culture in social work education. *British Journal of Social Work, 46*(4), 1–16.

Sen, A. (1999). *Development as freedom.* Oxford, UK: Oxford University Press.

Skegg, A.M. (2005). Human rights and social work: A Western imposition or empowerment to the people? *International Social Work, 48*(5), 667–672.

Staub-Bernasconi, S. (2010). Human rights: Facing dilemmas between universalism and pluralism/contextualism. In D. Zaviršek, B. Rommelspacher, S. Staub-Bernasconi (Eds.) *Ethical dilemmas in social work: International perspective* (pp. 9–23). Faculty of Social Work, University of Ljubljana.

Steiner, H. (2012). Human rights and the diversity of value. *Critical Review of International Social and Political Philosophy, 15*(4), 395–406.

Tester, K. (2007). Bauman's irony. In A. Elliott (Ed.), *The contemporary Bauman* (pp. 81–97). London: Routledge.

Williams, M. (2003). Rorty on knowledge and truth. In C. Guigon & D. R. Hiley (Eds.), *Richard Rorty* (pp. 61–80). New York, NY: Cambridge University Press.

Witkin, S. L., & Irving, A. (2014). Postmodern perspectives on social justice. In M. Resich (Ed.), *Routledge international handbook of social justice*. New York, NY: Routledge.

Wronka, J. (1998). *Human rights and social policy in the 21st century: A history of the idea of Human Rights and comparison of the United Nations Universal Declaration of Human Rights with United States federal and state constitutions*. Lanham, MD: University Press of America.

Wronka, J. (2007). *Human rights and social justice: Social action and service for the helping and health professions*. Thousand Oaks, CA: Sage.

4 Difference, Noticing, and Cultural Competence

Cultural competence is an example of an idea that was developed for the best of reasons: to help social workers become more aware of, knowledgeable about, and sensitive to ethnic and cultural differences between them and their clients (e.g., Johnson & Munch, 2009; Ortega & Faller, 2014). It also is an example of how problem construction and responses to those constructions are shaped by the dominant discourses of society and our profession; in this case, by a modernist worldview that considers, among other things, knowledge about something as equivalent to understanding, that reifies concepts (converts them into things) and assumes that those 'things' can be known by translating them into discrete units of information. Finally, it is an example of how well-intentioned responses to perceived problems can have unanticipated, less-desirable consequences.

In this chapter I will attempt to illustrate these themes. Fundamentally, cultural competency is about difference and how it should be addressed. Although only certain differences such as ethnicity and race tend to be addressed, it can be helpful to think more generally about difference, how we come to notice (or not notice) it, why some differences are regarded as significant while others are inconsequential, and how they are understood and valued.

Difference is essential to noticing. We can only notice something in relation to something else. For example, if everything was blue would we notice it? We do not notice 'what is there' but what is perceivable, discernable, and intelligible within a particular context. This position has implications for how we address particular kinds of differences, such as those addressed by cultural competence. I discuss this in more detail later in the chapter.

Cultural Competency and Social Work

The idea of cultural competency began appearing in the social work literature in the early to mid-1990s (e.g., Dana, Behn, & Ganwa, 1992; Manoleas, 1994; Pierce & Pierce, 1996). Weaver (1999) views this emergence as a shift from a concern about sensitivity to cultural diversity to competency – having appropriate skills, knowledge and values. Generally this entails learning about the normative or characteristic beliefs, customs, norms, and values that characterize people from a particular culture or ethnic group. For example, we might want to learn how common gestures in Western cultures like shaking hands might be interpreted differently in other cultures, what is the preferred language for addressing a person from a different culture, or how an authority figure like a social worker might be perceived. Although this information might be useful to know, this approach can also have serious drawbacks. First, it reduces the concept of culture to a relatively static body of information that characterizes a group of people. Second, this approach presumes a general, a priori expertise that can be applied to certain identified persons. Third, it assigns a kind of 'master status' (Goffman, 1963) to the person based on their presumed cultural or ethnic identity ignoring or minimizing the multiplicity and intersectionality of identities people carry. Fourth, it views cultural competence as more of an individualistic, knowledge issue than a relational, ethical one.[1] Fifth, it encourages an instrumental and strategic orientation (Christopher, 2007).

Despite these limitations and shortcomings, I am not arguing for the elimination of the concept of cultural competence. Rather, my task will be to show that there can be other ways of approaching the notion of difference and of thinking about these issues in the context of social work practice. Toward these ends, I will discuss the concepts of difference, noticing, and culture and link them to a relational–moral position regarding our work with others.

Difference and Noticing

Difference is a complex concept that has been understood in many ways. A century ago, the Swiss linguist Ferdinand de Saussure proposed that language itself is based on difference, that is, words gain meaning by identifying what things are not rather than what they are. This idea was further developed by the French philosopher Jacques Derrida who showed how difference was required not only for perception but for sensemaking. Talk of X would not be intelligible unless it could be distinguished from non-X. For example, would 'human' be intelligible without the contrasting concept of 'non-human'? Derrida also explored how binaries both enable difference and limit our thinking. For instance, binaries like male–female tend to simplify concepts (in this case gender) and create more and less favored alternatives.

Similarly, the anthropologist Gregory Bateson described difference as requiring 'two somethings' in a relationship that rendered them perceivable. Bateson referred to this perception as information. For Bateson, difference in the material sense did not exist but was an abstraction (Bateson, 1979).

This resonates with a social constructionist perspective in which difference (and sameness) are based on societal beliefs and available language rather than the things themselves, for example consider perceiving differences among certain dogs based on their breed compared to the group of dogs labeled as 'mutts'.

These views suggest that noticing difference is relational and that what is noticed, or following Bateson, what is meaning-fully noticed, will be relational and this in turn will be a function of language, culture, and context. I will try to illustrate this by inviting you to conduct a little experiment. For the next two minutes look around the room you are in – after putting this book down – and write down what you notice.

What did you write? When I did this exercise some of the things I noted were a book shelf, books, papers, a computer, a calculator, a box of paper clips, a lamp, a photograph and … the list could go on almost indefinitely depending on, among other factors, the time devoted to the task and the level of detail desired. In fact, without specific restrictions, it would be hard to know when such a task could be considered completed.

One observation about my list (and presumably yours) is that I noticed things for which I have names. In some cases I identified what I noticed using categorical language; for example, furniture instead of a chair and table. In many such cases it could be argued that it is the conceptual category that I have noticed. For instance, I wrote that I noticed a box of paper clips not a small cardboard container of numerous twisted pieces of metal all in the same shape.

We might also consider what was not noticed. For instance, I did not notice my skin, the erasers on the top of my pencils, or my act of noticing. The first example might be explained by my skin being taken for granted in combination with there not being an obvious binary (not skin). I may not have noticed the erasers because we generally think of them as part of pencils rather than something separate. Finally, not noticing my act of noticing may have to do with the difficulty of being self-aware in the moment. All of these examples will be extended to the case of cultural competence.

To a certain extent, what I reported noticing is related to my interpretation of the instructions to look around and report what was noticed. This encouraged me to notice visually and externally. Consider, for instance, if I asked you to look inward and report what you notice, or to listen instead of look. How might your responses have been different? What if you were in a different setting? For example, think of how your noticing might be differently directed in a classroom, a hospital, or a bar. What we noticed would likely depend, in part, on our knowledge of the setting and our purpose for being there.

What I hope is clear is that noticing is not simply an act of transcribing an already existing external world but a highly conceptual and contextual interaction mediated by language. An implication of this position (suggested on p. 73) is that noticing can never be exhaustive, that is, it is not possible to notice all that could be noticed. Being aware of this can have important implications. As the psychiatrist R.D. Laing has written, 'The range of what we think and do is limited by what we fail to notice. And because we fail to notice that we fail to notice, there is little we can do to change; until we notice how failing to notice shapes our thoughts and deeds'. For Laing, not being aware that we fail to notice – even if we do not know *what* we are not noticing – makes us vulnerable to the influence of the not noticed. This is reminiscent of Foucault's notion of how power works invisibly as when assumptions and beliefs are taken as expressing 'the ways things are' thereby suppressing the consideration of alternatives. Analogously, we may believe that what we notice is what exists – that it could not be something else, or, to put it another way, that we notice Reality rather than interpreted realities.

Not only will noticing vary across contexts, but the usefulness and importance of what is noticed may be judged differently even within the same context.[2] For example, noticing dark clouds when in a small boat on the ocean would likely be considered important whereas noticing – in the same situation – how stylish your sailor hat is would not be judged similarly. This reminds me of an anecdote about a camping trip taken by Sir Arthur Conan Doyle's great fictional detective Sherlock Holmes and his assistant, Dr. Watson. After a good meal and a bottle of wine, they lay down for the night and went to sleep. Some hours later, Holmes, renowned for his powers of observation, awoke and nudged his faithful friend.

'Watson, look up and tell me what you see'.
Watson replied, 'I see millions and millions of stars'.
'What does that tell you?' Holmes asked.
Watson pondered for a minute. Then responded:
'Astronomically, it tells me that there are millions of galaxies and potentially billions of planets. Astrologically, I observe that Saturn is in Leo. Temporally, I deduce that the time is approximately a quarter past three. Theologically, I can see that God is all powerful and that we are small and insignificant. Meteorologically, I suspect that we will have a beautiful day tomorrow'.
Feeling quite proud of his observational abilities, Watson said to Holmes, 'Why, what does it tell YOU?'
Holmes was silent for a minute, then spoke, 'It tells me ... that someone stole our tent!'

Clearly, noticing is not just a matter of magnitude (the more you notice, the better) but relevance to the situation. Cultural competence in social work focuses on noticing particular things in situations involving people called clients. Are these noticings more like Watson's or Holmes'? That is a question I will explore.

The Relation of Noticing to Cultural Competence

As noted, we come to perceive something as different when we can contrast it with something else. That something else always has a name. Interestingly, although the 'something else' functions as the reference point for perceiving difference, it may have previously been overlooked (not noticed) until the 'other' was identified. A relevant example is noticing skin color. I suspect that people tended not to notice skin color until there was a language of color differences and these differences were considered meaningful.[3] In other words, this difference was given meaning that went beyond mere color, in particular when it became a sign for a different social status, kind of person, or a racial category.[4] This interpretation changed people's noticing. Over time, people stopped noticing skin color per se, but race.[5] Consider, for example, how people differentiate between a 'white person' with a suntan and a 'black person' whose skin color is lighter, or consider how young, 'white' children, who have not yet learned the concept of race, see a 'black person'. As Stuart Hall (1987) has written, 'The fact is 'black' has never been just there either … . It, too, is a narrative, a story, a history. Something constructed, told, spoken, not simply found' (p. 45). Similarly, the African-American writer James Baldwin (1998) comments that, 'No one is white before he/she came to America. It took generations, and a vast amount of coercion, before this became a white country' (p. 178). However, because whiteness functions as the de facto standard, it remains unnoticed for many, 'seen' as a non-color. This provides another example of being unaware of what is not noticed, or even that not noticing is occurring.

The above also illustrates how our socially constructed sense of what is considered as trivial or significant will be instrumental to our noticing. For example, we do not usually notice differences in the size of people's ear lobes; however, we do notice differences in other facial features, for example, certain eye shapes. These differences are noticed because they are part of a constellation of differences that constitute a particular social designation that has significance in Western societies. These histories and their linguistic expressions influence our noticing – and our not noticing.

Noticing makes things available for our sensemaking (Starbuck & Milliken, 1988). Approaches like cultural competence training guides our noticing in particular directions. Things considered important become easier to notice, other things become more difficult. Remember, however, that as a socially constructed activity, noticing can always be reinterpreted and re-languaged to be something else. This seems particularly the case with social concepts. For example, what does it mean to notice anxiety or hyperactivity? Are we noticing something that exists independent of our interpretations? How could we even know if that was the case? The point is that such noticing can be renegotiated or revised depending on a multitude of factors. This seems true even with people whom we identify as sharing our own culture. Think how much more difficult it might be with those who do not share your general cultural knowledge or forms of expression.

Because we notice interpreted realities, there is an arbitrariness in noticing one thing rather than another. For example, if I notice 'anger' then I do not notice several related and possibly equally plausible states such as displeasure, alienation, estrangement, resentment, dissatisfaction, disappointment, or exasperation that have somewhat different mean-ings (particularly in a social work context) and might evoke different responses. Our interpretations will deflect or obscure our ability to notice other things. Although those promoting cultural competence may not intend to keep social workers from noticing particular things, the focus on particular normative characteristics will draw our attention to certain interpreted realities. While such reduction facilitates deliberative action, it is important – as Laing reminds us – to be aware that there is much that we are not noticing and that what we do notice could be otherwise. At a minimum, this awareness should encourage us to hold our perceptions loosely, treating them as expressing one of many possible perspectives.

Noticing that is considered meaningful also will prompt other, related noticing. For example, noticing 'ethnicity' will lead to noticings believed to be related to it. And because we act in relation to what we notice, these noticings may also *produce* other noticings. That is, if a social worker in an authorita-tive position relative to a client acts in a way consistent with her beliefs about some aspect of the client's ethnicity, then the client is positioned to act in a way that supports the worker's action. This sequence may then be seen as confirming the worker's original belief. While such interactions may provide workers with an appealing sense of 'knowing what to do', it may also impose restrictions on the relationship including who the other may become. An alternative position would be to maintain an uncertain, tentative, and ques-tioning approach that allows for multiple and changing noticing.

Other Issues Related to Cultural Competence

Not All Differences Are Equal. The association of certain differences with social disadvantage and their relative non-representativeness among social workers has provided justification for teaching social workers to notice various signs of such difference, for example, physical features, manners of speaking, and dress. This noticing is part of what it means to become 'competent' in the other's 'culture'. Learning things like different cultural norms about personal space and gender relations does not necessarily mean that these differences will be respected. In some cases, like personal space, practitioners would likely respect the difference, not wishing to 'violate' this different cultural norm. However, in the other cases like gender relations that may be deemed 'oppressive' in the host culture, clients may be encouraged to conform to the practitioner's beliefs.[6] Thus, knowledge of another culture does not mean abandoning one's own cultural values or even giving priority to another's practice that is experienced as offensive, nor am I arguing that one should or could do so. However, it seems to me that good practice would encourage practitioner transparency of her or his position. That is, it would require reflection on our own standpoint and cultural values and how they influence our understandings and responses. This might encourage explicitly acknowledging the cultural foundation of one's position rather than asserting its superiority.[7]

Individualism. Cultural competence can be viewed as a way of understanding the challenges that social workers face when working with people from different cultures, ethnicities, and races. By claiming a solution to this issue it also reinterprets it. Competency is an individual concept. To be competent at something means that you can perform a task well. As an individualistic concept, cultural competency underemphasizes the social, relational context of social work practice as the site where meanings are negotiated and realities generated. It seems to take the position that one can become competent through the acquisition of certain knowledge apart from the context in which such knowledge will be applied. Relationality from the perspective of cultural competency seems analogous to being computer literate. The alien Other is like a computer whose responses to a social worker will depend on the latter having the 'right' knowledge and applying it correctly. Relationship is secondary to individual knowledge.

Essentialism. From an individualistic, instrumental perspective, culture is reduced to something in which a social worker can become competent by acquiring the appropriate knowledge and skills. It becomes, in Park's (2005) term, 'commodified', 'classified as a body of knowledge which can be studied, disseminated, and acquired …' (p. 24). Culture is treated somewhat monolithically emphasizing sameness (and underemphasizing diversity) around a relatively fixed set of beliefs and values that are believed to characterize the essence of the culture. This position is known as essentialism. According to Holliday (2010), 'Essentialism presents people's individual behaviour as entirely defined and constrained by the cultures in which they live so that the stereotype becomes the essence of who they are' (p. 4). He goes on to note that despite essentialism's negative connotation, it remains a frequent aspect of cultural understanding. Such a perspective, supports the establishment of cultural competency training programs, an industry in its own right.

Essentialism leads to a cultural chauvinism in which the defining ethos of other cultures is viewed as inferior to one's own. Holliday (2010) illustrates this in the characterization of cultures as adhering to individualism or collectivism. The former, associated with Western cultures, is portrayed as superior. Park (2005) draws on the same example within the social work literature further arguing that allusions to notions that cultures change and that individuals identify differentially with cultural norms still assume 'a static core culture' around which these characteristics vary (p. 23).

Within the context of cultural competence, culture functions as a stand-in for racial and ethnic minorities in a way that positions these groups as inferior others. Using critical discourse analysis, Park (2005) also shows how the taken-for-grantedness of the concept 'culture' in the social work literature makes programs in cultural competence vulnerable to generating the very ideals that they claim to confront. It does this by leaving problematic assumptions unexamined, for example, 'the notion that culture is that which differentiates minorities, immigrants, and refugees from the rest of society' (p. 19).

This assumption produces another one: that the majority, ruling population is 'culturefree'. Culture becomes a concept that signifies a dividing line separating the normative non-cultured 'White' majority from the culture-bound Others (e.g., Perry, 2001). This is similar to the previous discussion about the invisibility of whiteness. As a trope, culture also entices by appearing to support social workers' sympathies for a non-victim-blaming approach: it is not you, but your culture, in which I must become 'competent'. Although Park does not provide alternative views of culture, others have. For example, instead of viewing culture as a fixed set of common meanings, Wedeen (2002) describes a semiotic perspective in which culture is considered as practices of sense making 'through which social actors attempt to make their world coherent' (p. 720). This standpoint foregrounds language's constitutive and performative functions and how meaning is connected to structural arrangements, historical processes, and 'changing relations of power' (p. 714). Thus, it is important to keep the concept of culture complex and inclusive of social workers and the people they serve.

Situational contexts. Social workers and clients interact within various settings (e.g., offices, homes) for particular purposes. These settings and purposes will likely have different meanings for each of them (based on myriad factors) and influence their orientation toward the encounter. As the encounter unfolds, each will likely attempt to position herself/himself and the other based on their ongoing interpretation of the situation (e.g., friendly, hostile, confusing, restrictive) in relation to their objectives (e.g., to obtain basic necessities, assign a diagnosis). *How* they do this also will be influenced by many factors such as their linguistic repertoire, beliefs, importance of their needs, and perceived differences in authority.

Given the complexity of these situations (the multiplicity of factors, their differential importance, varieties of their expression and interpretation, how they interact), it is not possible to predict how a particular encounter will develop. However, when increasing certainty (as implied in cultural competency approaches) is no longer a goal, and an appreciation of this complexity embraced, a reflective and open stance in relation to others and a receptivity toward alternative ways of approaching these encounters is invited. Some possibilities are taken up in the next section.

Going Forward

I have argued that difference and similarity are socially constructed, not dependent on 'what is there' but on various social, cultural, contextual, and relational factors. Thus, it is always possible to identify differences and similarities between social workers and the people that they serve just as, more generally, we can easily point out differences and similarities among everyone. Cultural competence focuses on particular categorical differences. Based on an understanding of those differences, social workers learn knowledge and skills intended to make a difference in the quality and effectiveness of services.

Knowledge of social categories can be helpful in understanding how these categories have influenced what people assigned to those categories believe, how they are treated, and how they may act. On the other hand, a categorical approach may make it difficult to notice how they are unlike their categorical descriptors or their ability to recognize and accommodate to different situations. It also minimizes the influence of structural factors, situational contexts, and relationship. More broadly, the very belief that we can understand or know another through any knowledge system may restrict others' uniqueness and potential particularly in relationships of unequal power. Thus, how we understand and approach relationships precedes what we think we should know about them and should be our first concern.

On Knowing the Other

As social workers, we have an obligation to help generate spaces in which people, particularly vulnerable people, can speak freely. As Krog (2011) puts it, 'We have to find ways in which the marginalized can enter our discourses in their own genres and their own terms so that we can learn to hear them'. We also 'have a duty to listen and understand them through engaging in new acts of becoming' (p. 384). This raises some pertinent questions: can this kind of communication occur within a context in which the social worker is an a priori knower of the other? What 'new acts of becoming' might facilitate a positioning where a different kind of listening and understanding might be possible? How can we practice a kind of 'radical relationality' in which 'the ethical ideal is to increase one's ability to enter into modes of relation with multiple others' (Braidotti, 2008: 16)?

One response to these questions is based on the work of Emmanual Levinas (e.g., 1979, 1981), a French philosopher (originally from Lithuania), Jewish theologian, and social theorist, whose work was deeply affected by the experiences – including his personal experiences – of the Second World War. These experiences led Levinas to develop a unique ethical philosophy based on a profound relational responsibility to the Other.[8] Although not widely known in social work, his work has been taken up by some social work scholars, notably Ben-Ari and Strier (2010) and Rossiter (2011) in ways that are directly relevant to the current discussion.

A fundamental assumption of Levinas's philosophy is that ethics precedes knowledge (Levinas, 1961/1979). That is, we first need to ask what kind of relationship is necessary for knowledge to be possible. This is the opposite of the cultural competency position, which assumes that knowledge of the Other is a prerequisite for an ethical relationship. Another fundamental difference is that whereas cultural competence is based on a knowable Other, Levinas argues the Other cannot be known. Finally, whereas cultural competency focuses on particular Others, primarily those assigned to certain ethnic and racial categories, for Levinas the Other is all people with whom one interacts.

According to Levinas, trying to understand the Other through the acquisition of knowledge is a form of violence. While on its face this sounds like a harsh position, for Levinas this violence is symbolic (although no less real) in that it denies the uniqueness of the Other. It does so by capturing them within a priori beliefs and concepts. Rossiter (2011) explains, 'For Levinas, the face of the Other looks at us and implicitly says 'Do not kill me', meaning *do not kill my singularity by making me an example of a pre-existing conceptual schema. If you do this, you murder my uniqueness*' (p. 985, emphasis in original). In other words, the seemingly reasonable desire to understand the Other through knowledge is an exercise in Western rationality that constructs a *noticeable* Other, but this very act of making the Other noticeable also makes them not noticeable while erasing awareness of our not noticing.

The concept of the Other is foundational to social work (Chambon, 2013). In contemporary analyses, the Other is viewed as subaltern, that is, as part of a group that is socially and politically marginalized and denied social mobility (e.g., Krishnaswamy & Hawley, 2008). From this perspective, the Other is viewed as a consequence of unjust social practices and proper knowledge is needed to restore ethical social relations (Todd, 2001). Levinas, however, sees knowledge itself as an ethical question and secondary to relationship.[9] Our encounters with Others are pre-cognitive and the proper relationship is one which acknowledges what he calls infinity – the recognition that the Other will always exceed our representations of them and that knowing, in a cognitive sense, is not possible (Rossiter, 2011).[10] In contrast, approaches like cultural competence, that assume knowing the Other through knowledge about them, are based on what Levinas calls totality: the reduction of individuals to cognitive categories and the imposition of a reality that attempts to transform otherness into sameness.

Levinas's concern about the Other and our relationship with them is germane to the broader questions of difference that I have raised. Human differences are commonly identified with socially significant categories such as race, ethnicity, culture, physical appearance, typicality, and so on. These identifications and the names we give to them will draw our noticing in certain directions. Particularly relevant within the context of this chapter is the identification of differences associated with social disadvantage. This broader perspective extends our analysis to people categorized in ways not usually identified within cultural competence discourse, for example people diagnosed with Alzheimer's and other disabilities. Although not identified as part of a culture in the usual sense of those concerned with cultural competence, these groups experience an extreme form of 'othering'. Not surprisingly, some of the issues and controversies in this field can enhance the present discussion.

One such issue is how knowledge (or discourses) pertaining to a particular group constructs relationships between helpers such as social workers and those being helped. In the case of Alzheimer's or people with other disabilities, and cultural competence, it can be argued that a certain understanding (e.g., medical model, essentialism) influences noticing of particular qualities and the non-noticing of others. Although specific issues may be highlighted in relation to differences associated with Alzheimer's (e.g., personhood) and 'culture' (e.g., ethos), in both situations Levinas's emphasis on relationship and his approach to difference is apposite. For example, Mitchell, Dupuis, and Kontos (2013) use Olthuis's (1997) Levinasian-informed concept of 'knowing other-wise' to radically reframe the perceived differences associated with people diagnosed with Alzheimer's as 'the space of emergent wisdom' (p. 13) and 'potential growth' that provides 'an opportunity for engagement and expansion of our own understanding ...' (p. 12). In other words, difference in this case is not viewed as an aberration to be fixed or pitied, but as an opportunity for expressing my responsibility to the Other and in doing so to transcend the limits of my understanding.[11] It entails a radical respect that goes beyond tolerating difference to the active embracing of the Other's singularity. This is a moral rather than an instrumental position remindful of Zygmunt Bauman's discussion of moral capacity,[12] which, as noted at the beginning of the chapter, 'consists in the capacity and the will to take the point of view of the other and the good of the other as seen in that view for one's prime concern even if no rule commands one to do so in a given case; and to take responsibility for one's responsibility for the other's good – also for one's responsibility for the other's right to define that good' (Bauman, 1998: 15). Like Levinas, Bauman emphasizes our responsibility to the Other but in a way that respects the Other's freedom 'to define that good'.

Similarly, Veck (2014), working from the context of special education, draws on Levinas to consider the differences between moral positions based on 'guidelines for action' that lead to applying effective practices to designated problems (i.e., those that engender the 'special' in special education), and those that precede knowledge and assume unknown possibilities. The former position is linked to Levinas's notion of intentionality (Levinas, 2006), which, in practical terms, refers to the imposition of one's knowledge of the Other, the consequence being the 'reduction of the Other to the Same' (Levinas, 2006: 139, cited in Veck, 2014: 455). Instead, following Levinas, Veck proposes a stance in which the Other 'precedes and goes beyond my knowing' and whose 'face' demands more than I can know, who is 'irreducible to any category' and exceeds my capacity to know. Knowing the Other is replaced by 'a radical alterity, totally exterior and inaccessible, and nonetheless acknowledg[ing] the obligation towards her and be[ing] able to hear her call for help' (Amiel-Houser & Mendelson-Maez, 2014: 206). How can such a relational stance be translated into practice in a manner that stays true to its precepts? It is to this challenge I now turn.

Applying Levinas

The complexity of Levinas's philosophy as well as its radical and transformative potential presents challenges for its application. Put succinctly, it does not fit within the assumptions of conventional pedagogy about learning and teaching, or the structures in which those assumptions are inscribed. We are left with the conundrum of fitting the square peg of Levinasian ethics into the round hole of knowledge-based pedagogy. The foundational presupposition of knowing about others through the acquisition of information contradicts a Levinasian-inspired training or education. Yet, dropping this presupposition may relocate a teacher in an unfamiliar landscape without navigational tools.

What remains, as Veck (2014) comments, is 'a strange form of *teaching* that adds nothing to the sum total of one's comprehension but instead teaches the Other's otherness to comprehension' (p. 457, emphasis in original).

How do we teach a way of respecting differences that is 'beyond knowledge' but relational (Ben-Ari and Strier, 2010: 2162)? Or 'a radical openness that is not seeking to 'understand' or 'know' the other …' (Todd, 2001: 70). Both Rossiter (2011) and Ben-Ari and Strier (2010) struggle to find a way to translate Levinas's philosophy into something that can be taught within the accepted epistemological parameters of education. Rossiter, for example, comes up with creative expressions such as 'razor's edge …' as a sort of acknowledgement of the difficulty of capturing Levinas's ideas in words that can be taught to others. Ben-Ari and Strier (2010) identify openness and humility but are vague on how these qualities would be taught.[13] In the field of education, Todd (2001) proposes three approaches that express a Levinasion orientation: (1) Education as applied ethics – rather than teaching about ethics, viewing education itself as a form of ethical practice. (2) The quality of relationality – shifting from an emphasis on content to the quality of relations and 'whether the Otherness of the Other is supported within these relations' (p. 72). (3) Teaching with Ignorance, or learning from the Other – approaching teaching with an openness and susceptability to learning from the Other and 'with our capacity to enter into a 'veritable conversation' that places us on ethical ground' (p. 73).

These struggles suggest the need for a complementary change in the 'culture' of education – a transformative shift from an individualistic knowledge-based orientation to one that is relational and morality-based. This shift would reorder priorities from what others need to know to our responsibility to the Other. Thus, although I will present some additional ideas about how some of Levinas's ideas may be appropriated to an educational context, I am mindful that there may be little institutional support for (or even opposition to) them. What follows are some ideas that resonate in part with Levinas's position that may have utility for education in social work and related fields.

Humility and Cultural Humility

In common parlance, humility is considered an individual quality or virtue characterized by self-abasement and modesty. Based on a literature review of humility in psychology, Tangney (2000) concluded that its key elements included accurate self-assessment, acknowledgement of limitations, openness to new information, even if contradictory, and maintaining perspective about one's abilities and accomplishments. To be humble (in this context) is to be aware that there is much about others that you do not know.

Although a Levinasion orientation encourages approaching others from a posture of humility rather than competence, Levinas extends these meanings beyond an epistemic (i.e., knowledge-based) humility. That is, our humility is not based on a rational assessment of our cognitive limitations, but is the expression of a relational ethic stemming from our non-reciprocal responsibility to the Other; the other's uniqueness and our dependence on them (Chiarenza, 2012). For Levinas (1979) the face of the Other 'opens the primordial discourse whose first word is obligation' (p. 201). It is a responsibility that compels us to care for and respect the Other.

The concept of humility as an alternative to cultural competence (that is, *cultural* humility) was first proposed by Tervalon & Murray-Garcia (1998) in a health services context. In contrast to competence, their approach stressed professionals' critical self-awareness, in particular of their own cultural identities and understandings and the power dynamics between them and their patients. They also stressed the importance of a commitment to lifelong reflection and learning. While not explicit about the primacy of the ethical relation between self and Other, their approach provides a beginning alternative to a predominantly knowledge- and skill-based approach.

Others have developed variants or additions to Tervalon & Murray-Garcia's ideas. For example, Ortega and Faller (2014), writing from a child welfare perspective, emphasized an understanding of the complexity of culture and the intersectionality of cultural identities as underpinning cultural humility. While also identifying self-awareness and openness as critical dimensions, they add, similar to Tangney's (2000) perspective, the idea of transcendence, 'the reality that the world is far more complex and dynamic then perhaps they can imagine' (p. 33).

Another interesting extension of Tervalon & Murray-Garcia is 'narrative humility' (DasGupta, 2008). The focus here is on 'acknowledge[ing] that our patients' stories are not objects that we can comprehend or master, but rather dynamic entities that we can approach and engage with, while simultaneously remaining open to their ambiguity and contradiction, and engaging in constant self-evaluation and self-critique about issues such as our own role in the story, our expectations of the story, our responsibilities to the story, and our identifications with the story – how the story attracts or repels us because it reminds us of any number of personal stories' (p. 981). The authors further argue that substituting narrative humility for cultural humility extends it to all people rather than only the culturally different and sensitizes us to the conditions that enable or inhibit narratives and shape the kinds of stories told (for an extended exposition of the latter, see Holstein & Gubrium, 2008).

Relationality

Adopting a posture of humility may invite the kind of relationship that approximates the openness and respect that Levinas envisions; however, this literature tends to focus more on the individual than the relationship per se. Rather, for Levinas humility is a relation in which the Other is engaged via supplication and uncertainty, and prior to any categorization (Clegg & Slife, 2005).

There is a certain congruence between this position and social constructionist perspectives although for the latter the justification may be more pragmatic than ethical. For social constructionists, relationships precede individuals. That is, relationships are not formed by separate individuals coming together, rather it is relational processes that form the basis for the emergence of selves (Gergen, 2011). There would be no self without relationships. Thus, the selves that are manifested in social interaction emerge and change within a contextual, dynamic interpersonal performance.

From this relational perspective, knowledge is not an individual possession used to thematize the Other, but generated within structurally bounded relationships. Thus, each encounter is an opportunity to co-construct what is taken as knowledge, however incomplete. Whatever knowledge I may hold from past relationships and the authority of my position is suspended in deference to my responsibility to the Other. This is coupled with the awareness that such relational encounters put into play each interlocutor's sense of personhood and life world within the 'local, historical, and discursive traditions that make certain ways of coordinating with others possible and eliminate other options' (McNamee, 2012: 153), and the power dynamics at play. We cannot be aware of all the forces influencing such encounters (although we can be aware that we are not aware) and therefore they cannot be overcome. Therefore, we approach encounters not with the aim of using knowledge to understand others, but with a curiosity about what might emerge. In this sense we retain an openness to unpredictability and surprise trusting in the relationship to lead us. Although having conceptualizations may be inevitable, they are held tentatively with the recognition that contextual and relationship dynamics will necessitate change (Slife & Wiggins, 2009). Through our efforts to model humility, openness, and self-reflection, we try to create a relational space in which interactants are free to assume different subject positions that are self- and other-affirming.

Both cultural humility and relationality as discussed are considered orientations to relationships with others[14] that are primarily ethical and relational rather than informational. Consequently, teaching such orientations invites going beyond knowledge-saturated approaches that depend on 'legitimized' information sources such as textbooks and research studies to alternative sources such as film, novels, poetry, narrative, performance, and first-person accounts that do not prescribe an intellectually right way to respond to others or what is necessary to know, but evoke affective responses, reflection, uncertainty, and ambiguity. Emphasis is on dialogue in which students can respond to the 'susceptibility to the other' (Sinha, 2010: 473), to go beyond the formalism of the rational, and to engage in open and risky ways that enable the possibility of transformation. As Sinha expounds

> the relational form of dialogue is ambiguous and risky. It indicates a movement towards the other where one's responsiveness to the other indicates the possibility of the disruption of conventional and comfortable ways of being, thinking and acting. Moreover, it can be understood to be driven by ambiguity from the very start. (2010: 472–473)

Although social work encounters often have a specific pragmatic aim – for example, to identify needed services, to help someone negotiate administrative procedures, to qualify someone for material assistance – this does not negate maintaining a relational, dialogical stance. Healy (2011: 165) articulates such an integrative approach

> ... we need to allow others to articulate their own positions in their own terms and accord them the status of equal partners in the conjoint exploration of a topic, to the extent that we are prepared to allow their views actively to challenge our own 'settled opinion', to modify our preconceptions when they are found wanting, and to learn from what they have to tell us rather than simply asserting the superiority of our own viewpoint ... to stop treating those who occupy different discursive standpoints either as mirror images of ourselves or as denizens of a deficient socio-cultural standpoint who need to prove themselves to us before we will accord them a respectful hearing, and instead recognise that they represent a position comparable in value to our own from which we can productively learn.

Concluding Thoughts

In this chapter, I have attempted to explore and analyze the concept and practice of cultural competence within the context of difference. I pointed out the limitations of taking a knowledge-based approach to difference drawing from the philosophy of Emmanual Levinas. According to Levinas, ethics must precede knowledge or we risk doing violence to others by reducing them to our conceptual categories and suppressing their singularity. Instead, we must be willing to live with uncertainty, prioritizing our responsibility to the Other, even while knowing it can never be fulfilled. Adopting this stance presents pedagogical challenges as it requires changes not typically supported by educational institutions or understood by students. In response, I briefly discussed two possible orientations – cultural humility and relationality – that accord with some aspects of Levinas's philosophy. These provide a beginning alternative to addressing the ubiquity of difference in a manner that is respectful of others' uniqueness and facilitative of unrealized potential. It should be noted that my critique of information and skills as the primary components of cultural competence does not mean that there is no place for them. Rather, my intent was to argue for an alternative perspective in which the emphasis would be relational and ethical. My hope is that consideration of this position will broaden and enrich readers' understanding of this important topic.

Notes

1 Cultural competency can be applied to different levels of service delivery. For instance, at the macro (policy) level it may refer to the kinds of services that are needed by different cultural and ethnic groups and their availability. Analyses may focus on the extent to which services are based on assumptions of the dominant culture. These are important issues; however, in this chapter my focus will be on interpersonal encounters.

2 There is a thornier issue of whether noticing and context are separable as both might be considered social constructions; however, I will leave this for you, the reader, to ponder.

3 Even in relatively homogeneous societies, people will have variations in skin color that likely will not be noticed until such variation is given social meaning. This suggests that noticing is an active process. Differences do not just impose themselves upon us. Rather, we construct them from our cultural and social beliefs.

4 Color rarely stood alone but was part of a constellation of differences that included physical characteristics and national origins.

5 Color itself is a concept as are the different names we have for colors. This is not to deny the biological basis for perceiving colors, but to emphasize how they become an inseparable aspect of the interpreted realities that we see; e.g., blue sky, green grass, red blood.

6 The issue of how we come to decide which differences should be respected and which should be ignored or opposed is an important one, but beyond the scope of this chapter.

7 I am not excluding the possibility that there might be multiple views within a culture about a particular practice. However, in this case the practitioner would still be responding as an outsider.

8   Since Levinas's position does not fit with the three major ethical theories – deontology, utilitarian, and virtue – there is some disagreement on whether it represents an ethical philosophy, a metaethics, or something different.

9   Social constructionists also view relationship as primary, not as an ethical necessity but as a precondition for understanding. For example, Gergen (2009) asserts that 'relationships stand prior to all that is intelligible' (p. 6).

10 Levinas's position is pre-cognitive, a fundamental imperative at the moment of encounter.

11 It is important to note that this position is not in opposition to the provision of activities designed to ameliorate the suffering of people or to enhance their social functioning.

12 Also influenced by Levinas (e.g., Bauman & Tester, 2001).

13 They also identify maintaining an anti-oppressive orientation; however, while appealing, it is hard to see how this would be an expression of Levinas's philosophy.

14 This orientation can be conceptualized in different ways. In the case of cultural humility as an attitude, a category of virtues, or a posture. In the case of relationality as the expression of an ontological position, a metatheoretical framework, a pragmatic positioning that aligns with values.

References

Amiel-Houser, T., & Mendelson-Maez, A. (2014). Against empathy: Levinas and ethical criticism in the 21st century. *Journal of Literary Theory, 8*, 199–218.

Baldwin, J. (1998). On being 'white' and other lies. In D. R. Roediger (Ed.) *Black on white: Black writers on what it means to be white* (pp. 177–180). New York, NY: Schocken Books.

Bateson, G. (1979). *Mind and nature: A necessary unity.* New York, NY: E.P. Dutton.

Bauman, Z. (1998). On universal morality and the morality of universalism. *The European Journal of Development Research, 10*(2), 7–18.

Bauman, Z., & Tester, K. (2001). *Conversations with Zygmunt Bauman.* Cambridge: Polity Press.

Ben-Ari, A., & Strier, R. (2010). Rethinking cultural competence: What can we learn from Levinas? *British Journal of Social Work, 40*, 2155–2167.

Braidotti, R. (2008). In spite of the times: The postsecular turn in feminism. *Theory Culture Society, 25*, 1–25.

Chambon, A. (2013). Recognising the other, understanding the other: A brief history of social work and Otherness. *Nordic Social Work Research, 3*(2), 120–129.

Chiarenza, A. (2012). Developments in the concept of 'cultural competence'. In D. Ingleby, A. Chiarenza, W. Deville, & I. Kotsioni (Eds.), *Inequalities in health care for migrants and ethnic minorities, volume 2* (pp. 66–81). Antwerp, Belgium: Garrant.

Christopher, J. C. (2007/2008). Culture, moral topographies, and interactive personhood. *Journal of Theoretical and Philosophical Psychology, 27*(2) & *28*(1), 170–191.

Clegg, J. W., & Slife, B. D. (2005). Epistemology and the hither side: A Levinasian account of relational knowing. *European Journal of Psychotherapy & Counselling, 7*(2), 65–76.

Dana, R. H., Behn, J. D., & Ganwa, T. (1992). A checklist for the evaluation of cultural competence on social work agencies. *Research on Social Work Practice, 2*, 220–233.

DasGupta, S. (2008). Narrative humility. *The Lancet, 371*, 980–981.

Gergen, K. J. (2011). The self as social construction. *Psychological Studies, 56*(1), 108–116.

Goffman, E. (1963). *Stigma: Notes on the management of spoiled identity.* New York, NY: Simon and Schuster.

Hall, S. (1987). Minimal selves. In L. Appignanesi (Ed.), *Identity: The real me: Postmodernism and the question of identity.* London: Institute of Contemporary Arts.

Healy, P. (2011). Situated cosmopolitanism, and the conditions of its possibility: Transformative dialogue as a response to the challenge of difference. *Cosmos and History: The Journal of Natural and Social Philosophy, 7*(2), 157–178.

Holliday, A. (2010). *Intercultural communication and ideology.* London: Sage.

Holstein, J. F., & Gubrium, J. A. (Eds.). (2008). *Handbook of constructionist research.* New York, NY: Guilford Press.

Johnson, Y. M., & Munch, S. (2009). Fundamental contradictions in cultural competence. *Social Work, 54*(3), 220–231.

Krishnaswamy, R., & Hawley J. C. (2008). Postcolonial and globalization studies: Connections, conflicts, complicities. In R. Krishnaswamy, & J. C. Hawley (Eds.), *The postcolonial and the global* (pp. 2–21). Minneapolis, MN: University of Minnesota Press.

Krog, A. (2011) In the name of human rights: I say (how) you (should) speak (before I listen). In N. K. Denzin, & Y. S. Lincoln (Eds.), *Handbook of qualitative research* (4th ed.) (pp. 381–385). Thousand Oaks, CA: Sage.

Levinas, E. (1979). *Totality and infinity: An essay on exteriority* (Vol. 1) (translation: Alphonso Lingis). Springer (original work published in 1961).

Levinas, E. (1981). *Otherwise than being, or, beyond essence* (A. Lingis, trans.). The Hague: Nijhoff (original work published in 1974).

Levinas, E. (2006). Diachrony and representation (M. B. Smith, & B. Haeshav, trans.). In *Entrenous: Thinking-of-the-other* (pp. 137–153). London: Continuum.

Manoleas, P. (1994). An outcome approach to assessing the cultural competence of MSW students. *Journal of Multicultural Social Work, 3*(1), 43–57.

McNamee, S. (2012). From social construction to relational construction: Practices from the edge. *Psychological Studies, 57*(2), 150–156.

Mitchell, G. J., Dupuis, S. L., & Kontos, P. C. (2013). Dementia discourse: From imposed suffering to knowing other-wise. *Journal of Applied Hermeneutics, 5*, 1–19.

Olthuis, J. H. (Ed.). (1997). *Knowing other-wise: Philosophy at the threshold of spirituality.* New York, NY: Fordham University Press, 1997.

Ortega, R. M., & Faller, K. C. (2014). Training child welfare workers from an intersectional cultural humility perspective: A paradigm shift. *Child Welfare, 90*(5), 27–49.

Park, Y. (2005). Culture as deficit: A critical discourse analysis of the concept of culture in contemporary social work discourse. *Journal of Sociology and Social Welfare, 32*(3), 11–33.

Perry, P. (2001). White means never having to say you're ethnic: White youth and the construction of 'cultureless' identities. *Journal of Contemporary Ethnography, 30*, 56–91.

Pierce, R. L., & Pierce, L. H. (1996). Moving toward cultural competence in the child welfare system. *Children & Youth Services Review, 18*, 713–731.

Rossiter, A. (2011). Unsettled social work: The challenge of Levinas's ethics. *British Journal of Social Work, 41*, 980–995.

Sinha, S. (2010). Dialogue as a site of transformative possibility. *Studies in the Philosophy of Education, 29*, 459–475.

Slife, B. D., & Wiggins, B. J. (2009). Taking relationship seriously in psychotherapy: Radical relationality. *Journal of Contemporary Psychotherapy, 39*, 17–24.

Starbuck, W. H., & Milliken, F. J. (1988). Executives' personal filters: What they notice and how they make sense. In D. Hambrick (Ed.), *The executive effect: Concepts and methods for studying top managers*. Greenwich, CT: JAI.

Tangney, J. P. (2000). Humility: Theoretical perspectives, empirical findings and directions for future research. *Journal of Social and Clinical Psychology, 19*(1), 70–82.

Tervalon, M., & Murray-Garcia, J. (1998). Cultural humility versus cultural competence. *Journal of Health Care for the Poor and Underserved, 9*(2),117–125.

Todd, S. (2001). On not knowing the other, or learning from Levinas. *Philosophy of Education Yearbook, 67*–74.

Veck, W. (2014). Inclusive pedagogy: Ideas from the ethical philosophy of Emmanuel Levinas. *Cambridge Journal of Education, 44*(4), 451–464.

Weaver, H. N. (1999). Indigenous people and the social work profession: Defining culturally competent services. *Social Work, 44*(3), 217–225.

Wedeen, L. (2002). Conceptualizing culture: Possibilities for political science. *The American Political Science Review, 96*(4), 713–728.

5 Social Work as Risky Business

Risk seems endemic to contemporary life. Hardly a day goes by where we do not hear about or consider the risk of taking – or not taking – some action. Whereas at one time the greatest dangers came from natural events over which people had no control, today it is primarily human-generated phenomena (e.g., technology) that engender our sense of risk.[1] Does this mean that life is riskier than in past ages? Not necessarily (e.g., Giddens, 1999). In fact, some would argue that we are safer now than ever before (e.g., Mythen & Walklate, 2006); however, our awareness, understanding, and acceptance of risk seem to have changed in ways that magnify its salience in our lives.

Some of these ideas are articulated in the risk society thesis, a view most closely associated with the work of German sociologist Ulrich Beck, particularly in his book *Risk Society: Towards a New Modernity* (1992). According to Beck, science, technology, and industrialization in the period of 'late modernity' have produced new kinds of risks that, until relatively recently (from a historical perspective), were unimaginable. Consequently, societies are unprepared to address them. The timing of Beck's book (i.e., its English translation), coming right after the Chernobyl disaster, was a dramatic illustration of the kind of consequences Beck was writing about and increased its impact. As Mythen (2007) wrote, '*Risk Society* (1992) served to document the deleterious environmental side-effects of economic development and tapped into the growing mood of public scepticism towards expert institutions gaining ground in the West' (p. 794).

There is an irony in Beck's thesis. The achievements of modernity, particularly science, were supposed to lessen risk; instead, they have generated it. Examples abound. Medicines to cure the ravages of disease produce side effects that seem equally dangerous or lead to the development of drug-resistant pathogens. 'Clean' and low-cost nuclear energy generates toxic threats to the environment and health. Beck comments, 'Manufactured uncertainties are those kinds of risks that emerged as answers to the uncertainties introduced by modernity. They produce a wide range of risks. And science, even good science, even the *best* science, is always producing numerous alternative risks' (cited in Culver et al., 2011: 8). For the sociologist

Anthony Giddens (1991), the ubiquity of risk and its accompanying uncertainty generates a sense of 'ontological insecurity', a loss of confidence in the continuity of the social order and a sense of uncertainty about the future. It also makes risk a central political issue of our time[2] engendering a tension between those who benefit from and wish to promulgate (and therefore defend) such change (e.g., genetically modified seeds) and the public's awareness that the impact of these changes cannot be absolutely predicted or controlled. Also, because risk is so connected to technology, it concentrates consequential knowledge – the knowledge that can produce technologies that impact the lives of many people – into the hands of experts and scientists. These people are not elected representatives of the populace and therefore not accountable in the ways of elected officials. Some argue that the enormous power of experts in our 'scientized society' poses a potential threat to our democratic ideals and freedom (see Ekberg, 2007). Commenting on this situation, Stoffle and Arnold (2008), drawing on Beck, write, 'Knowledge of the risks which are threats from 20th century techno-scientific civilization has only become established against massive denials and bitter resistance' (Beck, 1992: 58). They continue:

> One reason these risks have been denied is because the established leadership of modern society (political and scientific) neither has a way of fixing the risks nor of helping society be resilient against their challenges. So not only is contemporary society facing unimaginable risks but it is doing so without traditionally trusted leadership and knowledge providers to set these problems right. (Stoffle &Arnold, 2008: 2–3)

Exacerbating this situation are two other features of the contemporary landscape: globalization and the media. As implied in Beck's 'world risk society', risk in the contemporary world is not a local or regional phenomenon, rather the interconnectedness that characterizes the globalized world generates new risks that transcend national boundaries. Consider, for example, the reach of financial, terrorist, and ecological risks. Beck (2012) argues that such risks are characterized by three dimensions:

1. 'de-localization' – their causes and consequences are geographically transcendent;
2. 'incalculableness' – their consequences are in principle unknowable; and
3. 'non-compensability' – their global nature undermines the principle of compensation and leads to an emphasis on prevention. The limitations of the nation state to manage these issues further exacerbate the uncertainty experienced by institutions and individuals.

In an important sense, risk is a media product. Without the media, our awareness and understanding of risk would be greatly constricted. Kenny (2005) argues that the risk society would not even be possible without the media:

> our greater knowledge of risk derives not so much from the quest for knowledge, but from the way in which we are blitzed with the dangers of the world through the global mass media. From this perspective, risk society is only possible when we have global media, and risk is made all the more real through the instantaneous communication possible today, where we are confronted with stories about the riskiness of life. (p. 51)

Given the media's propensity to focus on the potential negative consequences of various products, actions, and events, it is not surprising that for those living the relatively affluent, techno-rational lifestyles of people in the West, these risk stories permeate the daily activities of living. Should I eat food with high fructose corn syrup? Will my extensive use of a cell phone lead to brain injury? Will vaccinations that protect my child from certain diseases create vulnerability to other maladies? Is my inability to remember names a sign of early onset dementia? Should I protect myself against global warming? Will taking an aspirin daily decrease my chances of heart disease? The list of questions seems endless. Interestingly, these risks are less dependent on whether something bad actually happens than on the belief that something bad *could* happen. Beck (2011) comments,

> Risks exist in a permanent state of virtuality, and only become 'topical' to the extent that they are anticipated. Risks are nothing without techniques of visualization, symbolic forms, mass media, and staging. In other words, it is irrelevant whether we live in a world which is "objectively" safer than all other worlds; if destruction and disasters are anticipated (in order to prevent them), then that produces a compulsion to act. (p. 665)

By keeping risk in the forefront of our consciousness, the media becomes part of the process that both constitutes and reflects the ubiquity of risk.

This 'compulsion to act', fed by the continuous and widespread reporting of potential dangers, leads us to consider preventive or defensive measures, for example, flu shots, escape routes for hurricanes, and airport screening. But since none of these are 100 percent effective, we are left with a background sense of unease or a need for vigilance to detect and act on potentially dangerous situations. Many also feel a responsibility to protect those such as children who are less aware of and more vulnerable to these risks. Thus, parents dutifully teach their children about the risks inherent in daily life and how to avoid or prevent them. 'Don't talk to strangers', 'wash your hands after using the bathroom', 'buckle your seat belt' are oft-heard admonitions of US parents trying to keep their children safe from potential harm. As safety is considered central to responsible parenting, maintaining this kind of vigilance and enforcing obedience to protective rules becomes a measure of parental competence. Additionally, the 'reality' of risk is socially transmitted across generations.

Meanings of Risk

The contexts and understandings of risk have changed over time from its origins in the Middle Ages when it was primarily associated with natural disasters having little to do with human actions, to its relationship with gambling in the 17th century, and to its modern expression in probability theory (Corbett & Westwood, 2005). An implication of these changes is that risk is not an objective characteristic of the world, but, as noted, can be understood as the anticipation of the possibility that something harmful could happen. Meaning, as Wittgenstein argued, is not inherent in the word, but is expressed in the doing which in turn is related to 'forms of life' – our background, often tacit, assumptions and beliefs. Thus, how risk is performed becomes its meaning.

Even within a particular context, risk can have multiple meanings. For example, within the context of human services, risk is understood as a way of preventing harmful future actions of certain categories of people such as the mentally ill as a justification for the use of actuarial methods as a classification method or their surveillance and control. In their research on risk and people with a cognitive disability, Eriksson and Hummelvoll (2012) view risk 'as a term describing some characteristics of contemporary society which impose difficulties for the individual and especially for those who already find themselves in a vulnerable position' (p. 595).

At least three points can be gleaned from this discussion. First, all meanings are contextual (see Mischler, 1979). Second, all meaning is perspectival; that is, meanings will vary depending on whose perspective is salient. People assigned to social categories considered risky often hold different meanings of their risk than the institutions that make these assignations. Third, some meanings focus on what constitutes risk, what it is, while other meanings emphasize function, how risk is performed. For example, in the previous example of people with a cognitive disability, risk functions not only as a probability concept, but as a moral one (cf., Stanford, 2009: 1071). Still, despite the multiplicity of meanings, some will be dominant. This leads to concern for those who are in more vulnerable positions and less able to influence its meanings and implications for them (e.g., being labeled as risky).

The preceding discussion suggests that risk will be experienced differently across contexts. Consider, for instance, how disparities in health care, vulnerability to the effects of technological and natural disasters, the impact of economic instability, and the safety of drinking water vary across social classes. These differences also will impact the perception of risk. For example, in many Western nations the availability and safety of tap water is assumed. Still, for some within these nations, drinking this water is perceived as risking the ingestion of contaminants that cannot be eliminated by conventional water treatment methods. This perception is exacerbated by the belief that public officials cannot be trusted to reveal the 'true' threat.[3] Responses include drinking bottled water or installing in-home filtering systems, options available only to the relatively affluent. In contrast, for people living in impoverished or drought-stricken regions of the world, having access to the kind of unlimited, flowing, drinkable tap water available in the West would be seen as an incredible benefit without concern for the perceived risks of the affluent.

The Social Construction of Risk

The above discussion suggests a social constructionist understanding of risk. That is, risk is considered a historically, culturally, and socially generated reality. This understanding has several implications. First, risk is not one thing (nor any-thing) but can be understood in different ways such as a material aspect of the world, a probability construct, or as a cultural response to global information networks. No particular understanding is required by the word risk. How it is taken up and understood will be influenced by cultural and social factors such as dominant discourses, knowledge traditions, and language use. Ewald (1991) comments that 'Nothing is a risk in itself; there is no risk in reality. But on the other hand, anything can be a risk; it all depends on how one analyses the danger, considers the event' (p. 199).

Second, each form of understanding will invite and justify different courses of action and discourage others; for example, compare risk as a probabilistic expression of danger compared to risk as an ideological expression of neo-liberalism. Third, how we 'language' and 'do' risk in particular contexts will constitute its meanings. For example, how risk is assessed within mental health, correctional, or social welfare systems will operationalize risk for those within those systems. Fourth, risk discourse creates risky subjects. This is an extension of the previous implication and would include assessment practices and other institutional and organizational practices such as the regulations governing the work of social workers. Fifth, given the plurality and contextual nature of meanings, our attention turns to who benefits and who is disadvantaged by dominant conceptions of risk and to possible alternatives. This brings up issues such as the justification of increased surveillance of certain categories of people, and how risk reinforces an ideology of individualism. These are some of themes that will be explored in the rest of this chapter.

Risk discourse functions recursively and evaluatively (Russell & Babrow, 2011). By recursively, I mean that our actions both generate and reflect perceptions of risk. By treating risk as an objective fact – rather than a social construction – these actions, including assessments, analyses, media coverage, and language use, lead to risk 'becom[ing] the explanations for actions that in turn produce risk' (Russell & Babrow, 2011: 244). This occurs in part because 'to see/say that something is a risk, we experience/express concern about *that something* among *all other possible somethings* that might concern us. To see a risk is to select it out of the welter of other possible cares' (Russell & Babrow, 2011: 248, emphasis in the original). Such identified risk is then inscribed in policies and practices further reifying them and inciting additional reaction to their 'existence'. Beck has been particularly emphatic regarding the role of science in this process. He states, 'Science is *one of the causes, the medium of definition and the source of solutions* to risks, and by virtue of that very fact it opens new markets of scientization for itself' (1992: 155, emphasis in the original). In other words, the authority of scientific discourse gives the notion of risk authenticity, a reality that seems incontrovertible while creating new areas for scientific expertise and support. Egner (2011), based on a recent interview with Beck, expands on this view:

> scientific risk research contributes to the staging of risk and encourages a self-amplification of the social risk debate. This leads to a paradoxical situation for scientists: on the one hand, risk researchers are hoping and trying to produce security with the results of their studies, on the other hand they contribute to the distribution of a risk perspective that identifies risk everywhere, insisting on the societal importance of their work and pointing out the need for action – not least to get funding for research projects. (Culver et al., 2011: 21)

This staging of risk includes such activities as airport security rituals and rehearsing evacuation plans. Such staging, while perceived as prudent, contributes to the perception of ubiquitous risk.

Discourses of risk function evaluatively in the ways that risk designations carry value judgments. Russell and Babrow (2011) state 'our constructions of risk also necessarily involve evaluative understandings; to judge something risky is to say that it is not merely possible, but also that some nontrivial (positive or negative) value is at stake' (p. 248). Thus, these constructions are constitutive and consequential (Bartesaghi, Grey, & Gibson, 2012); they matter. To label a person or an event as risky is to infer the potential for harm. Swift and Callahan (2009), drawing on the work of Mary Douglas, state that 'the risks we select to pursue depend on the identification of a person or group that is *socially* acceptable *to* blame' (p. 36, emphasis in original). People (or a socially designated category of people) at risk are considered a potential danger to themselves or others. This label functions somewhat like a master status overriding other qualities and justifying treating them in ways designed to prevent or reduce the alleged risk.

As the perception of risk has shifted from being associated with environmental/external causes to those generated by human actions, it has taken on a volitional dimension. That is, it involves decisions and actions made by people. As Zinn (2010) puts it, 'risks in practice have always something to do with decisions made by someone (or a social entity) and the victims or the people who are affected by such decisions' (p. 110). In the current context of individualism, this easily becomes an indictment of personal responsibility. Value judgments are justified when risks are seen as preventable and based on individual choice. This returns us to the difference between risk and danger. Whereas danger is seen to exist independent of persons, risk tends to be connected to decisions and therefore to human agency (Russell & Babrow, 2011; Zinn, 2010).[4] Again quoting Russell & Babrow:

> To see risk, to understand the future in terms of risk, to be the agents of risk decisions, and to embody "risky" behavior, we must be able to foresee potentially adverse consequences of our actions, we must be able to choose freely among alternative actions, and we must in fact choose and enact those choices (including inaction). Whatever is inevitable and whatever cannot possibly be foreseen lie beyond the realm of risk; such eventualities are instead dangers of existence. (p. 246)

The foregoing analysis of risk sets the stage for exploring the influence of risk consciousness on social work.

Social Work in the Risk Society

Social work is largely concerned with what Beck termed 'manufactured risks or uncertainties' – those that 'are dependent on human decisions, created by society itself, immanent to society and thus externalizable, collectively imposed and thus individually unavoidable ...' (Beck, 2009: 293). The pervasive sense of living in a risky world has influenced social workers' views of social life and individual responsibility. It has been taken up by governments and institutions and expressed in macro- and mezzo-level policies and micro-level practices. Social work has contributed to and been influenced by these activities.

Although social work publications about risk date back to the 1980s, a spate of publications have appeared in the last five years. Notably, much of this literature, in particular those taking a critical stance toward societal notions of risk and their relationship to social work practice, has emerged primarily from Europe and Australia.

Two interconnected logics underlie how social work is organized and practiced in relation to risk: that of the market (as embodied in neo-liberalism) and that of science (as the highest expression of rational thought). These will be discussed briefly including some of their implications for social work.

Neo-liberalism and Risk

The influence of neo-liberalism has been articulated by several social work scholars (e.g., Pollack, 2010; Stanford, 2011; Webb, 2006). In general, neo-liberalism can be thought of as an ideology with the market as its centerpiece. Unregulated economic processes are considered as the optimal blueprint for forming policy. 'Big government' such as expressed in the welfare state is viewed as a major obstacle to prosperity. Accordingly, social work is 'economized' (Stark, 2008) with competition, managerialism, and individual responsibility moving to the forefront of practice. Within this context, risk becomes a rationale for the regulation of those viewed as not contributing to or potentially undermining market forces. Typically, these include socially marginalized groups who do not exhibit the 'personal responsibility' characteristic of good citizens and therefore require external resources to regulate their actions and rehabilitate themselves. Thus, within social work, we see risk policies directed toward people involved with the penal, child welfare, public welfare, and mental health systems.

Within a neoliberal context, risk becomes personalized (Stanford, 2011). Emphasis is placed on individual responsibility to the neglect of the influence of structural inequalities. 'At the same time a moral programme of individual responsibility in public policy reinforces discrimination against disadvantaged groups, as social supports are withdrawn ...' (Zinn & Taylor-Gooby, 2006: 69). Thus, it becomes the individual's responsibility to 'practice and sustain their autonomy by assembling information, materials and practices together into a personalized strategy that identifies and minimizes their exposure to harm' (Pat O'Malley, 2000: 465, cited in Roberts, 2006: 56). This emphasis on individualism and responsibilism, when combined with a scientific logic form a pervasive, authoritative ideology that influences thinking about risk in relation to marginalized groups.

Scientific Rationality and Risk

The Enlightenment ideal of a reality that could be entirely known and controlled through the exercise of scientific reason remains a dominant discourse in much of the world. In its contemporary incarnation, reality is believed to be knowable through the rigorous application of scientific methods. These methods yield so-called objective information (i.e., the true nature of things) and, particularly when converted into numerical form, can be used to predict and control the future (Littlefield & Hawley, 2010). As noted previously, the development of statistics shifted understandings of risk from fate or chance to predictableness and, theoretically, control. It also brought risk into the realm of science giving risk discourse an authority that 'lies, in part, in its claim to an objective, empirical and predictive basis' (Pollack, 2010: 1274). Scientific discourse supports instrumental, actuarial, and quantitative approaches to risk. I comment briefly on each of these topics.

Instrumental Rationality

Within the human services, risk reduction tends to be viewed as an important, self-evident, uncontestable goal. The logic seems to go something like: risk is associated with the potential for harm, which is bad so its reduction is good. This leads to a means-oriented rationality in which the ends (e.g., risk reduction, safety) are taken for granted and emphasis is on the best way of achieving them. Best, in this context, usually means those technologies (methods) viewed as most authoritative, that is, considered scientific. This is reminiscent of instrumental or formal rationality, terms used by the sociologist Max Weber to indicate a privileging of means over ends and an emphasis on formal rules and calculations (Kalberg, 1980). Stephen Webb (2013) describes instrumental rationality as 'means-end driven, calculating, self-interested, predicting and regulative, ...' in which 'ends [are taken] as given'. This is contrasted with substantive rationality where emphasis and reflection are on the value-based articulation of ends. Substantive rationality, according to Webb, is 'a moral-practical rationality ...' that 'focus[es] on broader expressive values, affects and meanings' (3). Additionally, Weber (1921/1968: 85–86) states that substantive rationality 'is full of ambiguities' and 'not restrict[ed] ... to ... action based on 'goal oriented' rational calculation with the technically most adequate available methods ...'

It can be argued that social workers are oriented toward a substantive rationality. Ambiguity, values, reflection, and morality are the 'stuff' of practice and are employed in the development of appropriate, client-sensitive ends. Instrumental rationality inverts this orientation assuming a real, consensual aim and focusing on the means to achieve it.

The 'problem of risk' is, in large part, shaped by the authority of actuarial and probabilistic methods and the belief that their use can lead to risk prediction and control. In a sense ends are defined in probabilistic terms to conform to favored means. This 'instrumental logic' is 'based solely on calculation and utility' (Ugarte and Martin-Aranaga, 2011: 448) rather than on its ethical and value implications. Rational ends are, de facto, those that are congruent with the means (Gottschalk & Witkin, 1991). However, their inviolableness weakens when we consider the practice and consequences of risk reduction in the context of human services including how risks are defined (e.g., assessment instruments), their use (e.g., labeling people as risky), and their potential undesirable implications (e.g., increased surveillance).

Actuarialism

Actuarialism is 'the formal, statistical calculation of risk based upon aggregated data …' (Kemshall, 2010: 1254). It is concerned with preventing possible future dangers by classifying individuals and groups 'as particular bearers of risk who, once identified, can become the target of proactive intervention' (McLellan, 2012: 36). Although risk is generated by past and present understandings, its focus is on the possibility and probability of something negative happening in the future. This invites prediction. How well can we foretell the future? In this sense, it is a variant of the age-old question about what does the future hold for me? Hence our fascination with oracles, crystal balls, horoscopes, tea leaves, soothsayers, astrologers, and fortune tellers. Now we have become more scientific in our approach and look to statistics and actuarial tables. None are infallible. However, not unlike overreliance on the 'old-fashioned' ways of predicting the future, the current prominence of the actuarial approach to risk generates its own set of problems.

One issue concerns the difference between beliefs associated with the actuarial approach and how it is applied. Actuarialism leads to a belief that risk behavior can be known and predicted. A misunderstood analogy to the use of actuarial data in the insurance industry may buttress this belief. Unlike the human services, insurance companies aggregate risks. Littlefield and Hawley (2010) give the example of car insurance in which the insured are grouped into various categories such as age and car type. What companies do not attempt to do 'is to predict *which one of the insured individuals* over the ensuing year will have an accident in their car, or have their car stolen' (p. 214, emphasis added). In the human services, however, the goal is to predict individual behavior, whether a given individual will act in a certain way in some indefinitely defined time period, what Fitzgibbon (2007) calls the 'actuarial fallacy'.

Another problem with this approach is that social workers are most concerned with low base-rate events such as child abuse. In such cases, actuarial methods are less accurate and likely to result in frequent false positives (Fitzgibbon, 2007). Littlefield and Hawley (2010: 213) note that for low-base-rate events like sexual offenses, 'the next sexual offence which will occur is more likely to be committed by somebody who has no prior record of such offending than someone who has'. They also point out that further compromising such predictions is the incompleteness of the available data as most such offenses are unreported.

Quantification: The Risk of Eating Raw Oysters

The issue of actuarialism is part of a more general issue regarding quantification based, in large part, on the common belief that if we convert concepts or words into numbers, we gain precision and eliminate problems associated with language. What is overlooked is that numbers are also a language and a fairly restrictive one. An interesting example comes from the natural sciences, which are typically viewed as more precise in their predictions, concerning attempts to predict the risk of eating raw oysters (Danisch & Mudry, 2008). While this task might seem relatively straightforward compared to assessing the risk of someone committing a crime, abusing a child, or becoming mentally ill, the process turns out to be fraught with difficulties.

A primary reason for this situation is that risk assessment is not simply a straightforward application of numbers, but also involves semantic and rhetorical applications. Although the generation of tables and other mathematical expressions gives the appearance of objectivity and precision, the authors show that efforts to reduce uncertainty rely on the use of language, including seeking 'agreement on interpretations of objects or events, to influence human choices, and to coordinate social action in response to public exigencies' (p. 136). Put slightly differently, Ericson (2006: 350–51) proffers that 'risk management provides a rhetoric of reassurance, enacting myths of control, manageability, and accountability'.

The data provided by risk assessment does not eliminate uncertainty about whether someone should eat a raw oyster or whether someone will commit a crime. The assumption that computing statistical probabilities can 'tame uncertainty' (Wong & King, 2008) is misleading and potentially dangerous. This is seen in the 'non-knowledge' that is produced (e.g., 'I don't know') and in the paradox that comes from generating uncertainty when trying to reduce it. Ericson (2006: 350) notes that risk is reactive: 'every effort to refine it is also an exposure of its vulnerabilities that can be acted upon to create more risk'. In this regard Danisch and Mudry (2008: 137) ask: 'what do we know once we know that which is provided by a risk assessment? And the ironic answer is that we know that we do not know'. This conclusion is not confined to eating oysters as Danisch (2013) demonstrates in his analysis of the risk of bioterrorism. Rather than increase certainty, 'the purpose of risk assessment is to produce a kind of rational fear in the public mind' (Danisch & Mudry, 2008: 138).

When the risky objects are humans rather than oysters, the potential consequences for how such uncertainty is addressed can be of great concern. Framing risk as a statistical object tends to minimize 'contextual or non-probabilistic factors such as who and what is being singled out, level of uncertainty that is acceptable, moral judgments' (Zinn & Taylor-Gooby, 2006; Stanford, 2011). Thus, neo-liberal and scientific discourses legitimate the surveillance and regulation of people falling into risk categories (read: marginalized groups). These people are seen as being individually responsible for conforming to behavioral norms through engaging in self-surveillance and a decontextualized responsibilism (Powell & Wahidin, 2005). Clients get 'deconstructed' into sets of risk factors who are acted upon based on what they might do at some future time (Corbett & Westwood, 2005; Fitzgibbon, 2007). Pollack's (2010) study of women in the correctional system serves as a forceful example. Her interviews with women inmates revealed how their risk status was used to legitimate programs that focused on individual responsibility with little consideration of contextual factors. Also chilling was how concepts like empowerment (that are held in esteem by social workers) were coopted to the neo-liberal agenda. 'Premised upon notions of an independent, self-sufficient and entrepreneurial citizen, empowerment strategies in the neo-liberal context focus upon reworking the subjectivity of those who find themselves entangled within the state apparatus. Consequently, empowerment takes on a purely individualistic meaning, rendering structural/systemic factors irrelevant' (pp. 1267–1268; also, see Sáenz de Ugarte & Martin-Aranaga, 2011). Thus, the primary 'treatment' is therapy and attempts to resist this risk discourse are interpreted as further confirmation of one's risky persona.

It is not only clients who are blamed for their failure to exercise the proper steps to prevent their risky proclivities from being realized. Organizationally, a risk management environment can generate a 'culture of blame' (e.g., Littlechild, 2008; Parton, 1996) in which individual workers and agencies are held accountable for 'failure' to detect or take proper actions in regard to risk. This in turn generates a context permeated by fear; ironically, a new risk that fosters a risk-averse, justificatory, and limited exposure conservatism of audit trails, mechanization, and managerialism (Beddoe, 2010).

Relevant here is Stanford's (2010) distinction between being 'at risk' and 'a risk'. She argues that social workers too can be at risk as 'targets of blame' and "a risk' to clients by virtue of incorrect or overzealous risk assessments and management practices' (p. 1071). To follow procedures, utilize risk assessment instruments (Price-Robertson & Bromfield, 2011), and to document that one has done so, is to mitigate being blamed and held responsible for something going wrong. Thus, Parton (2010: 62) observes that at a time when the complexity of problems facing practitioners demand increased knowledge and skills and the ability to apply them in a contextual fashion, their ability to exercise discretion has been compromised, sacrificed to the demands of procedures and information and communications technology (ICT) systems. Herein lies yet another irony in which practitioners' efforts to manage risky clients positions themselves also as risky.

To summarize, in this chapter I have taken a critical perspective on risk assessment in the human services. My general position has been that the notion of risk, shaped by a neo-liberal ideology, has permeated our consciousness exerting a hegemonic influence over understandings of social reality. For those in the human services, this risk consciousness, and its enablement of individualism and responsiblism, has had deleterious effects for clients and practitioners, generating justifications for increased surveillance and control over marginalized groups and promoting managerialism and proceduralism within organizations. This is not a consensus view and there are counterarguments which claim, for example, that risk assessments represent an advance in our ability to prevent future harms (e.g., Swift & Callahan, 2009). Although I have contended that a risk orientation provides a false sense of certainty, debating the rightness or wrongness of different positions glosses over the implications of risk thinking for professional values and practices, for example the impact on social work's human rights and social justice agenda, advocacy on behalf of marginalized groups, and the ability for workers to maintain autonomy, professional judgment, discretion, and a relational focus.

What Can Be Done? Maintaining a Social Constructionist Orientation

The ubiquity of risk consciousness and its inscription in institutional settings presents daunting challenges for social workers. No particular action will change its influence in the short term. Moreover, an ironic aspect of increased risk consciousness is the dampening effect it seems to have on risk taking, arguably an important dimension of social work practice. Despite this, resistance to risk assessment and risk management in human service organizations may be more common than reported (e.g., Beddoe, 2010; Stanford, 2009). This is because such resistance risks punishment and therefore is often carried out covertly. For example, although practitioners may be required to administer risk assessment instruments to clients, how these measures are administered and how this information is used may be less controllable. In addition to such surreptitious practices, a social constructionist orientation toward risk encourages ways of troubling assumptions about risk that may inspire alternative practices, at least at the organizational or local level. Maintaining an understanding of risk as a product of particular historical, cultural, and social factors, keeps it from being reified, but contextual and open to multiple interpretations. This enables a critical analysis of how risk is constituted and how it operates. Taking an active, critically reflective stance on the dilemmas engendered by the construction of risk identities seems to enable social workers to resolve these dilemmas in a manner consistent with social justice (Stanford, 2012).

Interrogating risk discourse. Social workers can unsettle the inviolability of risk discourse by raising questions about the meanings of risk as it is used in their organization. They can ask about how this understanding came about, the factors that maintain it, about how it aligns with their professional obligations to the people they serve and to the larger society. Social workers can locate risk within the broader frame of attempts to reduce uncertainty and the implications of such attempts, for example, generating additional risks and creating a false sense of predictability. These types of inquiry may broaden the dialogue to consider alternative ways of understanding and addressing risk within organizations.

The framing of risk as socially constructed may lead to a shift from how to manage it to exploring the myriad ways it can be understood. For example, rather than focusing on controlling risk, we may turn to ways of working with uncertainty, ambiguity, and complexity (Bartesagh, Grey, & Gibson, 2012).

Risk as a social construction draws attention to the language of risk, for example, what does it mean to understand someone as risky? Is this another form of pathologizing without using medical terminology? I have discussed this idea previously in the context of the strengths perspective:

> When applied to people, the language of risks often sounds very similar to the language of deficits; consider, for example, 'ineffective parenting' as a risk factor for 'early-onset antisocial behavior' in children. Note too that

deficit labels also can be risk factors for further risks, for example, having a 'mental disorder' is a risk factor for 'substance abuse'. (Witkin, 2012)

Thus, risks become concatenated and self-perpetuating.

The measurement of risk. Considerable effort has gone into developing risk measurement instruments. One might say it is a flourishing business. These measures are based on assumptions that risks are real and can be predicted and prevented. When we measure risk we operationalize its meaning. However, as with all measurements, risk measures underdetermine the construct, that is, risk is reduced to whatever constitutes the measure. For example, the use of risk checklists can be questioned for their reduction of people to a set of decontextualized factors. Despite media sensationalism around horrific acts (e.g., the death of a child in the child welfare system), it is not clear whether formal, standardized assessments provide superior predictability or prevention potential than would be the case if practitioners were supported in developing meaningful relationships with their clients and given the autonomy to act on the knowledge gleaned from these relationships. In the context of litigiousness (especially in the United States), blame, and media spectacles, it may be relevant to ask to what extent are the use of such measures designed to protect children or to protect the organizations mandated to carry out this responsibility (Price-Robertson & Bromfield, 2011).

Narrative. Social workers tend to work (implicitly or formally) from a narrative perspective. This is congruent with social construction's position on narrative as 'a vehicle through which our world, lives, and selves are articulated and the way in which such narratives function within social relationships' (Sparkes & Smith, 2008: 298). Practitioner–client co-constructed narratives provide critical contextual information that enriches the meaning and understanding of risk. In contrast, technocratic, instrumental approaches tend to decontextualize clients' lives and generate narratives that accord with neo-liberalism, for example, by redefining concepts like empowerment to embody individual responsibility (Pollack, 2010; Sáenz de Ugarte & Idoia Martin-Aranaga, 2011). Risk is treated as an individual attribute, something akin to a personality trait, which invites interventions aimed at cognitive, behavioral, and personality change and strategies of self-regulation (Pollack, 2010). A social constructionist perspective helps keep risks relational. To be 'risky' is to attribute a trait-like characteristic to an individual. In contrast, riskiness can be viewed as generated from the interactions of people within particular cultural and societal contexts.

Dislodging the authority of science. In large part, risk management derives its authority from its association with science and its claims to be objective (Webb, 2006). However, science is never neutral. Its problems have to be conceptualized, articulated, measured, and generalized; its data must always be interpreted. All these processes will reflect cultural, societal, and personal values, beliefs, and preferences. Becoming conversant in the language and discourse of science and research can enable social workers to enter this discourse and question or contest its power to naturalize knowledge. Again, this has promise at the local level where those using scientific rhetoric (e.g., agency administrators) may have little methodological or substantive knowledge to back up their claims. Once the aura of science has been dimmed, alternative considerations such as structural factors and approaches to gathering information such as the aforementioned use of narrative may gain more credibility.

The pervasiveness of risk consciousness reflects and contributes to dominant neo-liberal and globalization discourses. These discourses are also expressed in the organization and functioning of social services and social work. It is difficult but not impossible to think outside of these contexts. Critically reflective analyses and alternative frameworks facilitate this task. My hope is that this chapter has contributed to this effort.

Notes

1   Although we are still subject to the forces of nature, these are experienced differently due to their interaction with human-made changes or creations; e.g., a typhoon in Japan destroys nuclear reactors, volcanoes in Iceland create risk to air travel, diseases that originate in one part of the world are carried to other parts.

2   Beck also shares this view.

3   Since writing this chapter, the contaminated drinking water crisis in Flint, Michigan, which was kept from the public by elected officials, has surfaced, sadly underscoring this lack of trust.

4   There is a similarity here to certain conceptualizations of stress and coping in which stress is experienced as threat, the anticipation of possible harm, leading to coping efforts to eliminate or reduce the threat.

References

Bartesaghi, M., Grey, S. H., & Gibson, S. (2012). Defining the concept of risk. *Poroi: An Interdisciplinary Journal of Rhetorical Analysis and Invention, 8*(1), article 6. Retrieved from http//dx.doi.org/10.13008/2151-2957.1112

Beck, U. (1992). *Risk society: Towards a new modernity*. London: Sage.

Beck, U. (2009). World risk society and manufactured uncertainties. *Iris 1*(2), 291–299. Firenze University Press.

Beck, U. (2011). Clash of risk cultures or critique of American universalism. *Contemporary Sociology: A Journal of Reviews, 40*(6), 662–667.

Beck, U. (2012). Redefining the sociological project: The cosmopolitan challenge. *Sociology, 46*(1), 7–12.

Corbett, K., & Westwood, T. (2005). 'Dangerous and severe personality disorder': A psychiatric manifestation of the risk society. *Critical Public Health, 15*(2), 121–133.

Culver, L., Egner, H., Gallini, S., Kneitz, A., Lousley, C., Lübken, U., Mincyte, D., Mom, G. and Winder, G. (2011). Revisiting risk society: A conversation with Ulrich Beck. *RCC Perspectives,* Issue 6, 1–31. Retrieved from www.rachelcarsoncenter.de

Danisch, R. (2013). Risk assessment as rhetorical practice: The ironic mathematics behind terrorism, banking, and public policy. *Public Understanding of Science, 22*(2), 236–251.

Danisch, R., & Mudry, J. (2008). Is it safe to eat that? Raw oysters, risk assessment and the rhetoric of science. *Social Epistemology, 22*(2), 129–143.

Egner, H. (2011). Enforced cosmopolitanization and the staging of risks. In L. Culver, H. Egner, S. Gallini, A. Kneitz, C. Lousley, U. Lübken, D. Mincyte, G. Mom, and G. Winder, Revisiting risk society: A conversation with Ulrich Beck (pp. 19–21). *RCC Perspectives,* Issue 6, 1–31. Retrieved from www.rachelcarsoncenter.de

Ekberg, M. (2007). The parameters of the risk society: A review and exploration. *Current Sociology, 55*(3), 343–366.

Eriksson, B. G., & Hummelvoll, J. K. (2012). To live as mentally disabled in the risk society. *Journal of Psychiatric and Mental Health Nursing, 19*(7), 594–602.

Ewald, F. (1991). Insurance and risk. In G. Burchell, C. Gordon, and P. Miller (Eds), *The Foucault effect: Studies in govermentality* (pp. 197–210). Chicago: Chicago University Press.

Fitzgibbon, D. W. (2007) Risk analysis and the new practitioner: Myth or reality? *Punishment and Society, 9*(1), 55–69.

Giddens, A. (1991). *Modernity and self-identity: Self and society in the late modern age.* Stanford, CA: Stanford University Press.

Giddens, A. (1999). Risk and responsibility. *Modern Law Review, 62*(1), 1–10.

Gottschalk, S., & Witkin, S. L. (1991). Rationality in social work: A critical examination. *Journal of Sociology and Social Welfare, 18,* 121–136.

Kalberg, S. (1980). Max Weber's types of rationality: Cornerstones for the analysis of rationalization processes in history. *American Journal of Sociology,* 1145–1179.

Kemshall, H. (2010). Risk rationalities in contemporary social work policy and practice. *British Journal of Social Work, 40*(4), 1247–1262.

Littlechild, B., & Hawley, C. (2010). Risk assessments for mental health service users: ethical, valid and reliable? *Journal of Social Work, 10*(2), 211–229.

McLellan, M. (2012). The loss of innocence in a risk society. Retrieved from SSRN: http://ssrn.com/abstract=2047453 or http://dx.doi.org/10.2139/ssrn.2047453

Mischler, E. G. (1979). Meaning in context: Is there any other kind? *Harvard Educational Review, 49*(1), 1–19.

Mythen, G. (2007). Reappraising the risk society thesis telescopic sight or myopic vision? *Current Sociology, 55*(6), 793–813.

Mythen, G., & Walklate, S. (2006). Criminology and terrorism: Which thesis? Risk society or governmentality? *British Journal of Criminology, 46,* 379–398.

O'Malley, P. (2000). Uncertain subjects: Risks, liberalism and contract. *Economy and Society, 29*(4), 460–484.

Parton, N. (1996). Social work, risk, and the 'blaming system'. In N. Parton (Ed.), *Social theory, social change and social work* (pp. 98–114). London: Routledge.

Pollack, S. (2010). Labeling clients 'risky': Social work and the neo-liberal welfare state. *British Journal of Social Work, 40*(4), 1263–1278.

Powell, J. L., & Wahidin, A. (2005). Ageing in the 'risk society'. *International Journal of Sociology and Social Policy, 25*(8), 70–83.

Price-Robertson, R., & Bromfield, L. (2011). *Risk assessment in child protection.* Melbourne: Australian Institute of Family Studies.

Roberts. C. (2006). 'What can I do to help myself?' Somatic individuality and contemporary hormonal bodies. *Science Studies, 19*(2), 54–76.

Russell, L. D., & Babrow, A. S. (2011). Risk in the making: Narrative, problematic integration, and the social construction of risk. *Communication Theory, 21*(3), 239–260.

Sparkes, A. C., & Smith, B. (2008). Narrative constructionist inquiry. In J. A. Holstein, & J. F. Gubrium (Eds.), *Handbook of constructionist research* (pp. 295–314). New York, NY: Guilford Press.

Stanford, S. N. (2009). 'Speaking back' to fear: Responding to the moral dilemmas of risk in social work practice. *British Journal of Social Work, 40*, 1065–1080.

Stanford, S. N. (2011). Constructing moral responses to risk: A framework for hopeful social work practice. *British Journal of Social Work, 41*(8), 1514–1531.

Stanford, S. N. (2012). Critically reflecting on being 'at risk' and 'a risk' in vulnerable people policing. In I. Bartkowiak-Theron, & N. L. Asquith (Eds.), *Policing vulnerability.* New South Wales: The Federation Press.

Stark, C. (2008). Neoliberalism and the consequences for social work. *IUC Journal of Social Work, 17*(4). Retrieved from http://www.bemidjistate.edu/academics/publications/social_work_journal

Stoffle, R. W., & Arnold, R. (2008). Facing the unimaginable: The limits of resilience and the risk society. *First international sociology association forum on sociology and public debate.* Barcelona, Spain.

Swift, K., & Callahan, M. (2009). *At risk: Social justice in child welfare and other human services.* Toronto: University of Toronto Press.

Webb, S. (2006). *Social work in a risk society.* Houndmills, Basingstoke: Palgrave Macmillan.

Webb, S. (2013). Bios and the function of social work. Retrieved from www.academia.edu/4115350/

Witkin, S. L. (2012). Forward. In D. Saleebey (Ed.), *Strengths perspective in social work practice* (6th ed.). London: Pearson.

Zinn, J. O. (2010). Risk as discourse: Interdisciplinary perspectives. *Critical approaches to discourse analysis across disciplines.* Retrieved from http://cadaad.net/journal

Zinn, J. O., & Taylor-Gooby, P. (2006). The challenge of (managing) new risks. In P. Taylor-Gooby, & J. Zinn (Eds.), *Risk in social sciences.* Oxford: Oxford University Press.

6 Re-constructing the Strengths Perspective[1]

Stories are a useful way of introducing and illustrating aspects of the strengths perspective. Dennis Saleebey, one of the primary architects of the strengths perspective, would often illustrate the basic principle of taking seriously the client's hope and dreams (see, for example, Saleebey, 2011) through a story about a student of his who worked with a man who loved airplanes and wanted to become a pilot. Despite her client's checkered employment history and lack of education, the student, mindful of this newly learned practice principle, dutifully took this seriously and worked with him to develop a plan for achieving his dream. In the course of their work together it became apparent to the client that choosing a related, more attainable goal would be a better place to start. This resulted in him becoming an airport baggage handler, a job which allowed him to be around airplanes and which he found satisfying.

Similarly, I often use the story of a young man named Martin living in a small town who spent much of his time simply 'hanging around' street corners and whose life prospects, according to many in the community, seemed bleak (Witkin, 2001). In this case, the turning point was contact with a vocational counselor whose relationship with Martin allowed for the emergence of other, more pro-social qualities and proclivities. She matched these potentials to community needs and marshalled community support to meet those needs resulting in her client becoming a successful businessman.

When social work students and practitioners first hear about the strengths perspective through stories like these, they tend to have three reactions: that the strengths perspective makes good sense, it is straightforward, and it is how I already practice (or would practice). These reactions likely stem, in large part, from the congruence between the strengths perspective and core social work beliefs and values. Martin's story, for example, illustrates the venerable tenet, 'start where the client is', the belief that people can change, and the value that everyone deserves to be treated with dignity and respect. The seamlessness of this fit makes the strengths perspective appear to be simply the expression of fundamental, well-established qualities of good practice (Witkin, 2001). Although this congruence may account for

the strengths perspective becoming a staple of social work education programs across the United States and in other parts of the world, it can lead
to an overly simplified understanding that reproduces limiting beliefs and
reduces the strengths perspective's potential as a radical alternative to mainstream practices. A primary source of this (mis)understanding is the (often
implicit) adherence to an individualistic model of the self as illustrated in
the emphasis on identifying internal assets and resources (e.g., intelligence
or courage)[2] and a correspondence model of language that overlooks its
constitutive properties.[3] In the first case, strengths are considered internal
qualities of persons. Whether traits, skills, or attitudes, strengths are understood as individual attributes that can be mobilized to help clients achieve
their goals. An alternative conceptualization, to be explored in this chapter,
considers strengths as relationally generated and variable across contexts.

To illustrate the second case, the correspondence model, consider the
arbitrariness of our naming conventions and that our observations already
are interpretations. Then consider, within the context of the human service
system, the language that informs those interpretations. It is a language
dominated by syndromes, addictions, pathologies, dysfunctions, disorders,
and the like. The 'conditions' such language engenders form the contexts
for our efforts to understand and help others. They define the field of possibilities available for our (and our clients') identification, consideration, and
imagination. Ironically, the very pervasiveness of this deficit language and its
embedded assumptions make these interpretations hard to detect. We may
overlook or fail to notice that the individuals, families, and communities
with whom we work are in part constituted by medically conferred labels
taken as facts. Entry into the service system may even *require* such labels.
Consequently, it is hard to see persons categorized as mentally ill or a child
abuser as something other than their labels, or to consider crime-ridden,
impoverished communities as wellsprings of resources. Negative situations
seem to cry out for negative explanations. We want to know what is wrong
when so little seems right (Witkin, 2001).

Strengths as Relationship

The desire to develop an approach to practice that did not rely on the
lexicon of individual pathology led, understandably, to a focus on individual
strengths. Rather than focusing on the elimination of pathology, the emphasis
shifted to identifying and/or activating internal qualities of individuals which
they could draw upon to achieve goals. Although this change was important,
weakening the totalizing and debilitating effects of pathological labels, it did
not challenge the individualist conception of the self that underlies this orientation (in the lexicon of Chapter 1, it was not transformative).

Going beyond identifying individual attributes or assets can be challenging given our culturally ingrained ethos of individualism. Even in cases like Martin's, it seems logical to consider his achievements as evidence of laudable internal qualities that were ignored or overlooked. Although Martin had help, *he* was the one who overcame negative expectations and stigma to attain what seemed like unreachable goals. While such individuals deserve praise, what was achieved can be understood as expressions of relationships, past and present, that generated and sustained Martin's positive qualities, and legitimated and enabled Martin's goals (Witkin, 2001). This understanding, I will argue, moves the strengths perspective in new and potentially useful directions.

Within Western cultural and intellectual traditions, selves have come to be conceived as singular, encapsulated beings separated from each other and the outside world. Within our interior lies a true self accessible, depending on the historical period, through religious practices or rational thought. Accessing this interior self enables us to exercise action relatively free from constraints (i.e., autonomously). In contrast, from a social constructionist perspective, relationships are prior to individual selves. The self (or selves) is viewed as a historically and culturally based social accomplishment formed and reformed through social relationships and interaction. Rather than searching within, attention shifts to how selves are constituted through discursive action and performance and shaped by language and social conventions (Gergen, 2011).

Viewed relationally, strengths and deficits are not distinct, internal properties but interdependent constructions, generated in interactions across varied contexts. What might be considered a strength in one context might be a deficit in another. From this standpoint, people do not *have* strengths or deficits; rather, they are products of social intercourse. Social and normative understandings form the parameters of such interactions. For example, labeling someone as mentally ill, an abuser, or a delinquent positions them in ways that pejoratively influences the meanings of their actions. Their standing to negotiate positive meanings (strengths) is weak; for example, behavior that could be considered imaginative is interpreted as delusional, being methodical and highly organized is considered obsessive, and assertiveness as oppositional.

As described in positioning theory (e.g., Harré, 2008; Harré et al., 2009) different discursive positions also restrict or expand people's right to interact with others in certain ways and obligates them to interact in other ways. For example, a person positioned as a 'welfare mother' may lose her right to talk about the virtues of employment and may be expected to listen to advice about managing child care and work. Similarly, people positioned as industrious or hard working – even if unemployed – may be associated with different story lines (e.g., the suffering hero) and afforded more expansive rights (e.g., to pursue their dreams). Relationally oriented, strengths practitioners are aware of the potential for multiple story lines in any episode of human interaction and how positioning can facilitate or thwart their expression.

Another way to think about a relational view is from the perspective of communal cognition. Harré (2008) writes, 'The domain of thinking is intrapersonal and interpersonal. Thinking is not only an Individual–Personal activity but also a Social–Public one' (p. 28). That is, acts of thinking such as remembering often involve interaction with others ('to decide what happened') or with artifacts (e.g., photographs). People positioned in certain ways – such as being mentally ill – may lose their right to participate in this kind of communal cognition. Their utterances may be dismissed or not taken seriously by others, in some cases losing even their right to define their own subjectivity (replaced instead by the language of psychiatry). From this standpoint the strengths perspective can be considered a positioning that enables participation in communal cognition and that invites positive storylines (e.g., a survivor of adversity). Such positioning enables people to exercise valued rights (e.g., to be heard) and duties (e.g., relational responsibility).

The Relational Self

Social constructionists tend to replace the dominant Western idea of a singular, encapsulated self composed of internal attributes with one of multiple selves. The particular selves most salient will vary depending on social and contextual factors. This 'multi-being' framework (to use Ken Gergen's term, 2009) is congruent with the strengths perspective: abusers are not always abusing, delinquents are not always breaking the law, heroes are not always engaging in acts of heroism. Thus, rather than focusing on the identification of internal, invariant personal qualities, emphasis is placed on relational positioning and its implications. When relationship takes center stage practitioners become integral to the strengths they seek to identify and enable. This positions them as allies and enablers rather than experts on the internal life of others.

Another illustration of interactive positioning is found in Karl Weick's (2001) discussion of adopting a 'naive' stance, which he describes as 'reject[ing] received wisdom that something is a problem', 'start[ing] with fewer preconceptions', and 'favor[ing] optimism' (pp. 238–239). This stance may require finding new words or ways of using words (for example, 'at promise' instead of 'at risk'), suspending belief in the taken-for-granted, and thinking counter to 'the evidence'. The value of such naivety lies in its potential to expand the space in which to generate new relational possibilities (Witkin, 2005).

The field of aging provides an illustrative example. Understanding aging as a process of decline characterized by diminished capacities and infirmities is deeply ingrained in our culture. Such a process seems to reflect 'the way things are'. Support for this impression can be found in gerontological research journals replete with reports 'documenting' the various declines associated with aging. In recent years, however, other voices have surfaced that question these 'facts'. For example, Ken Gergen and Mary Gergen in their *Positive Aging Newsletter* (2004) identified various limitations of the gerontological research literature (using the research on cognitive decline as an example) including: searching for deficits rather than positive characteristics, ignoring the influence of contextual demands, reporting trivial differences and capacities, attributing cause to aging rather than other plausible factors, and overgeneralizing findings to (and underestimating variability among) elders as a group. Given these limitations, other more positive interpretations may be equally likely (Witkin, 2005). It is hard to go against the grain of what seems to be the unfortunate facts of our developmental trajectory. However, if not challenged, even a strengths-oriented practitioner will be working in a delimited space trying to enact possibilities within the boundaries of the accepted reality of decline.

The point here is not that one interpretation is right and the other wrong but that the complexity of social life enables us to construe people and situations in multiple ways. Given the dominance of the deficit model, the strengths perspective provides an important, alternative way of interpreting human life in which unassailable truths and inevitable processes may be neither. This realization invites new stories of hope and refocuses our attention toward heretofore unrecognized resources. When strengths are the starting point or central theme for narratives about people's lives, new realities are generated. Like an ultraviolet light that makes visible previously unseen parts of the spectrum, the strengths perspective 'reveals' human potentialities that could not be perceived in the 'light' of current beliefs about human suffering (Witkin, 2001). It reminds us that the limits on someone's potential may be more cultural than existential.

Considering strengths as a relation integrates others (e.g., social workers) into the meaning-making process that generates them. It invites us to examine how we relate to the people we serve and to ask how we can coordinate our interactions to help them articulate and move toward their aspirations. Strengths relationships enable suppressed or potential selves to be acknowledged or expressed. They encourage a 'relational responsibility' (McNamee and Gergen, 1999) that reduces the alterity of our clients (Witkin, 2008).

There is an oft-quoted saying related to the strengths perspective that 'it is as wrong to deny the possible as it is to deny the problem' (Saleebey, 2008: 128). While there is wisdom in this assertion, I would rephrase it slightly to: it is as wrong to deny the possible as it is to deny someone's suffering. The advantage of this revision is that it does not imply accepting 'the problem', as defined or understood, which itself may be an expression of deficit thinking or pathologizing. To 'not deny the problem' in such circumstances might limit the range of relational positions and language that could be used. For example, to simply accept that a child has attention deficit disorder is to assume certain beliefs about the causes of her difficulties and to set certain parameters within which to employ a strengths perspective. 'The problem' is medicalized and individualized. Within this context, 'the possible' is limited and the position of naivety, described previously, is eliminated.

A variant of this issue relates to difference. Practicing from a relational strengths perspective does not mean denying or glossing over differences. However, it does influence what an identified difference is taken to mean or how it functions. For example, in their study of relationships of people with severe disabilities and their caregivers, Robert Bogdan and Steven Taylor (1989) note that their 'relationships are based not on the denial of difference, but rather on the absence of impugning the others' moral character because of it' (p. 278). Parents related to their children as unique, thinking individuals – as humans with the status of personhood. They also held an expanded understanding of reciprocity that enabled them to experience these relationships as mutually satisfying.

Identifying difference, rather than disability, as the problem can be difficult. In her dissertation research about visual representations of people with disabilities, Ann Fudge Schormans (2010) writes that 'The emphasis is still on taking care *of the problem* of disability instead of caring about, attributing value, and finding a place for people with disabilities' (p. 375, emphasis in original). In other words, there is no denial of the (socially constructed) difference associated with disability; however, this does not necessarily mean accepting the individual difference that is called disability as a problem. Rather, the problem can be located in social attitudes, beliefs, and institutional policies regarding people labeled as disabled or handicapped.

Not everyone gets to employ the strengths perspective. People who are ascribed pejorative labels or who are positioned as incompetent in certain ways may not have the standing to view their situation or enter into relationships from a strengths perspective. Can a person with a disability, a drug addiction, or a criminal record assess their situation from a strengths perspective? Would such a description/assessment have legitimacy? Could it counter the hegemony of pathology? I would suggest that it is within relationships, in this case practitioner–client relationships, that the strengths perspective can be realized. In an important sense there can be no strengths without a corresponding, legitimating response from someone positioned with the rights to make such a response. Social workers and other practitioners have such rights.

Keeping strengths relational helps to keep them contextual and functional. There can be no meaning without context and it is how we *use* language (not, for example, its meaning in a dictionary) that is most relevant. This may be why some programs focusing on skill training or affirmations detached from meaningful life circumstances may be of questionable benefit. On the other hand, recognizing strengths and building on them to make life changes can be powerful.

Mona Wasow (2001) provides a dramatic illustration in an article about her son, David, a young man with a chronic psychiatric disability (schizophrenia). Despite years of therapy, rehabilitation programs, and a variety of medications, David's condition had not markedly changed. He could not hold a job, was often asocial, and was deficient in 'daily living skills' like showering regularly. Efforts to teach him basic skills such as grooming and using public transportation were largely unsuccessful. As Wasow so poignantly put it, 'But where should he go on the bus? For whom should he shower? With whom should he make eye contact – with those fearful strangers on the street who he knows want no contact with him whatsoever?' (p. 1306). One day, out of frustration to the oft recounting of David's deficits, one of his therapists exclaimed, 'I don't want to hear all that again. That's his illness, and we have not been able to change that for years. Tell me about his strengths; we would do better to work with those' (p. 1306). This led to new efforts that built on David's love of music and guitar playing and his interest in pottery. Guitar and pottery lessons (relational activities) became the starting point for helping David. The daily living skills now were learned in the service of these interests rather than the other way around. Wasow notes, 'Learn to ride the bus to get to the pottery studio? You bet. Even make a little eye contact with the friendly pottery teacher, who laughed with pleasure at David's newly created ceramic bear sitting in a canoe' (p. 1306).

Strengths as Perspective[4]

Given that it has been about three decades since the first publications on the strengths perspective, readers might wonder why it has remained merely a perspective and not 'progressed' to a theory. In response, I want to suggest that there are good reasons for maintaining perspective (pun intended). Theory, in the formal sense, while potentially useful implies an esoteric type of knowledge that is not easy to understand and to which only 'experts' have access. In contrast, 'perspective' is a word of everyday language. It suggests a relationality and openness that theory lacks. Perspectives position us in a particular relation to other things. Unlike theories, which are *about* something, perspectives are locations of noticing. This makes them less substantive and more conditional and emergent than theories; for example, your understanding may change when you view something from a different perspective. Perspectives function as standpoints or orienting mechanisms; turning our gaze in a particular direction or tuning our senses to certain frequencies. Unlike theories, perspectives are easily changed. The word itself implies multiples, each with its own sensitivities. Thus, there is less embeddedness in content and more invitation to experimentation, that is, how do things look from this perspective?

The strengths perspective, as a perspective, reminds us that the way something appears is relative to where you are, not only physically, but culturally, historically, geographically, emotionally, and spiritually. These perspectives can also change in light of new information or experience; for example, 'I gained a new perspective on poverty after living in a public housing project'. There is nothing obligatory or sacrosanct about any particular perspective. Why some choices seem to make sense or are dominant has more to do with historical, cultural, and social factors than with the degree of correspondence between a position and 'reality'. There is choice. Adopting the strengths perspective is to recognize and enter this mélange of possibilities, not asserting the truth, but rather proposing that our attempts to help others may be enhanced.

Preserving the status of the strengths perspective as a sense-making framework helps us to remember that it is one of many possible perspectives for guiding our awareness and interpretations. Our interest shifts from questions about whether something is *really* a strength to how the strengths perspective functions in practice. For example: How does the donning of strengths-tinted lenses affect our noticing, understandings, and relationships? Does it move us in the direction of our visions of helping and world-building? Our responses to such questions will help us discover the functional meanings of the strengths perspective (Witkin, 2008).

The Language of Strengths[5]

There is a dynamic interdependence between what we take to be real and the language available to construe these beliefs. For many social workers the strengths perspective will provide an alternative language – of promise, resilience, generativity, and transformation – that enables them to reassess and, when necessary, 'talk back' to the dominant discourses of illness, pathology, and weakness. As an educator, I find it heartening to hear students' stories in which strengths discourse provides a context that enables them to question policies and practices and generate new, constructive possibilities for working with people. On the other hand, too often I have seen this language limited by assumptions about meaning or a priori beliefs about strengths, viewing strengths in a denotative rather than a connotative way.

To call something a strength is not to reveal an unassailable feature of reality, but to ascribe a value to a concept. For example, when I identify an individual's 'optimism' (a concept) as a strength, I am ascribing a value to some assumed quality, attribute, or characteristic (themselves social constructions). However, as literary theorists have pointed out, there is no necessary relation between a word and its referent. Nothing about a person or situation demands the words 'optimism' and 'strength'; it is one of many possible interpretations. What we call a strength (or a deficit for that matter) can be anything. This position frees us to expand our thinking about the ways in which people manage to survive and thrive in less-than-optimal circumstances. We need not limit our analyses to factors presumed to represent resources or resilience, but can entertain heretofore unconsidered possibilities. We can listen to others more openly in ways less fettered to theoretical screens.

Maintaining this openness helps keep the strengths perspective from becoming another 'universal good' that fails to recognize human diversity and how different perspectives function in different contexts. Despite the enthusiasm engendered by the strengths perspective, we must be mindful of how ostensibly positive concepts like social justice have been used to deflect or rationalize the perpetration of harms. Similarly, it is important that the strengths perspective not be reified, converted into a 'thing' with an enumerated list of defining characteristics that functions as a kind of virtue ethic or prescription for healthy living. To do so would diminish its power to transform and reproduce the reality-generating dimension of deficit discourses that strengths-oriented practitioners find so problematic. Practitioners can obviate these potential risks by retaining a perspective orientation and keeping strengths relational.

Positive Psychology

Fifteen years ago the term positive psychology might have been unfamiliar to most readers; however, this is likely no longer the case. In fact, for many in social work, positive psychology is probably seen as the new face of the strengths perspective, shoring up its foundations and extending its reach. Developed in the late 1990s by Martin Seligman, a psychologist previously most known for his work on 'learned helplessness', positive psychology has quickly become a widespread and highly influential, cross-disciplinary movement (e.g., Rusk and Waters, 2013). Not surprisingly, this rapid ascendance has drawn the attention of various analysts who, along with positive psychology's merits, point to its substantial funding and its ambitious program of information dissemination and development through numerous academic and lay publications, conferences, a dedicated research center, and graduate programs. Also noted as contributing to positive psychology's appeal is its congruence with the dominant Western, liberal view of personhood and, in particular, its rhetorical positioning as an important expression of US ideology. For instance, based on analyses of various positive psychology writings, Yen (2010) posits that positive psychology has constructed itself 'as an intellectual endeavor destined for this particular moment in American history – whatever that may be – and as a field whose values and purpose are intertwined with national and democratic ideals' (p. 72).

Interestingly, although publications on the strengths perspective preceded positive psychology by at least a decade (e.g., Weick, Rapp, Sullivan, and Kisthardt, 1989; Saleebey, 1992) the former's influence has been comparatively modest, largely confined to social work. Moreover, the strengths perspective is rarely acknowledged in the enormous positive psychology literature[6] and (in my opinion) never given adequate credit for its substantive contributions (for example, Saleebey's seminal work on the strengths perspective and social work practice originally published in 1992 and now in its 6th – 2012 – edition). This oversight or neglect may strike readers as puzzling given positive psychology's apparent congruence with the strengths perspective, particularly the former's critique of the emphasis on pathology and its aim to 'catalyze a change in the focus of psychology from preoccupation only with repairing the worst things in life to also building positive qualities' (Seligman and Csikszentmihalyi, 2000, p. 5). However, there also are differences that I suspect explain this situation. These include positive psychology's avowed scientific orientation in contrast to the general view of social work as not scientifically based and positive psychology's highly individualistic orientation. Additionally, positive psychology's ambitious agenda tends to emphasize its roots in the writings of famous philosophers (Yen, 2010), not social workers.

From my perspective, these differences reflect dissimilarities in orientations between social work and psychology and beliefs about what constitutes knowledge. Such differences are worth preserving and underscore the importance of a relational understanding of strengths.

While strongly proclaiming its scientific pedigree and adherence to the canons of conventional research (e.g., a detached attitude toward the objects of inquiry) may give positive psychology an aura of authority, this orientation also seems to blind it to certain limitations and biases.[7] For example, consistent with the conventional model of science, positive psychology claims to base itself on universal, timeless qualities that constitute the good life. Thus, Seligman and Csikszentmihalyi (2000) claim that positive psychology research can 'transcend particular cultures and politics and approach universality' (p. 5). This position leads to the enumeration and measurement of 'character strengths and virtues' that are believed to be cross-culturally valid. Such a position seems to minimize cultural variations in the meanings of these qualities and assumes a summative approach to the good life that is decidedly acontextual (Slife and Richardson, 2008). The use of words like 'objective' and 'descriptive' to characterize positive psychology research further obscures its ideological perspective. Thus, for example, while positive psychologists claim to be describing how people in other cultures identify their aspirations and values, they overlook the important historical, contextual and language differences that give these terms different meanings (Christopher and Hickenbottom, 2008). One result is that what is presented as an objective description of timeless truths can also be understood as an ideology that prescribes optimal (North American) values and goals.

A limitation of empiricist philosophy as expressed in conventional social science is its inability to step outside of itself and interrogate its own biases. In large part, this occurs because such biases (as I see them) are not considered biases, but truths. In the case of positive psychology, this blind spot is its individualistic, Western, view of the self as an encapsulated, interiorized entity. Becker and Marecek (2008) comment on how positive psychology's tacit endorsement of American individualism 'shapes its premises about human growth, fulfillment, and values, as well as its vision of the relationship between individuals and societal institutions' (p. 1170) in particular its embrace of self-improvement, which, I would add, is a representative expression of neo-liberal ideology. As Christopher and Hickenbottom argue, this view of the self 'is not a universal truth, but rather an interpretation ...' (p. 566) and one that is not shared by much of world's population. Rather, 'if identity is defined in a more extended or inclusive manner, as it is and has been for most of the world, the prized indicators of the good person tend to be interpersonal' (p. 568). Similarly, Slife and Richardson (2008) argue for a 'relational ontology' in which 'We are not first and fundamentally separated from one another, needing to find something (e.g., a shared belief or value to connect us). We are first and fundamentally related to one another in our most basic identities and roles' (p. 718).

It is these two areas, adherence to conventional science and individualism, where the strengths perspective (re)located in relationships can provide an important alternative. Such positioning encourages the problematizing of dualisms such as objective/subjective, emphasizes a contextual orientation, and maintains a dynamically interpretative and explicitly moral and value-based approach.

Some of this is wishful thinking. Although the strengths perspective is not based on the strict conventional scientific/research stance as positive psychology, calls for its validation or effectiveness through such research are not uncommon and probably inevitable given the current climate around evidence and outcomes. There is nothing inherently wrong with conventional research. My concern is that when the strengths perspective is thought of in terms of 'dependent and independent variables' and the 'effectiveness of the strengths model on different consumer populations ...' (Rapp, Saleebey, and Sullivan, 2005: p. 87) its important contextual, relational, and moral dimensions are minimized. As Goldstein (2002) has written, 'it is not the staid human sciences but the vital humanities and its literature – the novel, autobiography, poetry, and drama – that best tells us about the resilience and strength and their implicit moral persuasions that one calls on to become a person' (p. 25). We must not cede these rich sources of understanding to the authority of narrow scientific metatheory.

By sharing the same philosophical tenets and methodological approaches to knowledge production as those who favor pathological perspectives, positive psychology may be less alternative than claimed (Becker and Marecek, 2008). Although their foci might look different, their assumptions about the nature of reality and how to know this reality and its implications are identical. Thus, arguments tend to focus on which side is 'right' and may never extend to questioning, for example, how they generate the very realities that they claim to discover, the model of the person that is assumed, or the cultural biases inherent in their findings. This is somewhat like using the same tools to build houses. In one case, the builders focus on building square houses and in the other round ones. Both have similar views of the tools that should be used, how to use them, and what constitutes a house (although its shape may differ).

In contrast, the strengths perspective with its roots in the lived experiences of disenfranchised and marginalized people and their narratives of personal and community survival and achievement can offer a more expansive vision of change and flourishing. One that does not claim nor seek to claim a universal template of virtues to which all should aspire, but that simply re-directs people to identify and utilize whatever resources and assets make sense within their social and cultural contexts. Befitting its social work foundation, there is more attention to context; that is, the person-in-environment perspective, interest in people who are disadvantaged by oppressive social arrangements, sensitivity to the social character of life, and respect for differences. Still, as suggested previously, individualism often trumps relationality and it is here that I am suggesting that the strengths perspective can be 'strengthened'.

Concluding Thoughts

Despite encouraging inroads into practice, education, and inquiry, understanding people in terms of their deficits, diseases, and failings is still going strong. Three brief examples illustrate what I mean. First, the latest version of the DSM (Diagnostic and Statistical Manual of the American Psychiatric Association), still the de facto standard of diagnosis, contains a new list of diagnostic labels identifying individual pathologies, syndromes, and disorders that will be used to define and categorize people. Second, psychotropic medications are now taken regularly by millions of people, including children. Overwhelmingly, the rationale for prescribing such medications is to alleviate the symptoms of some disorder or their presumed cause.[8] Third, is the ascendance of what might be called the actuarial perspective (see Chapter 5). We live in a time of heightened awareness of risk. Almost everything, from natural phenomena to human inventions to individuals, is viewed in terms of the possible damage or harm it might cause. Such thinking contributes to a pervasive sense of uncertainty and fear. When applied to individuals, the language of risks often sounds very similar to the language of deficits; consider, for example, 'ineffective parenting' as a risk factor for 'early-onset antisocial behavior' in children. Note too that deficit labels also can be risk factors for further risks, for example, having a 'mental disorder' is a risk factor for substance abuse. Although a focus on harm reduction and probability tends to be viewed as less pejorative or stigmatizing than an overt focus on pathology, a risk orientation calls us to look for what is wrong, missing, or deviant. In doing so, it fosters relationships of mistrust, caution, and suspicion (Witkin, 2012).

The strengths perspective provides an important counterbalance to all three of the preceding examples. It does so by offering an alternative frame and language by which to understand people's challenges and struggles which in turn encourages different ways of 'social working'. For instance, we are invited to supplement the dialogue of risk with the dialogue of promise. Yes, the world can be a dangerous place where people do hurtful things to themselves and others. But it is also a place where acts of kindness, altruism, compassion, heroism, and generosity happen. What we notice is influenced by our perspective. A strengths perspective helps us to 'see' potentialities and to relate to others in ways that acknowledge and validate them. To consider the potential ramifications of such an approach when conducted en masse is to begin to gain a sense of the power of the strengths perspective (Witkin, 2012).

Is there a particular way to practice the strengths perspective? I would argue, no. To prescribe how to do so would transform the strengths perspective from a perspective to a practice approach. While it can be argued that this would preserve the fidelity of the approach, it has the drawback of limiting its creative possibilities and of narrowing its scope to a particular point of view and reducing it to a set of methods. Despite this, there have been attempts to identify key components of the strengths perspective. Rapp, Saleebey, and Sullivan (2005) identify six 'hallmarks' of the strengths perspective: a goal orientation, a systematic assessment of strengths, environment as a resource, using explicit methods for using strengths to attain goals, inducing hope, and providing meaningful choices for clients. As I see it, the potential value of this enumeration is as a platform for further dialogue about the strengths perspective and how it may be used; the potential drawback is its use as a litmus test of what is or is not the strengths perspective or even worse, its operationalization into something like a checklist.

The various ways in which the strengths perspective is understood and practiced make it vulnerable to critiques. Some of these can be helpful. Consonant with this chapter's themes, Dybicz (2011) argues that a modernist orientation toward the strengths perspective leads to its misunderstanding and misapplication. Gray (2011) warns of the possibility of the strengths perspective serving as another expression of neo-liberalism in which responsibility for change is placed on individuals rather than structural factors. Similarly Guo and Tsoi (2010) argue that the strengths perspective does not adequately address power relations and the social conditions (e.g., poverty) that affect those relations and overly depends on a model of 'pure rationality' (p. 238). They propose an expanded understanding of strengths that goes beyond resilience to include resistance and rebellion.

To some extent, these critiques are addressed by adopting a relational stance. If strengths are constructed within relationships, we all bear some responsibility for their generation (as we do for deficits and pathology). The onus of change is not shifted onto individuals qua individuals but onto the social processes that engender problems and that might enable new ways of relating. Similarly, rationality is no longer located in the individual mind but in historical, cultural, and social processes.

It takes courage for social workers to practice from a strengths perspective and to challenge or unlearn past truths (Saleebey, 1996). Inventing new expressions risks obfuscation. Questioning the self-evident or the 'scientifically documented' risks charges of irreverence or extremism. Strengths-based practitioners are challenged to not deny the 'reality' of disease and dysfunction, or to delay providing needed assistance. In a world that increasingly requires that clients be assigned formal diagnoses and where poverty is considered a personal failing, resisting these challenges is difficult. However, the strengths perspective helps us understand that reality is equivocal: a world in which deficits are salient is one reality, one in which strengths prevail is another. As noted previously, this latter position need not deter practitioners from acting to relieve suffering or prevent harm. We can accept the reality of others' pain without assuming their 'disease' and the social implications that such formulations entail. For the strengths-based practitioner or researcher, the key question becomes not what is Real (capital R intended), but what are the implications of the ways that we construct the real? For example, strengths-based practitioners believe that when reality is constructed in collaboration with clients, when their stories are combined with, not subjugated to, professionals' stories, we generate useful realities. They also believe that focusing on the qualities and actions of people and communities that enabled them to surmount difficulties or even just 'get by' in difficult circumstances leads to practices that are more in line with our professional values and beliefs than those developed from focusing on their deficits and failures (Witkin, 2001).

As experienced practitioners know, in the process of trying to change others, we also change. Thus it is not uncommon for those who work from a strengths perspective to report that over time they experience themselves and their relationships differently. There's nothing magical about this. The social world is highly variegated and complex. It 'offers itself up to [our] imagination' (Oliver, 1986). The strengths perspective invites us to imagine a world in which all people are treated with respect and dignity: in which difficult situations are opportunities for growth, where the marginalized and disadvantaged can teach the rest of us about resourcefulness, resilience, and heroism; in which our focus is on how people thrive and endure rather than how they deteriorate and fail; and in which our bootstraps are interlaced and lifted by us all.

In hindsight, it may have been unfortunate to have named this alternative vision the strengths perspective. Although it provided an easy-to-discern contrast with the dominant approach to human struggles, it got too easily subsumed by the foundational ideologies of these same approaches. At this point, adding the word 'relational' before strengths may have some benefit, at least as a reminder to not limit the strengths perspective to an individual perspective and to reclaim the social that is part of its heritage.

Notes

1 This chapter is dedicated to the memory of Dennis Saleebey, a brilliant and pioneering voice in the development of the strengths perspective. Parts of this chapter have been taken or adapted from Witkin, 2001, 2005, 2008, 2012.

2 Although resources external to the person such as family may also be identified, their function – in addition to possible material support – is similar to the

practitioner's: to help the individual recognize and develop their internal positive qualities.

3 There are other related issues such as a modernist model of science that minimizes the role of historical, social, and cultural factors that are taken up briefly later in the chapter.

4 Also, see Witkin (2005).

5 See Witkin (2008).

6 One exception is the *Encyclopedia of Positive Psychology*, Vol. 2, (Lopez, 2009) which contains entries on the strengths perspective in social welfare to distinguish it from another entry on the strengths perspective in positive psychology and on Dennis Saleebey, who is probably most responsible for awareness of the strengths perspectives in social work. It should be noted, however, that as an encyclopedia these volumes offer a compendium of terms – including social work – that are considered having any association with positive psychology.

7 Positive psychology has also been criticized for its inconsistency regarding its scientific grounding, seemingly disregarding these evidentiary criteria in certain publications (see, for example, Wong's 2011 review of Seligman's recent book on 'flourishing').

8 In some cases, these 'disorders' (e.g., depression) are said to be engendered by the constant demands of finding one's 'authentic self' (e.g., Petersen, 2011).

References

Becker, D., & Marecek, J. (2008). Dreaming the American dream: Individualism and positive psychology. *Social and Personality Psychology Compass, 2*(5), 1767–1780.

Bogdan, R., & Taylor, S. J. (1989). Relationships with severely disabled people: The social construction of humanness. *Social Problems, 36*, 135–148.

Christopher, J. C., & Hickinbottom, S. (2008). Positive psychology, ethnocentrism, and the disguised ideology of individualism. *Theory and Psychology, 18*, 563–589.

Dybicz, P. (2011). Interpreting the strengths perspective through narrative theory. *Families in Society, 92*(3), 247–253.

Gergen, K. J. (2009). *Relational being: Beyond self and community.* New York, NY: Oxford University Press.

Gergen, K. J. (2011). The self as social construction. *Psychological Studies, 56*(1), 108–116.

Gergen, K., & Gergen, M. (2003).Questioning cognitive decline in aging. *The Positive Aging Newsletter*, No. 22, www.healthandage.com

Goldstein, H. (2002). The literary and moral foundations of the strength perspective. In D. Saleebey (ed.) *The strengths perspective in social work practice*, 3rd edition (pp. 23–47). Boston: Allyn and Bacon.

Gray, M. (2011). Back to basics: A critique of the strengths perspective in social work. *Families in Society: The Journal of Contemporary Social Services, 92*(1), 1–7.

Guo, W., & Tsoi, M. (2010). From resilience to resistance: A reconstruction of the strengths perspective in social work practice. *International Social Work, 53*(2), 233–245.

Harré, R. (2008). Positioning theory. *Self-Care and Dependent Care Nursing, 16*(1), 28–32.

Harré, R., Moghaddam, F. M., Pilkerton Cairnie, T., Rothbart, D., & Sabat, S. R. (2009). Recent advances in positioning theory. *Theory and Psychology, 19*(1), 5–31.

Lopez, S. J. (ed.) (2009). *Encyclopedia of positive psychology, Vol. 2.* London: Blackwell.

McNamee, S., and Gergen, K. J., & associates (1999). *Relational responsibility.* Thousand Oaks, CA: Sage.

Oliver, M. (1986). Wild geese. *Dream Work.* Boston: Atlantic Monthly Press.

Petersen, A. (2011). Authentic self-realization and depression. *International Sociology, 26*(5), 5–24.

Rapp, C. A., Saleebey, D., & Sullivan, W. P. (2005). The future of strengths-based social work'. *Advances in Social Work, 6*(1), 79–90.

Rusk, R. D., & Waters, L. E. (2013). Tracing the size, reach, impact, and breadth of positive psychology. *The Journal of Positive Psychology, 8*(3), 207–221.

Saleebey, D. (Ed.) (1992). *The strengths perspective in social work practice.* White Plains, NY: Longman.

Saleebey, D. (1996). The strengths perspective in social work practice: Extensions and cautions. *Social Work, 41,* 296–305.

Saleebey, D. (2008). The strengths perspective: Putting possibility and hope to work in our practice. In Karen M. Sowers, & Catherine N. Dulmus (Eds.), *Comprehensive handbook of social work and social welfare* (pp. 123–142). Hoboken, NJ: John Wiley and Sons.

Schormans, A. F. (2010). *The right or responsibility of inspection: Social work, photography, and people with intellectual disabilities.* PhD Dissertation, University of Toronto.

Seligman, M. E. P., & Csikszentmihalyi, M. (2000). Positive psychology: An introduction. *American Psychology, 55,* 5–14.

Slife, B. D., & Richardson, F. C. (2008). Problematic ontological underpinnings of positive psychology: A strong relational alternative. *Theory and Psychology, 18,* 699–723.

Wasow, M. (2001). Strengths versus deficits, or musician versus schizophrenic. *Psychiatric Services, 52*(10), 1306–1307.

Weick, K. (2001). *Making sense of the organization* (pp. 438–439). New York, NY; Oxford: Basil Blackwell.

Weick, A., Rapp, C., Sullivan, W. P., & Kisthardt, W. (1989). A strengths perspective for social work practice. *Social Work, 34*(4), 350–354.

Witkin, S. L. (2001). Foreword. In D. Saleebey (Ed.), *The strengths perspective in social work practice* (3rd edition, pp. xiii–xv). Boston, MA: Pearson/Allyn and Bacon.

Witkin, S. L. (2005). Foreword. In D. Saleebey (Ed.) *The strengths perspective in social work practice,* 4th edition. Boston, MA: Allyn and Bacon.

Witkin, S. L. (2008). Foreword. In D. Saleebey (Ed.) *The strengths perspective in social work practice,* 5th edition. Boston, MA: Allyn and Bacon.

Witkin, S. L. (2012). Foreword. In D. Saleebey (Ed.) *The strengths perspective in social work practice,* 6th edition. Hoboken, NJ: Pearson.

Wong, P. T. P. (2011). Big money, big science, big names, and the flourishing of positive psychology. *PsycCRITIQUES, 56,* Release 49, Article 1.

Yen, J. (2010). Authorizing happiness: Rhetorical demarcation of science and society in historical narratives of positive psychology. *Journal of Theoretical and Philosophical Psychology, 30,* 67–78.

7 Social Work from a Global Perspective

Social work in the 21st century is a global profession. This globalism references a marked growth in the number of social work programs worldwide and the increased awareness of the impact of global factors and conditions on issues of concern to social workers. More specifically, political changes over the past 25 years have led to the development or re-development of many social work programs in Eastern Europe, China, and Africa. Additionally, there is widespread recognition of the worldwide impacts of advances in communication and transportation technology and the interdependencies and global nature of issues affecting people across the globe. For instance, issues related to the environment, health, violence, and economics transcend the arbitrary borders of nation states. Also of importance for social work is the awareness that these issues do not affect people equally but tend to have their most adverse impact on those who are poor, disadvantaged, and marginalized.

These developments have highlighted the need to re-consider social work from a global perspective. It invites us to question whether social work's traditional (i.e., Western) intellectual frameworks and practices are the most useful and relevant for addressing the complexity and diversity of a global context. In other words, the central issue is not *whether* social work should adopt a global perspective, but *how*. I will argue that to respond to these changes without radical changes to our analytical frameworks and understandings is to risk reproducing Western hegemony on a broader scale. In response, I will propose an alternative approach to these developments.

Before delving into this issue, there are some matters of terminology that need to be addressed. I do this not to come up with correct definitions, but for the sake of clarity – to enable you, the reader, to understand how I am using particular terms. These usages also constitute, in part, my analyses and positions.[1]

First, you will notice that I favor the terms social work from a global perspective or social work in a global context over the more popular and concise term, 'international social work'. Although this latter term has wide recognition, it suggests the notion of nation states and relations between them; that is, to be inter-national. In contrast, global implies a more transnational perspective. Additionally, the term international social work invites definitions that treat it as an entity. This tends to concretize and narrow its meanings. Definitions inevitably reflect the position and interests of the definers, legitimating certain views and practices and marginalizing others. Using global perspective or global context seems to me to be a less restrictive entrée into this area. Lastly, 'international social work' implies a particular kind of social work, a specialization. Specializations are optional. They are chosen based on interest. In contrast, I view all social work as global and, therefore, a necessary perspective that must be integrated into our understanding of social work.

Second, I want to provide some clarity among globality, globalism, and globalization as they are terms frequently encountered in the literature.[2] My brief explication does not imply that these terms are always used in the way expressed here or that there is consensus on their meaning so it is still necessary to understand their usage within different contexts. Simply put, globalism can be thought of as a representation of interconnectedness, the '… networks of connections spanning multi-continental distances, drawing them close together economically, socially, culturally and informationally' (Das, 2011: 18). Globalization refers to processes by which globalism is augmented or diminished, usually the former. Both globalism and globalization can have many dimensions, for example, economic, cultural, political. Also, there is sufficient ambiguity in their use such that it is not always clear which term applies in a particular statement. Given its active nature and importance in understanding social work from a global perspective, globalization will be taken up in some detail. Finally, globality seems more an existential state, referring 'to the consciousness of living in one world' that is often considered as a consequence of globalization (Guillén 2001).

Donning Global Lenses

Adopting a global perspective has the potential to change our understanding of social work, the issues that are important to address, and how to go about doing so. On the positive side, a global perspective can increase awareness of global issues, policies, and institutions, and sensitize us to their impact. For instance, interconnections between the global and local and interdependencies such as environmental, health, and economic issues may become more visible. A global perspective may also deepen appreciation of differences arising from different histories, geographies, and cultures. It extends our domain of concern beyond localities and national borders to people perceived as different. These changes may, in turn, enrich social work's knowledge base and practices and bring needed services to more of the world.

Discussions of global or international social work tend to have five foci:

1. social justice and human rights particularly as articulated in international documents and covenants such as the UN Declaration of Human Rights;
2. problems that are defined by their cross-border dimension, for example, refugee issues or child trafficking;
3. problems that are viewed as having global ramifications or significance, for example, poverty or environmental issues;
4. the impacts of globalization; and
5 knowledge of other cultures both within a nation state (often linked to 'cultural competence', see Chapter 4) and outside of it.

These topics are important and worthy of attention; however, it is *how* they are addressed that concerns me. As suggested previously, I would contend that without a shift in our interpretive and analytical frameworks, there is a risk of enabling positions that we might oppose and reproducing the kinds of relations we might wish to change; for instance, when 'international social work' becomes a way of extending a particular ideology such as neo-liberalism or a positivist-oriented science that functions as a form of dominance or exploitation. This also can happen when concepts like social justice and globalization are taken up as universals without critical analysis. Despite the hard-to-resist appeal to promote social justice, without critical analysis of its meanings or uses, we risk advocating for something antithetical to social work values.

Conventional understandings and the intellectual frameworks on which they are based tend to assume the reality of the extant world. This limits the range of responses and keeps change 'within the paradigm'. Adopting a global perspective can be a transformative move. Whether or not this is so will depend on whether this perspective is used to challenge foundational beliefs and assumptions and spur imaginative, alternative understandings and practices, or whether 'global' is simply tacked onto existing frameworks.

How might we address this? One possibility is to use the concept of discourse as an interpretive and analytical framework. Holliday (2010) states, 'It is at the level of discourse that individuals are able to negotiate, make sense of and practice culture; and it is within this process that imaginations about culture are generated and ideology is both experienced and manufactured' (p. 1). As noted in Chapter 1, discourse, in the Foucauldian sense, can be thought of as a system of knowledge, a way of *constituting* the world through the ways we have to understand, talk about, ,and represent it (Miller, 2008). The important points to re-emphasize here are, first, that discourses are more than just representations or descriptions, but constitutive. As I will argue, globalization discourse not only describes a phenomenon, but generates it, reflecting and creating global realities. Second, discourses do this through language, through the institutions that inscribe their tenets, and through the practices that enact them. Third, the embedded and pervasive qualities of dominant discourses give their representations a naturalism or common-sense appearance that protects them – to some extent – from critique and influences how we understand and respond to their 'problems'. For example, Edward Said's idea of orientalism (1978) was meant to show how commonly-assumed representations of the Orient were not descriptors, but a way of depicting Eastern cultures as alien and inferior to those of the West. This type of understanding is extended by representing Eastern and Western cultures using so-called neutral categories of collectivism and individualism (Holliday, 2010).

Typically, however, there exist alternative discourses that offer competing understandings. These alternatives discourses can be a resource for social workers who represent interests and people not always embodied in the dominant discourses of a society. Consider, for example, the construct of 'family'. Instead of viewing it as a thing, we can view it as a 'discursive field', a site in which different family discourses (e.g., nuclear family, extended family, non-biologically related persons) vie for legitimation.

Globalization

The concept of globalization provides a useful platform for illustrating the potential uses of adopting a discourse perspective. What do you think of when you hear the word 'globalization?' A world economy? Interdependence? Greater opportunities? Multinational capitalism? Paradoxes? McDonald's? These are typical of the responses students give when I pose this question to them. Such diversity is not surprising as the complexity of globalization invites many definitions. Definitions of globalization often emphasize its economic aspects (Wiebelhaus-Brahm, 2002), particularly the global proliferation of free-market capitalism; however, other aspects such as culture or politics may also be identified. Other definitions focus on generic features of globalization such as increased interdependency or interconnectedness, or the compression of time and space. So numerous are the definitions, that debate over the meaning of globalization has become its own subfield (e.g., Al-Rodhan & Stoudmann, 2006).

The breadth and ubiquity of globalization (as a concept) also enables it to be used as shorthand or code for multiple trends or changes, as an inevitable force, and as a deterministic explanation for myriad events or phenomena. This boundless application can nevertheless limit its usefulness.

As Van Der Bly (2005) notes, when globalization explains everything it explains nothing, that is, it becomes a tautology.

Although globalization as the exchange of goods or cultural influence among nations is not new, what does seem different in the contemporary era is its scope and intensity. Regarding scope, Das (2011) writes, 'Never in history had global integration involved so many people, both in absolute numbers and as a percentage of the global population' (p. 16). Intensity as I use it here refers to the concept of supraterritoriality and space–time compression. Supraterritoriality refers to the transcendence of territorial distance and borders and even time primarily as a result of technology. Scholte (2005a) states that 'global connections often also have qualities of transworld simultaneity (that is, they extend anywhere across the planet at the same time) and transworld instantaneity (that is, they move anywhere on the planet in not time)' (p. 18). Place is de-linked from territory and distances are traversed almost instantly. This does not mean that territoriality is unimportant, connections originate from somewhere; however, territorial boundaries no longer impede or prohibit contact and territorial issues are understood differently (Scholte, 2002). This has implications for how people experience the world. 'With globalization people become more able – physically, legally, linguistically, culturally and psychologically – to engage with each other wherever on the planet Earth they might be' (Scholte 2005b: 59). These supraterritorial relations connect people in complex ways that influence their actions, experiences, and life choices. 'In participating and acting in these connections, individuals and communities see the world increasingly as one place and imagine new activities and roles for themselves in this world' (retrieved from www.globalautonomy.ca/global1/global_guide.jsp).

While recognizing this new connectivity, it is also important to recognize that not everyone shares in this experience. That is, globalization is not equally global nor does everyone benefit. For example, many countries in sub-Saharan Africa have experienced an increase rather than a decline in poverty (Das, 2011). Similarly, the notion of global consciousness (i.e., globalism), viewing the world as one place or identifying as a citizen of the world, is not evident among many people and as Kennedy (2007) observes, 'those who appear to exhibit it often do so ambivalently, inconsistently and erratically' (p. 269). He cites research by Norris (2000) based on World Data Survey from 1996/1997 and covering 70 nations that 'found that only one-sixth of the sample pointed to their continent or the world as a whole as their primary geographical unit of identity, rather than nation, region or immediate locality' (p. 277). Thus, we might think of globalization in the plural – globalizations – as a way to sensitize ourselves to the fact that not everyone takes up or participates in global discourse in the same way (if at all).

This differential sense of globalism extends to globalization. Various factors such as geographic location, economic position, cultural/ethnic identity, political ideology, or 'on whether one gains or loses from it' (Ritzer, 2003) will shape our views. Given globalization's perceived significance, different views about its benefits, and its unequal impact, it is not surprising that it has become a political issue with both proponents and detractors.

How then should globalization proceed, that is, how should we do globalization? A problem is that both advocates and critics can cite data to support their positions. These differences are further complicated by political assessments of whose power rises and whose suffers under currently prevailing practices of globalization and to consider whether alternative policies could have better political implications' (Scholte, 2002: 32). When coupled with the notion that globalization does not have to be understood as a singular force but as a covering concept that can be expressed in multiple ways, it becomes clear that the struggle is not confined to what is the case, but to how 'the case' is understood and judged. It is within this context that a discourse perspective can be helpful.

A discourse perspective invites us to understand globalization in a way that shifts the focus from determining which definition or position is true to considering it as a site in which competing discourses (e.g., neoliberalism, social justice, cosmopolitanism) compete for dominance. This shift has several implications. Rather than focusing on questions about what globalization is, emphasis is placed on how different understandings of globalization (as a deterministic force, as a social construction) have different consequences. Such a shift increases the possibilities for multiple conceptualizations and ways of enacting globalization. Awareness of multiple perspectives can dislodge the authority of any one position and make visible beliefs that are implicit or taken for granted thereby rendering them available for analysis. Additionally, examining different understandings and representations, how they function, and the kinds of worlds they generate, broadens choice and suggests an agentive dimension to how globalization is experienced.

Maintaining the breadth and complexity of the global frustrates reductionist attempts to create a single, uniform understanding or to express it in a quantitative form. Rather, as Fiss and Hirsh (2005) assert, globalization becomes 'a grand contest of social constructions … that enables conflicting claims to coexist and coevolve. Because the material facts at hand are ambiguous, the public discourse that develops to support and legitimate particular interpretations of these ambiguous data is of great importance' (p. 32). In a similar vein, Kalyan (2010) argues that the global becomes 'actualized in discourses that affirm certain images and representations, while excluding others' and that these discourses 'produce the very thing[s] they are supposed to re-present'

(p. 546). In other words, globalization does not refer to an independently exist-ing reality that is then revealed through representations and images as much as it is produced by them. This production also occurs on a micro level through participation in global communication processes that utilize and build inter-connectivity and community through technological infrastructures and virtual networks (Monge, 1998).

Collectively, these representations, images, and practices shape how we understand and experience globalization, forming a backdrop against which events are noticed (or not), interpreted, and evaluated. Thus, globali-zation discourse becomes an exercise of power by enabling and justifying certain beliefs and actions and discouraging others. For example, Bau-man (2000/2011) describes a new class of haves and have-nots which he terms 'tourists' and 'vagabonds' that are defined by their mobility. Tourists represent those who feel they must keep moving, whereas vagabonds are those who want to move but cannot. Bauman also ties these ideas to ways of controlling vagabonds through, for example, strict immigration policies and prisons. Thus, within the discourse new boundaries of inclusion and exclusion are created.

The Commodification of Children

Another illustrative example of this power is the shaping of children's iden-tities by market forces that seek to exploit their potential as consumers.[3] Children in affluent countries are subject to a multibillion dollar advertis-ing and marketing campaign that attempts to influence their desires and how they understand themselves. These efforts include television and print advertising, as well as social networking sites that use tracking technology to identify particular interests that are used in targeted advertisements. Regarding the latter, Phoenix (2011) writes,

> They also, arguably, encourage commercially-defined constructions of identity since users are required to define themselves through their consumer preferences, and through specific acts of consumption. They are, for example, encouraged to use branded resources to design their personal profile pages, and to engage in communication with others; and they are effectively forced to 'advertise' and 'promote' themselves, or rather particular versions of themselves. (p. 21)

As Henry Giroux (2009) puts it, 'Children now inhabit a cultural landscape in which they can only recognize themselves in terms preferred by the market' (p. 714). Although much focus has recently been placed on the adverse health consequences of food and beverage marketing (e.g., Harris,

Pomeranz, Lobstein, & Brownell, 2009), a less acknowledged issue concerns how children come to regard themselves, their desires, and their needs, in ways that conform to commercial interests. As the reach of these interests continues to expand globally to younger and greater numbers of children, these desires, needs, and self-images seem less the result of manipulation and more like 'natural' attributes.

Interdependence

Another dimension of globalization discourse is the notion of increased interdependence (see, for example, Healy, 2008) commonly expressed through categories such as the environment, culture, economics, security, and politics.

Environmental interdependence is a function of humanity's dependence on the Earth's finite resources and the competition over their acquisition and use. From a global perspective, environmental interdependence can be depicted by the concepts of global footprints and global shadows (Dauvergne, 2005). Briefly, a global footprint is a measure of the amount of natural resources required to sustain an individual's lifestyle: food and water, clothes, shelter, transportation, and consumer goods and services. Global shadows refer to a nation's environmental impact beyond its own borders. These concepts illustrate how resource use and its environmental effects have consequences that extend beyond individuals and nation states. For example, the United States draws heavily on global resources to sustain the lifestyle of it citizenry, while the ozone depleting 'shadows' of China and India extend to many parts of the globe.

Cultural interdependence became salient as supraterritoriality associated with communications technology and travel obscured geographic boundaries making cultural contacts frequent and intense. In some cases, culture itself is destabilized leaving its meaning ambiguous. This is illustrated in the following commentary (Dahl, 2014):

> A Norwegian student can sit on the tram in Oslo and 'chat' by the help of her mobile phone with an Australian friend in Sydney, or with a Brazilian student in Rio de Janeiro, who has the same admiration for the same pop idol. They can even exchange photos and music links. The youths have developed a language of 'chatting' and a special jargon, which works well for the communication purposes of the young. They like the same hip-hop music, watch the same (American) movies, drink the same Coca-Cola, and eat the same burger at McDonald's wherever they live in the world. What 'culture' do these young people belong to? On the same day the Australian student can surf the waves of Manly Beach in Sydney; the Norwegian can

do skiing in Nordmarka or visit her own grandmother who does not know up and down of the cell phone. Do the grandmother and the student have the same culture? Or is it the student and her friend in Sydney who have the same or share the same culture?

Economic interdependence has become manifest in the global nature of markets and in the production, distribution, and sale of goods and services. International economic policies aimed at increasing global economic integration coupled with technological advancements have connected national economies in unprecedented ways (Das, 2011). This interdependence was succinctly illustrated by Martin Luther King's observation that 'Before I finish breakfast I have depended on half the world' (cited in Healy, 2008). Moreover, half the world's largest economic units are not nations but multinational corporations.

Security interdependence refers to the perception that acts of aggression are not limited to territorial disputes but to ideological, ethnic, religious, or political issues that transcend national boundaries. This perception is linked to the increase in terrorism, which is by definition extra-territorial (Bauman & Gałecki, 2005: 4). Potential threats are both everywhere and nowhere. Nations anywhere in the world are seen as potential breeding grounds for terrorism. This globalizes regional conflicts as their outcomes are often seen as favoring or thwarting the aspirations of terrorist groups. Another consequence has been a complex of 'globe-straddling military and strategic alliances of power as well as parallel alliances among the neutrals and the non-aligned countries' encompassing much of the world (Das, 2011: 26).

Political interdependence reflects (and constitutes) how a nation's policies concerning its own citizenry and its relations with other nations are influenced by global issues. It also may refer to how the policies or political turmoil in one nation may influence the policies in other nations, for example trade agreements, perceived terror threats, or droughts.

Interdependence occurs not only within these categories (consider, for example, the global economic impact of the euro crisis or the economic recession in the U.S.) but among them. Environmental issues provide striking examples of the latter. As competition over finite resources (e.g., water, oil, food), perceptions of growing disparities, and environmental degradation increase, the potential for violence escalates, economic policies are altered, and political relations are strained (Najam, Runnalls, & Halle, 2007).

It is also important to recognize that not all interdependence is the same. For instance, entities can be positively or negatively interdependent in relation to goals. In the case of positive interdependence, the goals of different parties are positively correlated so that the success of one contributes to the success of the other. This tends to encourage cooperation and facilitation of the other's efforts (a 'win-win' situation). Negative interdependence, on the other hand, describes a situation in which the success of one party entails the failure of the other (as in a zero-sum game). Such a situation encourages competition and efforts to undermine the other's efforts.

Interdependence can also be considered on two related dimensions: as a continuum ranging from total dependence to total independence and in terms of relational symmetry – the relative possession and control of desired or needed resources (economic, military, environmental). Generally, the greater the dependence the more asymmetric the relationship. This in turn may affect the means of influence that are used, for example, economic benefits or sanctions, threats or use of violence, and appeals to values.

Implications of a Discourse Perspective for Social Work

If we take globalization discourses as integral to how globalization comes into being – how it is experienced, understood, and acted upon, then social workers need to enter or engage with these discourses. They also need to help others to do so, particularly those for whom these discourses are inaccessible or a negative force. In part this will entail identifying alternative discourses that generate new realities. These aims will require analyses of how these discourses operate (e.g., who benefits and is disadvantaged) and the realities they generate (e.g., consumerism); to decide which discourses or aspects of discourses to support and which to challenge. This engagement can occur at multiple levels and in multiple ways: at the interpersonal level through dialogue, at the meso level through organizational change, and the macro level through policy development and advocacy, writing, and research. Of course, these levels are neither mutually exclusive nor independent. It is possible to engage at all levels and each may affect the other.

Let's look briefly at two examples: consumerism and colonialism.

Example One: The Ideology of Consumerism

Until relatively recently, the acquisition and consumption of goods in amounts significantly exceeding what was needed to live was limited to the wealthy classes representing small segments of the population. Today, this practice has shifted to the masses on a global scale (Sklair, 2002). This change, which Sklair (1998) calls the 'cultural-ideological project of consumerism', is driven by global capitalism whose aim is to perpetuate its own continuance by persuading people that the meaning of life is to be found in the things that we possess. When coupled with advances in mass media technology, the message that 'To consume, therefore, is to be fully alive, and to remain fully alive we must continuously consume' becomes an important theme about how to live. Equating happiness and well-being with material possessions transforms people into consumers driven to acquire the resources necessary to accumulate goods and to value their acquisition above other values. Even our sense of acting ethically or progressively can be understood as occurring within a consumerist and neo-liberal frame; for example, the idea of being an 'eco-activist' based on corporate narratives of individualistic ethical consumerism and displacing macro interventions into economic and labor issues (Thompson, 2012). As noted previously, children are particularly vulnerable as they lack the knowledge or experience to understand the motives underlying these messages. For example, in her study of 300 American children, Juliet Schor (2004) found 'that television 'induces discontent with what one has, it creates an orientation to possessions and money, and it causes children to care more about brands, products, and consumer values" (cited in House, 2011: 67). Unfortunately, one of the largest product categories is food, in particular sweets, snacks, and beverages, a multi-billion dollar industry (Schor & Ford, 2007) that contributes substantially to the obesity problem and its associated health issues among children in the United States.

Example Two: Colonialism

Colonialism refers to the subjugation of one people by another. It is usually associated with 'the project of European political domination from the sixteenth to the twentieth centuries' (Kohn, 2014). From a discourse perspective, colonialism is expressed through the exportation of Western assumptions and beliefs and their associated practices. These beliefs and practices are thought to reflect transcendent truths and therefore to represent a superior way of living compared to indigenous practices.

Although social workers reject the more obvious practices of colonialism, they may unwittingly participate in colonizing discourses by uncritically accepting the superiority of their own assumptions and beliefs or by overlooking how these beliefs are historical-cultural products. Jim Ife (2007) describes this as 'spreading the dominant way of looking at the world and, in the process, marginalising and devaluing other world views, and, by implication, those who hold them' (p. 9). This type of *'benevolent colonialism'* (Martinez-Brawley, 1999: 334) may be hard to detect as it is an expression of the dominant social science and research discourses that operate 'below the radar' of many social workers. Shrouded in good intentions, the importation of Western social work theories and practices to non-Western cultures may undermine indigenous beliefs and prove to be more destructive than helpful.

Practice Implications: Entering the Discourse

A discourse-based conceptualization of globalization and its associated problems suggests possible courses of action for social workers. In general, it suggests identifying how these discourses operate and the realities they generate. Additionally, it invites us to find ways of entering these discourses in order to strengthen or change them and to help others do so.

Globalization from Above and Below

The breadth of globalization discourse creates multiple access points. At one end, multinational corporations employ the tools of global technology to enact a neo-liberal agenda. This so-called 'globalization from above' is driven by corporate capitalism and instruments of the capitalist state such as the World Trade Organization. It is characterized by a consumerist ideology and a Westernized world view. Some of these same tools may also be available to those who are left out or disadvantaged by global processes. They may use these tools to enact a 'globalization from below' and to resist global developments promulgated by dominant groups. More affirmatively, it also refers to how groups 'use the institutions and instruments of globalization to further democratization and social justice' (Kellner, 2002: 293). For example, Radcliffe, Laurie, and Andolina (2002) argue that one way in which globalization operates discursively is in the ways that indigenous peoples who have been constituted by 'deracialized, apolitical discourses' maintain their disadvantaged social positions, for instance, by focusing on their impoverished condition. Counter discourses by indigenous groups 'reverse this discourse, displacing lack away from themselves and highlighting issues of racism and political economy' (p. 5).

Counter discourses are also expressed through practices that appropriate global tools such as the internet to promote locally controlled economic development. For example, Holland (2005) describes how the distribution of 500 old computers to remote rural villages in Nicaragua enabled teenaged daughters of poor, illiterate peasants to use the internet to track price fluctuations in the global corn market. Using email to connect with each other, these girls formed a marketing cooperative that helped them determine the best time to market their product and eliminated the need for traditional regional brokers. 'As a result, the peasants ... doubled the sale-price of their harvest' (p. 11). Although dualisms like globalization from above and below can be limiting if taken too literally, they can highlight alternative understandings of globalization and new pathways into its discourse.

Global, Local, or Glocal?

Related to the recognition of different entrée points into globalization dis-course is an understanding of 'global' and 'local' as neither in opposition nor independent, but as interdependent social designations. This counter-acts the tendency to reify and essentialize these terms and describing them as fundamentally positive or negative. Regarding reification, Scholte (2002) writes, 'The global is a dimension of social geography rather than a space in its own right.... . we must not turn the global into a "thing" that is separate from regional, national, local and household "things" (p. 27). Regarding essentialism, he notes that

> there is nothing inherently alienating about the global and nothing intrinsically liberating about the local.... . the two qualities are insepa-rable in social practice; so terming one circumstance 'local' and another 'global' is actually arbitrary and confusing. A social condition is not positive or negative according to whether it is local or global, since the situation is generally both local and global at the same time. (pp. 28–29)

From this perspective, local and global are social constructions that can be construed in different ways for different purposes. Some authors use the term 'glocal' to signify a blending of local and global spheres. This construal is particularly evident in social relations. Beck (2002) com-ments, 'Sociability is no longer dependent on geographical proximity. It thus becomes possible – as recent studies have already shown – for peo-ple who live isolated from their neighbours in one place simultaneously to be tied into dense networks stretching across continents. In other words: the sphere of experience, in which we inhabit globally networked life-worlds, is *glocal*, has become a synthesis of home and non-place, a nowhere place' (p. 31).

A discourse perspective can help social workers avoid the limitations of reified or essentialized conceptions and broaden their interpretations of these concepts. Rather than simply decrying the effects of global forces on the plight of their clients or working solely on the local level, social workers can work to reconfigure the global–local matrix in ways that assist people to influence and partake of the benefits of global processes and resist their negative aspects. In the previous example of the Nicaraguan girls, a key task was getting resources (computers) into the hands of people and help-ing them learn how to use them. In some ways, this is a variation on well-known social work functions of connecting people with needed resources and helping them form empowering alliances. By operating with global/local/glocal awareness, we can use these skills in new ways.

Moving Toward a Discursive Practice

The previous section illustrates some of the ways in which social workers might become sensitive to and engaged in global issues and globalization from a discourse perspective. Numerous understandings and practices are possible. Therefore, rather than a prescriptive approach to global social work which would decontextualize practice and dampen the creative initiatives that might emerge from social interactions, I conclude with some general suggestions for how we might take up this issue.

Problematize and Challenge the Assumed and Taken-for-granted

Examples might include that globalization is a unitary force, that it is a contemporary phenomenon, that it is either good or bad, or that it fosters homogenization or hybridization. The point is that globalization will be whatever people, particularly those in authority, decide to call it. It is more important to understand how the concept is being used (e.g., to explain, to justify) and its implications (e.g., create a division between people, leave people feeling hopeful or hopeless) than what it is. The latter tends to reify globalization and to characterize its features and value according to certain interests. While definitions have their value, it seems preferable to leave this somewhat open with the understanding that there is nothing that demands this particular label.

Interrogate Our Own Understandings of Globalization and a Global Perspective

It is important to be vigilant in the application of our own understandings and their impact on allowing others to 'express their own cultural realities in their own terms' (Holliday, 2010: 15). Embracing a global perspective is not adequate if that perspective is immune from critical analysis. To claim neutrality or objectivity is to mask values and ideology and as noted in the discussion of 'benevolent colonialism', to perpetuate what is professed as objectionable.[4] Along these same lines it may be useful to retain the notion of a global *perspective*. A perspective implies understanding from a particular vantage point; there can be other vantage points as well. No one is necessarily right but all may be assessed regarding their utility and congruence with cherished values. Therefore, multiplicity is encouraged.

Incorporate Values into Globalization Including Issues of Inequality and Oppression

Often, the debates about the benefits or harms of globalization sidestep these issues focusing, for example, on whether the rich are getting richer and the poor are getting poorer. However, as Amartya Sen (2002) notes, 'Even if the poor were to get just a little richer, this would not necessarily imply that the poor were getting a fair share of the potentially vast benefits of global economic interrelations' (5 of 8). Rather, as he argues, the central issue is 'the massive levels of inequality and poverty that exist in the world'.

Another way of considering values is to assign them equal status with other more commonly understood aspects of globalization. Howard Zinn (2007) suggests including cherished values into our notion of global commerce, loosening the barriers to their implementation as we have done with commercial goods. He poses the question, 'If national boundaries should not be obstacles to trade – some call it 'globalization' – should they also not be obstacles to compassion and generosity? Should we not begin to consider all children, everywhere, as our own?' (p. 119). Such a strategy capitalizes on accepted practices to help bring about other kinds of change.

Engage In and Foster Dialogue

This recommendation is the most ubiquitous and accessible since it is the modus operandi of social workers. In the current context, however, the emphasis is on dialogue that enacts counter discourses. This can be broadly understood as countering modernist discourses of truth (right/wrong), universalism, absolutism, and acontextuality that are salient in global practices. Or it can be more focused, such as counter discourses to consumerism like those that support 'green' social movements, sustainability, and valorize non-exploitive lifestyles.

It is also important to remember that dialogue itself is an alternative discourse to those of debate and authority in which the aim is to win, convince, or enlighten others about what is correct or true. Instead, dialogue aims to understand and respect differences, even over resolving them. In some cases of moral conflicts, resolution may not be the most desirable end. Rather, as Rorty notes, the goal is 'continuing the conversation rather than at discovering Truth' in a way that 'engendered new social practices, and changes in the vocabularies deployed in moral and political deliberation' (cited in Koopman, 2013: 99).

The importance of dialogue within a global context is emphasized by Ife (2008) who sees it as 'a precondition for international work, as it is the only way we can learn from rather than learn about other people and cultures, and the only way we can work with rather than work for people internationally' (p. 10). In my view, this stance of learning from and working with cannot be overstated and one in which a discourse perspective can be helpful.

Concluding Thoughts

As noted at the beginning of this chapter, a globally informed social work has the potential to facilitate transformative change if we are open to critically examining the foundational assumptions and beliefs that justify and maintain current ways of thinking. For instance, universalist notions of truth and the belief in the necessity of agreement may tacitly influence assessments and relations. An alternative perspective, presented here, does not view adopting identical beliefs or practices, or obtaining consensus on issues of import as necessary for understanding and practicing social work from a global perspective. Rather, it is difference that must be respected. Specifically, social work must be based on respect for different cultural and knowledge traditions and a willingness to engage in constructive dialogue across those differences. Such constructive dialogue cannot come from an orientation whose aim is to demonstrate the 'rightness' of one's own position and the 'wrongness' of others' positions, but from an appreciation of the rich resources that such dialogue makes available to us and a commitment to use these resources to co-construct better futures.

Notes

1 I want to acknowledge my location in the United States. Despite advocating for a global perspective, I, like everyone, am grounded in a particular place and time. I have been educated and socialized in the United States. and have undoubtedly internalized, to varying degrees, its historical narratives, social mores, and cultural assumptions. Therefore, I make no claims that my position is neutral or a 'positionless' position. What I try to do is to be reflective and reflexive about my analyses and proposals.

2 Again, my aim here is not to provide definitive definitions, but to provide an understanding of how I use these terms in this chapter.

3 The concept of children as commodities is often used in relation to the buying and selling of children as in surrogate parenting or adoptions from countries and people who are poor. In this chapter, I use it to discuss how children's identities are shaped by commercial interests. In this sense, they are commodified in that their needs, desires, and sense of self is being shaped and 'sold' to the market.

4 Holliday (2010) refers to this as neo-essentialism in which liberal ideas about diversity, truth, and fairness conflict with the belief in the neutrality of description and chauvinistic description.

References

Al-Rodhan, N. R. F., & Stoudmann, G. (2006). Definitions of globalization: A comprehensive overview and a proposed definition. *Geneva Centre for Security Policy*, 1–21.

Bauman, Z. (2000/2011). Tourists and vagabonds: Or, living in postmodern times. In J. E. Davis (Ed.), *Identity and social change* (pp. 13–26). New Brunswick, NJ: Transaction Publishers.

Bauman, Z., & Gałecki, Ł. (2005). *The unwinnable war: An interview with Zygmunt Bauman*, December 1. Retrieved from www.openDemocracy.net

Beck, U. (2002). The cosmopolitan society and its enemies. *Theory, Culture & Society, 19*(1–2), 17–44.

Dahl, O. (2014). Is culture something we have or something we do? *Journal of Intercultural Communication, 36* Retrieved from http://search.proquest.com.ezproxy.uvm.edu/docview/1703413192?accountid=14679

Das, D. K. (2011). Conceptual globalism and globalisation: An initiation. Centre for the study of globalisation and regionalisation, University of Warwick (Working paper no. 275). Permanent WRAP. Retrieved from http://wrap.warwick.ac.uk/49071

Dauvergne, P. (2005). Globalization and the environment. In J. Ravenhill (Ed.), *Global political economy* (pp. 371–395). Oxford: Oxford University Press.

Fiss, P. C., & Hirsch, P. M. (2005). The discourse of globalization: Framing and sensemaking of an emerging concept. *American Sociological Review, 70*(1), 29–52.

Giroux, H. A. (2009). Youth in the empire of consumption: Beyond the pedagogy of commodification. *JAC*, 691–756.

Guillén, M. F. (2001). Is globalization civilizing, destructive or feeble? A critique of five key debates in the social science literature. *Annual Review of Sociology*, 235–260.

Harris, J. L., Pomeranz, J. L., Lobstein, T., & Brownell, K. D. (2009). A crisis in the marketplace: How food marketing contributes to childhood obesity and what can be done. *Annual Review of Public Health, 30*, 211–225.

Healy, L. M. (2008). *International social work: Professional action in an interdependent world*. New York, NY: Oxford University Press.

Holland, J. (2005). The regeneration of ecological, societal, and spiritual life: The holistic postmodern mission of humanity in the newly emerging planetary civilization. *Journal of Religion and Spirituality in Social Work, 24*(1/2), 7–25.

Holliday, A. (2010). *Intercultural communication and ideology*. London: Sage.

House, R. (2011). Children's well-being and the commercialization of childhood: Some ethical considerations for business. *Interconnections*, Issue 7, 63–71.

Ife, J. (2007). The new international agendas: What role for social work. Inaugural Hokenstad International Social Work Lecture. Presented at the Annual Program Meeting of the Council on Social Work Education, San Francisco, October. Retrieved from http://ifsw.org/statements/the-new-international-agendas-what-role-for-social-work/

Kalyan, R. K. (2010). Ghostly images, phantom discourses, and the virtuality of the global. *Globalizations, 7*(4), 545–561.

Kellner, D. (2002). Theorizing globalization. *Sociological Theory, 20*(3), 285–305.

Kennedy, P. (2007). Global transformations but local, 'bubble' lives: Taking a reality check on some globalization concepts. *Globalizations, 4*(2), 267–282.

Kohn, M., (2014). Colonialism. In E. N. Zalta (Ed.), *The Stanford encyclopedia of philosophy* (Spring 2014 Edition). Retrieved from http://plato.stanford.edu/archives/spr2014/entries/colonialism/

Koopman, C. (2013). Challenging philosophy: Rorty's positive conception of philosophy as cultural criticism. In A. Groschner, C. Koopman, & M. Sandbothe (Eds.), *Richard Rorty: From pragmatist philosophy to cultural politics.* New York, NY: Bloomsbury Academic.

Martinez-Brawley, E. E. (1999). Social work, postmodernism and higher education. *International Social Work, 42*(3), 333–346.

Miller, L. (2008). Foucauldian constructionism. In J. A. Holstein, & J. F. Gubrium (Eds.) *Handbook of constructionist research* (pp. 251–274). New York, NY: Guilford Press.

Monge, P. (1998). Communication structures and processes in globalization. *Journal of Communication, 48*(4), 142–153.

Najam, A., Runnalls, D., & Halle, M. (2007). *Environment and globalization: Five propositions.* International Institute for Sustainable Development. Retrieved from www.iisd.org/publications

Norris, P. (2000). Global governance and cosmopolitan citizens. In J. S. Nye, & J. D. Donahue (Eds.), *Governance in a globalizing world* (pp. 155–177). Cambridge, MA: Brookings Institute Press.

Phoenix, A. (2011). *Review of the recent literature for the Bailey Review of commercialisation and sexualisation of childhood.* Childhood Wellbeing Research Center. Retrieved from http://eprints.ioe.ac.uk/16179/1/CWRC_commercialisationsexualisation_review_final_version_2June2011_MasterA.pdf

Radcliffe, S., Laurie, N., & Andolina, R. (2002). *Indigenous people and political transnationalism: Globalisation from below meets globalisation from above.* Oxford: University of Oxford, Transnational Communities Programme, Working Paper WPTC-02-05. Retrieved from www.transcomm.ox.ac.uk/working_papers.htm

Ritzer, G. (2003). Rethinking globalization: Glocalization/grobalization and something/nothing. *Sociological Theory, 21*(3), 193–209.

Scholte, J. A. (2002). What is globalization? The definitional issue-again. Working Paper. Coventry: University of Warwick. Centre for the Study of Globalisation and Regionalisation. Retrieved from http://wrap.warwick.ac.uk/id/eprint/2010

Scholte, J. A. (2005a). The sources of neoliberal globalization. United Nations Research Institute for Social Development, Programme Paper Number 8, 1–30. Retrieved from http://unrisd.org/UNRISD/website/document.nsf/ab82a6805797760f80256b4f005da1ab/9e1c54ceeb19a314c12570b4004d0881/$FILE/scholte.pdf

Scholte, J. A. (2005b). *Globalization: A critical introduction.* London: Palgrave Macmillan.

Schor, J. B. (2004). *Born to buy: The commercialized child and the new consumer culture.* New York: Scribner.

Schor, J. B., & Ford, M. (2007). From tastes great to cool: Children's food marketing and the rise of the symbolic. *The Journal of Law, Medicine & Ethics, 35*(1), 10–21.

Sen, A. (2002). How to judge globalism. *The American Prospect, 13*(1), 1–8. Retrieved from www2.econ.uu.nl/users/marrewijk/pdf/ihs/geo/sen%202000%20judge%20glob.pdf

Sklair, L. (1998). *Transnational practices and the analysis of the global system.* Seminar delivered for the transnational communities programme seminar series, 22, London School of Economics and Political Science. Retrieved from http://163.1.0.34/working%20papers/sklair.pdf

Sklair, L. (2002). The transnational capitalist class and global politics: Deconstructing the corporate-state connection. *International Political Science Review, 23*(2), 159–174.

Thompson, S. (2012). The micro-ethics of everyday life: Ethics, ideology and anti-consumerism. *Cultural Studies, 26*(6), 895–921.

Van Der Bly, M. C. (2005). Globalization: A triumph of ambiguity. *Current Sociology, 53*(6), 875–893.

Wiebelhaus-Brahm, E. (2002). *Globalization, modernity, and their discontents.* Retrieved from SSRN: http://ssrn.com/abstract=1666871 or http://dx.doi.org/10.2139/ssrn.1666871

Zinn, H. (2007). *A power governments cannot suppress.* San Francisco, CA: City Lights Books.

8 Knowledge and Evidence: Exploring the Practice–Research Relationship[1]

We live in a time when demonstrating effectiveness is considered an important criterion for the justification and support of different practice approaches and programs. Both ethical and pragmatic rationales are used to justify this positon. Specifically, it is argued that clients of social workers and related professionals have a 'right' to know about and receive treatments or interventions that have been shown to be the most efficacious in preventing or ameliorating their situation or problem (e.g., Barber, 2008; Myers & Thyer, 1997; but see Witkin, 1998, for a rejoinder). Practitioners therefore have a corresponding responsibility to be informed about, communicate, and employ such approaches. Further supporting this position is the claim (e.g., from government sources and health insurers) that in a context of finite resources it is imperative to be able to differentiate effective from less effective programs so as to optimize benefits and minimize cost. These economic justifications are particularly persuasive within the current neo-liberal climate in the United States and Europe.

Claims of program or practice effectiveness are seen as credible to the extent that they are backed by 'evidence', typically in the form of research-generated, quantitative data. It is not sufficient to opine about the value of a program or approach, or to argue for its virtue; empirical data are required. These data, in turn, are seen as the constituent elements of 'knowledge' – a kind of truth bearing information that will enable us to understand and respond to issues in the most effective ways.

In this chapter, I will address these ideas especially as they underlie and justify the influential movement called evidence-based practice (EBP). Despite being founded on the laudable desire to improve the human condition by integrating scientific (i.e., research-based) knowledge with practice, I will attempt to show that this movement (and its offshoots such as empirically supported treatments (EST)) is based on assumptions and beliefs that limit the possibility for transformative change and in some instances have been taken up in ways that may perpetuate systems of oppression.

My plan is to begin with a brief overview of the relationship of social work with science (as expressed through social research) and to show how this relationship led to the profession's current embrace of EBP. Next I will interrogate some of the basic notions of EBP and identify various issues for readers to consider. Third, I will examine three key concepts that underlie EBP: evidence, effectiveness, and knowledge. I will attempt to show how particular understandings of these concepts support EBP and that these understandings are expressions of wider social and political forces dominant in contemporary Western societies. Finally, based on my analysis, I will propose a different model of knowledge generation that is centered in practice relationships, a change I will argue is potentially transformative.

Social Work and Science: Professional Aspirations

The story of social work's early aspirations to become a recognized profession is linked to its relationship with science. Basing social work practice on scientifically generated knowledge was a way to distinguish it from charity, altruism, and the expression of religious philanthropy. For example, as far back as the late 1800s advocates of the scientific charity movement looked to systematic data collection and causal analyses of science as a model for charity efforts (Kirk & Reid, 2002; Lubove, 1965).

These professional ambitions were influenced by societal changes (e.g., industrialization) that led to new challenges for managing populations, in particular vulnerable citizens who were dependent on outside assistance and the 'dangerous classes' perceived as posing a threat to the state. Social work arose as a mediating profession occupying an 'intermediary zone or space between the public space of the state and wider society' (Parton & Kirk, 2010: 25). Claiming this space required social work to separate itself from other efforts such as charity to address similar concerns. One way to do this was to redefine itself as a profession that required a university education and that looked to research as a model for practice and as a source of authoritative knowledge (Kirk & Reid, 2002). The model for this redefinition, particularly in the United States, was the field of medicine, which in the early part of the 20th century was developing its science-based curriculum.

In 1915, Abraham Flexner, the chief architect of medical education reform, was asked to speak to the National Conference of Charities and Corrections on the topic 'Is Social Work a Profession?' (Flexner, 1915/2001). Although Flexner began his talk by acknowledging his limited knowledge of social work, he nevertheless proceeded to answer the question in the negative. Flexner's assessment, however uninformed it might have been, has reverberated across the history of social work and been used to argue for social work's need to become more scientific. My own reading of Flexner's actual speech suggests that he was more concerned about social work's lack of specialization and its mediating role in relation to other professions like medicine and law. He considered a social worker 'not so much an expert ... as the mediator whose concern it is to summon the expert' (p. 163). In fact, although he alluded to the importance of science in his speech, he also stated that 'No question can be raised as to the source from which the social worker derives his material – it comes obviously from science and learning ...' (Flexner, 1915/2001: 162).[2]

Despite differences in the interpretation of Flexner's speech, the belief that social work needs to be scientifically based (like medicine) in order to be a 'real' profession, has strongly influenced its relationship to science and its expression in research. Science, medicine, social work research, and professionalism became further intertwined as the fields of psychiatry and psychology came into prominence in the early 1900s, particularly after Freud's lectures at Clark University in 1909. However, this entwinement was not a smooth one. As Austin (1983) wrote, 'While Freudian theory appeared to satisfy one element of the Flexner model [a systematic, transferable body of knowledge], it did not deal directly with the model's strong emphasis on the importance of laboratory and experimental science' (p. 370). Eventually this led to the divergence of psychiatrically/psychologically oriented (later, clinical) social work practice from the development of a systematic, 'scientific' research orientation. In contrast, the field of medicine continued to develop its scientific evidentiary base (see Witkin & Iversen, 2012).

These divergent directions in social work did not reconverge until the scientist–practitioner movement (in the United States) of the early 1970s. Although space restrictions do not allow a full exposition of this movement, in many ways it could be considered the forerunner of what is now known as evidenced-based practice (EBP). Briefly, in the period of relative economic austerity that followed President Lyndon Johnson's 'Great Society' initiative of the late 1960s, social work found itself increasingly competing for dwindling resources for social programs. Publications such as Joel Fischer's 'Is Casework Effective?' (1973) questioned the efficacy of social work practice thereby increasing the need to develop a convincing argument for allocating resources to social workers. Once again, scientific research was seen as the best, even necessary, response. However, exhortations to do more research had limited success. What was needed was a new approach. This was found in a methodology called single-case designs based on B. F. Skinner's behavior modification research and extrapolated to clinical research in psychology (e.g., Hersen & Barlow, 1976). Single-case designs, which used repeated measurements of an individual's behavior over time and under varying conditions, were seen as a way to integrate the logic and components of experimentation into practice, thereby generating scientific data on treatment effectiveness.

Within social work, these developments helped energize what came to be known as empirical clinical practice (ECP). This approach had two components: the use of empirically supported practices and the implementation of research designs (e.g., single-case designs) by practitioners to evaluate their own practice (Thyer, 1996). The ECP movement evoked vociferous debate regarding the congruence of its values with social work and the future directions of the profession (e.g., Heineman Pieper, 1981; Ivanoff, Blythe, & Briar, 1987; Witkin, 1991). Although ECP never achieved the prominence that its proponents had hoped, the political climate of the 1990s with its demands for privatization, accountability, efficiency, and effectiveness of outcomes along with the widespread availability of technology for accessing information, provided an environment favorable for its current incarnation as EBP (Gibbs, 2001).[3]

The Evidence-based Practice Movement in Social Work

Whereas ECP was derived primarily from psychology, EBP originated in medicine, specifically as part of a new program in clinical epidemiology developed at McMaster University in Canada (Zimerman, 2013).[4] At the time, the late 1980s, the idea of evidence-based medicine was seen as revolutionary, a 'paradigm shift' in medical practice from using 'intuition, unsystematic clinical experience, and pathophysiologic rationale as sufficient grounds for clinical decision making [to] ... stress[ing] the examination of evidence from clinical research' (Evidence-Based Medicine Working Group, 1992: 2420).

Although there is no question that those originally involved in developing this approach thought of themselves as progressive thinkers who were changing medical practice for the better, controversies arose around the philosophy, ethics, and pragmatics of Evidence-Based Medicine (EBM) (e.g., Wyer & Silva, 2009). These included, for example, concerns about a routinized approach to practice, the importance given to patient preferences and values, the role of practice experience and expertise, and the support for a hierarchy of study designs that privileged randomized trials (e.g., Sackett, Rosenberg, Gray, Haynes, & Richardson, 1996; Sackett, Straus, Richardson, Rosenberg, & Haynes, 2000).

Has Social Work Strayed from the 'Real' EBP?

Within social work as well as medicine a particularly salient controversy has been about whether the implementation of EBM (or in the social work case, EBP) is representative of the concept or philosophy of those who originally coined the term and described its features. This issue is analogous to what is called content validity in measurement. A measure is said to have content validity to the extent that it is judged to adequately represent its intended construct. For example, if I have a measure of depression, its content validity would be judged based on how adequately the dimensions of depressions (e.g., negative thoughts, feelings of sadness) were represented in the measure. This judgment will be based on whatever theory of depression is being used as a standard. Similarly, applications of EBM/EBP (essentially its operational definition) have been criticized for not being adequately inclusive of some of its original principles such as client preferences. In support of this position, critics often quote a definition of EBM by Sackett et al. (1996) as 'the conscientious, explicit, and judicious use of current best evidence in making decisions about the care of individual patients' (p. 71), adding their caution that 'evidence' is multifaceted, requiring 'a bottom-up approach that integrates the best external evidence with individual clinical expertise and patients' choice' (p. 72). Within social work, Gambrill (2011) has been particularly critical of how EBP has been understood and implemented decrying its rigid and narrow application of evidence. She blames this situation, in large part, on an overreliance on secondary rather than original sources (like Sackett et al.) that provide skewed or incomplete descriptions of EBM/EBP.

Is this emphasis on the original descriptions of EBM or the intent of its originators warranted? In my view, yes and no. There are at least three questions germane to this issue:

1. Who has the authority to define EBM/EBP? For instance, should definitions be confined to those credited with developing the approach or coining the term?
2. Is there a 'pure' form of EBM or EBP articulated in a conceptual definition, or does its practice constitute its meaning?
3. Is the original philosophy fixed and inviolable? Practice approaches or philosophies like EBM/EBP are rarely static but change in relation to social and political factors, organizational contexts, and experience. In fact, the emergence of EBM can itself be viewed as an example of such a response to changing contexts. For instance, Gordon Guyett, a 'founder of EBM', has noted the increased emphasis on client values since his original 1992 publication (Smith & Rennie, 2014).

There is no doubt that the originators of EBM had a vision of medical practice that would be improved through the integration of research-based evidence. And it is appropriate for promotors of EBM/EBP to cite these writings in support of their position and to critique others for their misinterpretation or misrepresentation. However, fidelity to the origins of

EBM has its limits. As noted, contexts will shape the meanings of concepts such as evidence that constitute the approach (Mishler, 1979). Meanings will be further influenced by the ways in which these concepts are applied. That is, it can be argued that the dominant applications of EBM/EBP are, de facto, their meaning. Similarly, these understandings and applications will continue to change in ways that are differentially responsive to these contexts. Such tensions are not uncommon. For instance, the arguments regarding the appropriateness or authenticity of EBM/EBP are analogous to disputes in the United States about the true meaning of the US constitution. So-called constitutionalists argue for the original meanings of the 'founding fathers' (the originators), others argue that such meanings should be adapted to contemporary life.[5] I suggest that rather than argue about the 'real' meaning of EBM/EBP it may be more useful to allow for several EBM/EBPs based on, for instance, different understandings and uses of evidence and their inclusiveness of clients' interests.

Gambrill may be correct that there is overreliance on secondary sources. Still, there is a lot of interpretive 'wiggle room' between EBM as a conceptual approach and its translation into practice as EBP. Although Gambrill (2015) is sensitive to the impact of the socio-political context on practice, she nevertheless appears to believe that EBP can transcend this context. This does not seem to be the case. For example, Arnd-Caddigan and Pozzuto (2010) describe how some states in the United States are mandating a narrow version of EBP (i.e., symptom relief) for Medicaid clients. Ironically, it may be that the vulnerability of EBP to such political manipulation is based on its avowed scientific foundations and the associated myth of neutrality, its minimalizing of the cultural and social complexities of practice, and its congruence (intended or not) with the growth of proceduralism and managerialism. Thus, while I concur with Gambrill's desire to make EBP more client-centered, I doubt whether urging a return to the 'originators'' intent will prove effective or whether it will negate other issues associated with EBP that I discuss later in this chapter.

Other Relevant Issues

Although there are many issues of contention about EBP, I will highlight some that seem particularly pertinent to social work. The first concerns the claim (sometimes implicit) that practitioners who base their practice on EBP will be more effective (have better outcomes) than those who do not. In the spirit of EBP we might ask whether the evidence supports this claim. My answer would be it depends on such factors as what counts as evidence, the meaning applied to 'effective', what it means to base one's practice on EBP, the range of problems to which this question is applied, and so on. There are multiple ways to define and assess client improvement. Depending on a researcher's theoretical orientation, improvement can mean such things as a desired change in the frequency of a behavior, symptom relief, insight about one's childhood, or an understanding of how societal practices are implicated in an individual's problem. If improvement is asserted, there still is the question of whether such improvement can be attributed to their program, treatment, or other factors. Also, even if clients of practitioners using EBP improve on some measures, it would need to be shown that they improve significantly more than those who do not use EBP. Such comparisons may be further complicated by the use of different understandings or measures of improvement.

As discussed previously, it is not always clear what is meant by EBP. For some, it means the use of empirically supported treatments (ESTs); for others it is more of a philosophy of practice. However EBP is defined, its typical expression in practice settings compared to studies of practice in research contexts will always involve more than the narrow and rigid application of a highly specific treatment. Some of these additional factors, like the client – practitioner relationship, may be identified, while others remain unnamed.

Researchers have tried to address some of these issues by conducting comparative studies of different treatments and by investigating the specific factors responsible for client improvement. The overall picture, at least regarding psychological treatments, suggests that no particular therapeutic approach is significantly more effective than any other, nor is any technique in itself effective (Wampold, 2001, 2005). Rather, it appears that client improvement can be best accounted for by so-called common factors – aspects of treatments that are shared across different approaches (Elkins, 2007; Laska & Wampold, 2014; Wampold, 2001). For example, Laska and Wampold (2014) note that 'One of the aspects of all treatments is that the patients are provided an explanation for their disorder and that there are treatment actions consistent with that explanation' (p. 520).

Interestingly, the existence of these data seems to have had little impact on advocates of ESTs. In their response to critics of their article advocating for common factors as an evidence-based approach (Laska, Gurman, & Wampold, 2014), Laska and Wampold (2014) state,

> … we were unclear about what evidence would be sufficient to cast doubt on the specificity of ESTs … . it appears that an equivalence of outcomes of theoretically diverse treatments is not sufficient, nor is the fact that treatments devoid of theoretically hypothesized ingredients are effective, or that removing the ingredients fails to attenuate the benefits of the treatments. We ask: What evidence would be sufficient for advocates of particular therapeutic ingredients to abandon their belief that these

particular ingredients are remedial and consider an alternative explanation for how psychotherapy works? (p. 521)

Conversely, we may ask how much and what kind of evidence qualifies a
treatment as an EST?

Finally, there is the persistent problem of generalizability; that is, the stability of treatment effects across settings, persons, measures, and time. It cannot
be assumed, for example, that results obtained in research settings will be the
same in practice settings. For instance, Weisz, Ng, and Bearman (2014) use
the term 'the implementation cliff' to refer to the 'fall off' in the magnitude
of effects of treatments between research and practice settings. Typically, the
latter will have less control of extraneous factors such as outside influences
and a more heterogeneous mix of practitioners, clients, and settings. There
will also be less concern about the uniformity of treatment implementation.

Added to these differences is the challenge of interpreting the results of
research, typically reported as mean scores on specific measures. Assuming
a normal distribution of outcome scores (a bell-shaped - curve), this means
that about 68 percent of the participants will fall within one standard devia-
tion (plus or minus) from the mean. It also means that about 32 percent will
fall outside of these parameters; that is, their scores on the outcome measures
may differ substantially (better or worse) than the average score of the group.
For practitioners the challenge is determining how likely is it that their *particular* clients will benefit from a treatment, for example how similar are they to
research participants whose scores were on the positive side of the mean? They
must also assess whether other differences might make a difference in their
confidence about the research. Examples include differences in their training
and practice orientation from those in the research studies and differences in
when and where the practice was and will be carried out.

In most cases, accepting research results involves a leap of faith that a
study's findings or a summary of studies will be representative of practice
settings and clientele. This position is somewhat ironic given the EBP
emphasis on data-based treatment. Despite awareness of these issues for
decades and the hope that research would progress to the point where a
practitioner could confidently make such an assessment, that is, which
treatment is best for which problem for which practitioner in which context
at which time, it seems questionable whether this will ever happen.

The Ethical Argument

A common argument for the use of EBP or ESTs, noted previously, is that
practitioners have an ethical obligation to rely on the best available evidence
for particular problems. A primary rationale for this position is the claim

that such practices will lead to better outcomes than practices that are not empirically based (Goodman, 2003), a position that I have previously questioned. Another widely held position (beyond EBP) is that clients should be informed participants in practice (e.g., Gambrill, 2014). Therefore, professionals have an obligation to be knowledgeable about the most efficacious practices (according to EBP criteria).

I will briefly address these latter two issues: the responsibility of practitioners to be knowledgeable about ESTs and their obligation to inform their clients about the most effective treatments for their problems. In the first case, it is a normative expectation that professionals will be knowledgeable in their areas of purported expertise. However, in the EBP or EST case, being knowledgeable is complicated by the following assumptions: (1) the assumed superiority of research-based knowledge over practice experience, (2) adherence to restrictive kinds of knowledge (discussed previously), (3) having the necessary resources and expertise to assess the quality and magnitude of the available evidence, and (4) the ability to judge the relevance of the available evidence for a particular client. I have already addressed the first three assumptions (the first will also be discussed in more detail later in the chapter). Regarding assumption 4 (and to some degree 3), most social work practitioners have neither the time nor the expertise to review and methodologically assess individual research studies or meta-analyses. Indirect acknowledgement of this situation is found in the development of various organizations whose business is to provide summaries and generic analyses of the extant research on various practices, in some cases providing a list of those practices considered evidence based. For example, on the website of the Campbell Collaboration, one of the best known of these organizations, it states, 'The purpose of a systematic review is to sum up the best available research on a specific question. This is done by synthesizing the results of several studies' (www.campbellcollaboration.org/what_is_a_ systematic_review/index.php).

Often these summaries are written so as to be accessible to those without research expertise. Wyer and Silva (2009) comment that the EBM movement has led to the development of new sources of information (e.g., databases) 'all aimed, in different ways, at making information from clinical research available to clinicians and to health policy makers in appropriately synthesized, pre-digested and conveniently accessible form' (p. 892).[6] For example, the Social Work Policy Institute lists 37 websites that provide information on EBPs (www.socialworkpolicy.org/research/evidence-based- practice-2.html).

Although these reviews are often accepted at face value by organizations and practitioners, they too need to be subject to critical analysis. For example, Gorman and Huber (2009) reanalyzed data from their study of a drug prevention education program (DARE). Using 'basic data dredging techniques' they we able to change the conclusions to now be evidence based. They note the considerable latitude of researchers to conduct several and different types of analyses and to selectively report results, arguably not an uncommon practice within a confirmation-oriented research culture. They suggest that not only social problems but 'social solutions ... are also socially constructed, with program evaluators and the developers of evidence-based lists performing the role of claims makers' (p. 410).

The irony here is that to accept the summary analyses and conclusions of others is to take a knowledge-by-authority approach, one of the problematic kinds of knowledge sources that has been used to justify the need for EBP (Gambrill, 2006). As Goldenberg (2009) comments in relation to evidence-based medicine, 'authoritarianism seems to be restored by the creation of 'expert' EBM sources that proliferate clinical guidelines, meta-analyses, educational products, electronic decision support systems, and all things worthy of the brand name 'evidence-based medicine' to a captive and paying audience of clinicians who desire to be 'evidence-based practitioners' (p. 180).[7]

It should be noted that these summary reviews tend to be limited to randomized controlled trials or quasi-experimental designs, thereby adhering to the hierarchy of evidence in which randomized controlled trials (RCTs) are at the top and practice wisdom is near the bottom. Also, given their somewhat narrow focus on evidence, other relevant issues that may be of particular interest to social workers such as the meaning and social implications of particular categorizations or diagnoses, or the ethical issues associated with certain treatments, tend to be overlooked or ignored.

Respect

Treating clients with respect is a non-controversial ethical mandate. Its meaning, while variable, generally includes informing clients about how their problems were assessed and their treatments determined so that they can be informed participants in their own treatment. These values have been used by EBP proponents as ethical justifications for clients' right to be provided with evidentiary information about treatment decisions. For example, Gambrill (2015) writes that 'Treating clients with respect includes accurately informing them of the evidentiary status of recommended assessment and intervention methods and means of evaluating outcome. This applies both to voluntary and to involuntary clients' (p. 6). Such disclosure also is viewed as fulfilling the venerable ethical principle of informed consent. As Barber (2008) expresses it, 'evidence-based practice is ultimately about informed consent. It is about the client's right to know what is recommended and why, and it is also about treating the client as a collaborator rather than a recipient' (p. 444).

These statements express laudable aims; however, once again, their expression within the context of EBP tends to generate a truncated version of these ethical principles that omits or oversimplifies crucial information. Most central is the ethical mandate of informed consent as other mandates such as collaboration depend on it. For the EBP-oriented practitioner, the emphasis, not surprisingly, is on evidence. Although relevant, evidence per se is only part of the picture. It is also important to consider the form and manner in which such information is presented. For example: How authoritative is the presentation? How much further editing of the evidence – which itself is likely to be known only in summary form – is deemed to be needed in order for clients to comprehend the information presented? Responses to such questions will affect the extent to which the spirit of the identified ethical principles are carried out.

Informed consent is necessary for clients to be meaningful collaborators in their own treatment or service plan and for them to be aware of potential risks. This requires transparency from practitioners *and* the sharing of information. For instance, in most cases transparency would require practitioners to inform their clients that the evidentiary data for their decisions is based on their paraphrasing of a third-party summary. They might also add how factors such as funding issues, agency policies, and caseloads have influenced their assessments and treatment options. Other relevant topics of disclosure might include their ability to evaluate the relevant research (e.g., the soundness of the methodology and analyses, not generally noted as a strength of social work practitioners), their confidence that a particular treatment will 'work as advertised' for a particular client (e.g., their similarity to researched populations), their beliefs and practice experience, and their knowledge of alternative viewpoints that do not accept EBP doctrines.

Although the complexity of this issue can seem overwhelming, that does not justify providing information as if it were comprehensive or authoritative. At the least, practitioners should be candid about how they are editing and truncating the information being presented.

Evidence

In the EBP model, the status of evidence is related to how it is generated. For example, information generated from randomized controlled trials is considered to be more evidentiary than information from various forms of qualitative inquiry. This so-called hierarchy of evidence (e.g., McNeece & Thyer, 2004; Reid, Kenaley, & Colvin, 2004) is not independent of the conceptual bases of EBP but reflects its epistemological and ontological foundations. Thus, acceptance of this hierarchy concedes, a priori, central underlying assumptions of EBP, for example, about reality, causality, and measurement. Similarly, the foci of EBP evaluation such as operational definitions of individual problems are constituted, in large part, by the methodologies associated with its philosophical positions, for example the measurement of a problem by recognized means. Thus, the same 'theory' constitutes the problem and how it is evaluated. An example would be when depression is conceptualized in terms such as irrational thoughts that conform to its operationalization in a recognized psychological measure such as the Beck Depression Inventory. Depression as a construct (e.g., the social processes that render it sensible, the forces that maintain it) is essentially outside of this exercise. Its reality is taken for granted.

EBP focuses on the achievement of identified outcomes, as demonstrated by empirical indicators, due to particular treatments. While this has value within the model, it does not address alternative conceptualizations or issues such as the appropriateness of the outcomes and how they were determined. Thus, a potential limitation of EBP is that the range of questions, perspectives, and outcomes considered will be truncated or modified in order to accommodate the requirements (e.g., measurement, experimental manipulation) of evidence (Griffiths, 2005). Webb (2001) expresses the concern that 'evidence-based practice entraps professional practice within an instrumental framework which regiments, systematizes and manages social work within a technocratic framework of routinized operations [like three pills a day]' (p. 71). In effect, persons are reduced to their diagnoses to which evidence-based therapeutic interventions are targeted.

What is the fate of other practice approaches from the perspective of EBP? For example, Goldstein (2000) sees practice as engaging clients' moral narratives, the 'morass of goods and bads, rights and wrongs, evils and virtues, bearing little resemblance to the diagnostic labels or the balance sheet of assets or liabilities that the client inevitably earns' (p. 349; also see Goldstein, 1987). Can this view of practice coexist with EBP? The answer will depend, in part, on the political context in which evidence is constructed and used.

The Political Context of Evidence

Despite its myth of neutrality, research is never value free. The questions posed, the topics researched, even the methodologies employed express values about what is important to know, the kinds of information needed, and how to best obtain it. When these values are combined with research's authoritative status, its impact on the understanding and organization of social life and the allocation of resources can be considerable. Not surprisingly, the conduct and control of research and its findings are part of the machinations of political life.

As an expression of research, EBP also can be construed as a political activity (Ladson-Billings, 2003; Witkin & Harrison, 2001). One way this gets expressed is in what is considered evidence and how it is understood and used. As Denzin (2009) expresses it,

> the politics and political economy of evidence is not a question of evidence or no evidence. It is rather a question of who has the power to control the definition of evidence, who defines the kinds of materials that count as evidence, who determines what methods best produce the best forms of evidence, whose criteria and standards are used to evaluate quality evidence? (p. 142)

Methodology matters. The kind of information that is considered evidence and how much it is valued influences what we believe.

One response to this issue has been to advocate for broadening the meaning of evidence to include many types of information from various sources; however, research-based information remains the standard (Anastas, 2014) and research evidence as a necessary justification for programs or treatments remains sacrosanct. This position minimizes other criteria such as authenticity, inclusion, or conscientization that might be used to assess program or treatment viability and value. Justification is often expressed as accountability. However, here again there can be other ways of addressing this issue than by research-based evidence.

One possibility is decoupling accountability from effectiveness and considering alternatives such as

> the extent to which one's practice challenges existing forms of oppression within the social order, treats clients with dignity and respect (for example, by validating their life experiences, honoring their language, and working with them as collaborators), uses a strengths rather than a pathology perspective (Saleebey, 1992), engages in emancipating practices (for example, by helping clients see themselves within a broader historical and social context, helping them identify options to change that context, and facilitating action toward those changes), and is grounded in fundamental human rights. (Witkin, 1996: 73–74)

Another political concern, particularly for social workers, is how EBP has been taken up and used to shape organizational and governmental policies. The adoption of an evidence-based approach by the state of North Carolina (Arnd-Caddigan & Pozzuto, 2010) is an example of how EBP gets expressed in the political arena. By mandating 'a list of approved manualized treatment approaches aimed at behavioral symptoms and diagnoses' (Arnd-Caddigan & Pozzuto, 2011: 123), or risk losing federal funding, the state is using a narrow interpretation of EBP to justify policy and limit the range of problems treated, how such problems are identified, and the types of treatments permissible.

Lastly, is the issue of how policies and resource allocation may be used to support stereotypical views of marginalized groups or maintain an ideological context that supports dominant groups while disadvantaging others. For example, in an analysis of the political effects of qualitative research in the area of health care, Mykhalovskiy et al. (2008) note 'the way new evidence-based ways of knowing health care were aligning with managerial discourses of efficiency, helping to coordinate neo-liberal health restructuring' (p. 198). More broadly, within social work, Parton (2007) has expressed concern about how EBP has been used to reinforce 'the political instrumentalism and aspirations for greater central control which are being implemented by the modernization agenda' (p. 155; also see Webb, 2001). Similarly, Carey and Foster (2013) write of 'an altruistic ideological veneer' 'that draw[s] significantly from a scientific knowledge-base ... to articulately mask or dismiss the structural causes of disadvantage, exclusion and poverty' (p. 261).

In other words, the influence of EBP is not confined to practitioners, but extends to policies and ideologies that shape understandings of marginalized groups, the challenges they face, the organization of human services, and the kinds of programs and treatment approaches used. However well-intentioned the proponents of EBP may be, the socio-political-economic context of its utilization largely accounts for what it 'is'.

In an important sense, a foundational belief underlying EBP is that increased knowledge through research will improve social conditions and enhance people's well-being. But as I have just argued, knowledge per se is not necessarily beneficial. However, because the very notion of knowledge carries the presumption of truth and therefore authority, it can be a powerful means of justifying policies and actions. In the next section, I explore the topic of knowledge and how different understandings about its meaning and generation relate to EBP.

Information and Knowledge

Evidence in the EBP/EST context is considered a form of knowledge, that is, it is research-based and has truth value (Tarlier, 2005). Evidence can also be viewed as a function of knowledge. Knowledge functions as evidence when it is used to justify a claim, in this case, that a particular program or treatment is effective in addressing a specific problem. Thus, knowledge production underlies the EBP/EST movement.

In this final section, I problematize the notion of knowledge: first, by distinguishing it from information and second, by considering how information is transformed into knowledge. Although this transformational process may occur in many settings and in many ways, they are not equally recognized or valued. Specifically, research is privileged. As an affirmative alternative, I propose an expanded understanding of knowledge production that includes practice.

The importance of this topic stems from Michel Foucault's writings about power/knowledge: 'power and knowledge directly imply one another; that there is no power without the correlative constitution of a field of knowledge, nor any knowledge that does not presuppose and constitute at the same time power relations' (Foucault, 1977: 27). Much of what is taken as knowledge is assumed to be 'the way things are' or 'what is' and therefore has considerable influence over our interpretations and interactions. These beliefs (implicit or explicit) form the backdrop for further knowledge generation, for example the belief that mental illness exists (is real) functions as a knowledge context for producing further knowledge about this 'self-evident truth'.

Knowledge in the EBP Context

In general, research is regarded as the primary site and most powerful means of knowledge production. In contrast, practice is viewed as the primary site and means of knowledge utilization. This distinction provides the basis for the oft-used metaphor of a 'gap' between research and practice, which, in turn, invites efforts to bridge this gap (Witkin, 2011). Bridging efforts tend to be expressed in three ways: (1) how to make research knowledge usable in practice (or in contemporary jargon, how to 'translate' that knowledge); (2) how to provide incentives to practitioners to use this knowledge (e.g., Gray & Schubert, 2012); and (3) how to get practitioners to modify their practice to resemble research (as in the use of single-case designs). To date, the results of these efforts have been less successful than simply mandating practitioners to be 'evidence based', a position that, as noted previously, has its own problems.

Knowledge is considered as justified, true belief (e.g., Dawson, 1981; Gill, 1985). People who hold such beliefs about a particular topic are said to be knowledgeable. Knowledge may also be viewed as an entity that exists apart from persons as in a body of knowledge or knowledge base.

Consistent with this position, the general line of reasoning underlying EBP is that:

1. Research produces knowledge using standard processes (i.e., research protocols) and benchmarks (e.g., p<.05).

2. Knowledge is truth-bearing and justified by the conditions of its production.
3. Once produced, knowledge is reified – treated as an entity that has a
reality beyond the context of its production.
4. Therefore, practitioners should be knowledgeable about research-generated knowledge pertaining to their practice and to use that knowledge in
their work. That is, they should know what and they should know how.
5. Knowledgeable practitioners have an ethical obligation to inform clients
about those programs and practices for which they have knowledge.

In the EBP context, justified, true beliefs are research-based. Applying the
methods and methodology of research is how information becomes knowledge.[8] This tends to restrict knowledge to those beliefs that are research-
able. In other words, beliefs and the criteria for their justification are not
independent. A belief that cannot be researched is, a priori, not a candidate
for knowledge. Rather, it will be identified by other names such as opinion
or value.

These ways of understanding knowledge (knowledge about knowledge)
lead to the kinds of issues that characterize the EBP literature (e.g., the
practice–research gap, arguments about what kinds of research should
count as producing knowledge, the hierarchy of evidence) and the rationale
for advocating for the use of ESTs.

In contrast, I propose not confining knowledge production to research
or assuming it exists as a kind of independent, free-floating entity but recognizing that knowledge also is produced in practice through dynamic processes of social interaction. Such knowledge is contextually dependent. This
alternative understanding changes the focus from *solving* the 'gap problems'
identified above to *dissolving* them, in this case by showing that practice
offers a viable, more useful context for knowledge generation.[9]

Distinguishing Information and Knowledge[10]

The word 'knowledge' is widely and somewhat indiscriminately used in
the social work literature. As noted, in general usage knowledge refers to
information that is considered justifiably true (although these terms are
often conflated). In contrast, information does not require justification and
may be true or false. Also, information tends to be given – the recipient of
the information is relatively passive. In contrast, knowledge requires an
active knower who processes the information (i.e., interprets it relative to
the context, its potential use, and the knower's existing beliefs and commit-
ments). From this perspective, we receive information that has the potential
to *become* knowledge.

Knowledge also implies understanding. For example, consider the difference between having information about tomorrow's weather (e.g., 'There is a 50 percent chance it will rain') and understanding this information (i.e., the bases for this prediction). In the latter case, we would say that the person is knowledgeable about weather prediction. Or consider the difference between knowing that a car needs an engine to run and understanding the workings of a car engine. Again, the latter information, if true, would be called knowledge.

Knowledge is contextual in at least two senses. In one sense, context refers to the social warrant for knowledge, that is, the norms and traditions of the relevant knowledge community: networks of individuals, often associated with a particular field, who more or less collectively accept, explicitly or implicitly, certain epistemic assumptions, norms, standards, processes, and goals by which to justify, produce, and legitimate knowledge. Knowledge communities can be found within science, education, academic disciplines, and religion. For example, in the case of research knowledge those norms and traditions concern 'the scientific method'. Thus, knowledge is social and relational. It is produced through relationships that give it meaning and authorize its status. No information is inherently knowledge without legitimation within some community. Oeberst, Kimmerle, and Cress (2016) write that 'in the case of knowledge, acceptance of the truth of a belief and its justification always count only within the context of the knowledge-related system from which it originates' (p. 116). As an expression of a particular knowledge community, what is called knowledge in one community may be interpreted differently (e.g., as information) in other communities.[11]

Context also refers to conditions of use, for instance the constraints on knowledge-generating processes and aims to which potential knowledge will be used. In the practice context knowledge cannot be generated by randomly assigning clients to different study conditions. Additionally, the nature of the presenting problem might dictate the processes and kinds of knowledge most favored.

A related issue is the relation of knowledge production to knowing. Does being able to recite research results qualify as having knowledge? This is where understanding comes into play. For example, from my perspective, although I might be able to recount the findings of different studies about adolescent alcohol use, if I did not know how these findings were derived (beyond simply stating 'research'), or their relevance to adolescents outside of the research setting (e.g., the community in which practice is being carried out), I could hardly be said to be knowledgeable. Rather, it would be more appropriate to say that I had information about adolescent alcohol use. In contrast, within the EBP/EST context, such information is treated as knowledge that is potentially available to practitioners. In other words, it is the process that produces knowledge and this knowledge, once produced (usually in textual form), exists independently of knowers.

Another issue with the research view of knowledge in the context of EBP is that it tends to conflate what the philosopher Gilbert Ryle called knowing that and knowing how (Ryle, 1949). Roughly, this can be thought of as analogous to theoretical knowledge (knowing about something) compared to practical knowledge (knowing how to do something). Conventional research focuses on discovering the characteristics or patterns of the extant world – knowing that. It does not focus on how to utilize that presumed knowledge in a particular situation. To continue with the previous example, learning about the correlates of adolescent alcohol abuse does not provide knowledge about how to apply this knowledge in a program or treatment in a context-sensitive manner.

There are areas where research and practice use both knowing that and knowing how; however, each context will emphasize and value them differently (Tenkasi & Hay, 2004). For example, researchers will need to know about the current literature in their field of study, research methodology, and protocols. They will know how to do things like analyze data and design a study. Social work practitioners will know about local issues relevant to their work, organizational policies, and what approaches have been useful in the past. They will know how to do things like complete an assessment, empathize with a client, and explain regulations. These different 'knowledges' help each to accomplish the tasks required by their contexts.

Even research about practice, while more closely aligned with application, does not provide knowing how. Rather it attempts to show that a particular way of doing something is likely (other things being equal) to bring about certain outcomes conceived in a particular way. When working in practice settings, however, the more standardized the instructions (as in treatment manuals), the more likely they are to underrepresent the complexities and dynamics of practice. Again, this is information that has yet to be transformed into knowledge.[12]

Knowing how seems to be based more on experience (e.g., trial and error, apprenticeship) than on cognitive comprehension. That is, the process of knowing how involves the additional element of doing. Research can judge the success of that doing in certain contexts but it cannot 'do' the doing. Although practitioners may accept the view that research produces knowledge, this does not negate that knowledge also is produced within practice settings in ways that enable it to be contextually responsive and useful.

Practitioner-generated Knowledge

As noted, the putative meanings of research and practice denote the former as a knowledge-generating activity and the latter as a knowledge-applying activity. These differences are arbitrary. Practitioners also generate knowledge; however, from a research perspective it tends to be viewed as unsystematic, impressionistic, and idiographic – closer to information and skills. In contrast, research is believed to produce generalizable knowledge that is stable and broadly applicable. Consequently, research-generated knowledge is thought of as more valuable to practice than practice-generated knowledge. However, from the perspective of knowledge described above, practice is considered the primary site for knowledge generation.

There are advantages to this shift. First, practitioners generate actionable knowledge (Argyris, 1996) that is usable toward change efforts. That use requires active interpretation and judgment about its relevance in the context and the ends for which it is employed. Second, practitioners can develop kinds of knowledge that are outside the scope of most research yet critical for successful practice. An example is tacit knowledge, which Webb (2002) describes as 'personal, context specific, and therefore hard to formalize and communicate as it essentially represents "know how" ...' (p. 4). (Also, see Berg, 2008; Imre, 1985; Martinez-Brawley & Zorita, 2007, for a discussion of the importance of tacit knowledge in social work.) Third, instead of being dependent on research methodologies and methods, knowledge is produced through practices that constitute practice itself. As Austin (2013) notes, the act of execution not only makes ideas actionable, but transforms them. Context and execution are inseparable from the knowledge-creation process.

Researchers tend to assemble information into units of measurement, practitioners tend to organize information into narratives. Donald Polkinghorne (1988) describes practitioners as 'concerned with people's stories: they work with case histories and use narrative explanations to understand why the people they work with behave the way they do' (p. x). Knowledge generation in this context is related to ideas such as story lines, coherence, and outcomes. By transforming information into knowledge in the same context in which it will be used, the problem of translating knowledge is dissolved.

Transcending the Research–Practice Binary

The assumption of a research–practice binary supports many of the issues involved in the EBP debates (e.g., how to bridge the assumed gap). However, it is possible to engage in inquiry without assuming this binary. For example, participatory action research (PAR) (e.g., Reason & Bradbury, 2007) generates actionable knowledge by focusing on solving practical problems in collaboration with stakeholders (e.g., practitioners and clients). The democratization of research roles in all phases of the inquiry process and the focus on addressing problems identified by those most affected by them obfuscates the research–practice binary. In many ways PAR epitomizes the right to knowledge that some EBP advocates see as integral. Also, its broad acceptance of various forms of knowledge and a flexible methodology 'that privileges the voices and lives of participants' make such participation accessible and meaningful (Billies, Francisco, Krueger, & Linville, 2010: 279).

A related approach is to redefine research *and* practice so they are expressions of each other. For example, McNamee and Hosking (2012) argue that what practitioners do *is* research and what researchers do is practice. They base their position on the idea that both research and practice are relational activities that intervene into the lives of participants/clients as well as researchers and practitioners.

Contesting the research–practice binary (and to some extent the researcher–researched binary) also expands the range of potential knowledge-generating approaches to more liminal forms of inquiry such as autoethnography (e.g., Witkin, 2014), performative approaches (Denzin, 2003), and narrative. In these approaches the aim is not the discovery of Truth, but openness to multiple ways of understanding, increasing sensitivities, expanding consciousness, or empowering others.

The decoupling of research from a conventional view of science enables greater acknowledgement of practitioners' knowledge-generating activities. From my perspective, practitioners generate potential knowledge when they interrogate, contextualize, reflect on, and critically interpret information leading to understandings that are relevant and sensitive to the values, aims, and exigencies of practice. Exemplary in this regard are critically reflective practitioners (Fook, 2004, 2012; Karvinen-Niinikoski, 2009; Rusch, 2009). Using interrogation, contextualization, and critical analysis. critically reflective practitioners locate information in multiple historical, social, and cultural contexts. They also consider how their own social location within, for example, gender, ethnicity, and social class, has shaped their exposure to and acceptance of certain kinds of knowledge. Importantly, they extend this consideration to structural realities and how power operates through knowledge to maintain these structures and suppress or marginalize others. Finally, critically reflective practitioners recognize that knowledge production is not confined to codified methods in highly structured situations, but can be created through multiple means in their emergent interactions with people. Thus, they are cognizant that knowledge is being created in these interactions and strive to become aware of these processes, for example, how implicit theories are operating (see Fook, 2012, for a more detailed discussion of these topics).

Approaches like critically reflective practice are important sources of knowledge production. Recognizing them as such requires that we eliminate the research–practice binary as separate sites of production and application and broaden the range of processes and types of knowledge acceptable to different knowledge communities.

Additional Thoughts Addressing the EBP Framework

In addition to becoming aware of and advocating for alternative forms of inquiry and expanding knowledge production from the research to practice setting, there are two other things practitioners can do to alter the discourse that maintains the dominance of EBP. These are briefly discussed below.

Enter the Dominant Discourse (in this Case on Research and EBP) from a Critical Perspective

For some, this may require learning more about research – not to become a true believer, but to become a critical consumer and interpreter. Generate dialogue by raising questions (such as those raised in this chapter) that dislodge the authority of EBP. Broaden discussions about evidence by bringing in the perspective of social work values and ethics and maintaining a contextual orientation, for example, identifying structural issues and political contexts. Research is never neutral and ethics are not separable from research or practice.

Decouple Accountability from Effectiveness

Accountability has been appropriated by EBP to mean quantified outcomes of research that show the effectiveness of a treatment or program. Accountability from this perspective is a way of legitimizing and maintaining the authority of research-generated knowledge. But there is no reason why this view should not be challenged or alternatives considered. For example, back in 1996 I suggested considering alternative meanings of accountable practice such as

the extent to which one's practice challenges existing forms of oppression within the social order, treats clients with dignity and respect (for example, by validating their life experiences, honoring their language, and working with them as collaborators), uses a strengths rather than a pathology perspective, engages in emancipating practices (for example, by helping clients see themselves within a broader historical and social context, helping them identify options to change that context, and facilitating action toward those changes), and is grounded in fundamental human rights. (Witkin, 1996: 73–74)

As social workers it is important that such meanings remain visible in our dialogue.

Should We Retain EBP?

The short answer is yes, but take it down a notch or two. However critical this chapter might seem, I am not advocating that we get rid of EBP but that we keep it from being the ultimate or automatic justification for what we do or a justification for eliminating alternative approaches. As social workers, we need to use our unique location between those in authority and those on the margins to ask tough questions, propose alternative and generative (potentially transformative) forms of understanding, and to promote the values that undergird our profession. This chapter on EBP is one small illustration of this position.

Concluding Thoughts

The aims of this chapter were to critically explore the research–practice relationship particularly as represented in the EBP movement and to propose a new understanding of knowledge as the transformation of information in a way that legitimates practice as an equal site of knowledge production. Practitioners have always learned from their practice. However, at some point this learning became devalued in favor of research-generated information. A primary theme of this chapter has been to recognize the advantages of knowledge production in the same context in which it is to be used and to acknowledge and further enhance the ways in which practitioners learn from their experiences. Approaches like critically reflective practice enable practitioners to generate knowledge and make it actionable. Shifting the site of knowledge generation to practice and conceiving of knowledge as requiring the transformation of information in accord with various community standards, dissolves the perennial issues of EBP and opens new avenues for learning from and with practitioners about how they generate and derive knowledge from their practice. Finally, it is important to note that my position is not intended to eliminate research about practice, but to redefine and enlarge the field in which such activities take place.

This was a difficult chapter to write. The issues are multifaceted and complex. I hope that I was able to communicate ideas in an accessible way that helped illuminate some of the challenges practitioners are facing in today's evidence-based environment and to provide an alternative vision that affirms the centrality of practice and provides a way forward and its potential as a site of knowledge generation.

Notes

1   This chapter further extends some ideas that I have explored in earlier publications (Witkin, 2011, 2015; Witkin & Harrison, 2001; Witkin & Iversen, 2012).

2   Flexner listed six criteria for a profession: 'intellectual operations with large individual responsibility; they derive their raw material from science and learning; this material they work up to a practical and definite end; they possess an educationally communicable technique; they tend to self-organization; they are becoming increasingly altruistic in motivation' (p. 156).

3   Although there is no consensus on whether ECP and EBP represent different movements, Okpych and Yu (2014), based on their historical analysis of these two movements, view 'EBP as the second attempt to take hold of the field as an empirically grounded practice paradigm …' (p. 38).

4   Although Gordon Guyett, part of the McMaster group, was the first to popularize the evidence-based medicine, the roots of this approach can be traced to earlier times (see, for example, Smith & Rennie, 2014).

5   There are other difficulties with this position. For example, how are original sources determined? Is it those that first used the term or others who laid the foundation for this term? How far back do we go and how long do we continue to rely on them? Also, even if we could identify the originators, there is no guarantee that they would agree on the meanings of EBM/EBP (assuming, of course, that they were still alive to respond to such queries). Using original sources as a source of insight or enrichment is useful but different than a litmus test of whether something is or is not EBP.

6   For example, the California Evidence-Based Clearinghouse for Child Welfare (www.cebc4cw.org/ratings/scientific-rating-scale/) ranks various topics using a rating scale based in large part on the results of randomized control trials.

These include:

1. Well-Supported by Research Evidence

2. Supported by Research Evidence

3. Promising Research Evidence

4. Evidence Fails to Demonstrate Effect

5. Concerning Practice

6. NR. Not able to be Rated

It seems to me that the very existence of these ratings suggests the inability of practitioners to access and evaluate the research literature. It also raises questions about the extent to which the more extensive information available on their website about their rationale and processes is utilized or critically evaluated.

7 I want to be clear that my comments are not meant to be disparaging of these organizations or the potential value of their reviews. My point is that their very existence supports the notion that even self-identified evidence-based practitioners are unlikely to review original research, but rely on outside reviews to inform them of what treatments or approaches are evidence-supported.

8 In this view, knowledge is true in the sense of representing reality. The issue of truth is important but complex especially for a social constructionist who subscribes to the idea of multiple truths. For reasons of space, relevance, and complexity, I will focus on the justification part of this perspective.

9 Knowledge is a complex and contested concept in fields like philosophy and psychology. Although I will make some reference to some of the issues discussed, I will not attempt to tackle them in any comprehensive way. Interested readers who wish to delve further into these issues should follow up on some of the references provided.

10 See Witkin (2015) for an earlier view of this topic.

11 Getting us to treat this information as knowledge, a priori, is a political achievement.

12 Interestingly, within the EBP model, 'knowledge how' relies on rigidly holding to certain operational definitions of practices, problems, and outcomes, that is, by constructing a social reality that approximates a material one.

References

Anastas, J. W. (2014). When is research good evidence? Issues in reading research. *Clinical Social Work Journal, 42*(2), 107–115.

Argyris, C. (1996). Actionable knowledge: Design causality in the service of consequential theory. *Journal of Applied Behavioral Science, 32*(4), 390–406.

Arnd-Caddigan, M., & Pozzuto, R. (2010). Evidence-based practice and the purpose of clinical social work. *Smith College Studies in Social Work, 80*(1), 35–52.

Arnd-Caddigan, M., & Pozzuto, R. (2011). The politics of 'twoness': Policy, clinical judgment, relationship, and evidence-based practice. *Social Work in Mental Health, 9*(2), 122–136.

Austin, D. M. (1983). The Flexner myth and the history of social work. *The Social Service Review,* 357–377.

Austin, J. R. (2013). Making knowledge actionable: Three key translation moments. *Journal of Organization Design, 2*(3), 29–37.

Barber, J. G. (2008). Putting evidence-based practice into practice. In B. W. White (Ed.), *Comprehensive handbook of social work and social welfare, the profession of social work* (Vol 1, pp. 441–450). Hoboken, NJ: John Wiley and Sons.

Bauman, Z. (1993). Postmodernity, or living with ambivalence. J. P. Natoli (Ed.), *A postmodern reader* (pp. 9–24). New York, NY: SUNY Press.

Berg, E. M. (2008). Clinical practice: Between explicit and tacit knowledge, between dialogue and technique. *Philosophy, Psychiatry, and Psychology, 15*(2), 151–157.

Billies, M., Francisco, V., Krueger, P., & Linville, D. (2010). Participatory action research: Our methodological roots. *International Review of Qualitative Research, 3*(3), 277–286.

Carey, M., & Foster, V. (2013). Social work, ideology, discourse and the limits of post-hegemony. *Journal of Social Work, 13,* 248–266.

Dawson, G. (1981). Justified true belief is knowledge. *The Philosophical Quarterly, 31*(125), 315–329.

Denzin, N. K. (2003). *Performance ethnography: Critical pedagogy and the politics of culture.* Thousand Oaks, CA: Sage.

Denzin, N. K. (2009). The elephant in the living room: Or extending the conversation about the politics of evidence. *Qualitative Research, 9*(2), 139–160.

Elkins, D. N. (2007). Empirically supported treatments: The deconstruction of a myth. *Journal of Humanistic Psychology, 47*(4), 474–500.

Evidence-Based Medicine Working Group. (1992). Evidence-based medicine: A new approach to teaching the practice of medicine. *Journal of the American Medical Association, 268,* 2420–2425.

Fischer, J. (1973). Is casework effective? A review. *Social Work, 18*(1), 5–20.

Flexner, A. (2001/1915). Is social work a profession? *Research on Social Work Practice, 11*(2), 152–165.

Fook, J. (2004). Critical reflection and transformative possibilities. In L. Davies & P. Leonard (Eds.), *Social work in a corporate era: Practices of power and resistance* (pp. 16–30). Farnham: Ashgate.

Fook, J. (2012). *Social work: A critical approach to practice.* London: Sage.

Foucault, M. (1977). *Discipline and punish: The birth of the prison.* New York, NY: Random House.

Gambrill, E. (2006). Evidence-based practice and policy: Choices ahead. *Research on Social Work Practice, 16*(3), 338–357.

Gambrill, E. (2011). Evidence-based practice and the ethics of discretion. *Journal of Social Work, 11*(1), 26–48.

Gambrill, E. (2015). Integrating research and practice: Distractions, controversies, and options for moving forward. *Research on Social Work Practice, 25*(4), 1–13.

Gibbs, A. (2001). The changing nature and context of social work research. *British Journal of Social Work, 31,* 687–704.

Gill, J. H. (1985). Justified true belief, period. *International Philosophical Quarterly, 25*(4), 381–391.

Goldenberg, M. J. (2009). Iconoclast or creed? Objectivism, pragmatism, and the hierarchy of evidence. *Perspectives in Biology and Medicine, 52*(2), 168–187.

Goldstein, H. (1987). The neglected moral link in social work practice. *Social Work, 32*(3), 181–186.

Goldstein, H. (2000). Joe the king: A study of strengths and morality. *Families in Society, 81*(4), 347.

Gorman, D. M., & Huber, Jr, J. C. (2009). The social construction of 'evidence-based' drug prevention programs: A reanalysis of data from the drug abuse resistance education (DARE) program. *Evaluation Review, 33,* 396–414.

Gray, M., & Schubert, L. (2012). Sustainable social work: Modelling knowledge production, transfer, and evidence-based practice. *International Journal of Social Welfare, 21*(2), 203–214.

Griffiths, P. (2005). Evidence-based practice: A deconstruction and postmodern critique: Book review article. *International Journal of Nursing Studies, 42,* 355–361.

Heineman Pieper, M. (1981). The obsolete scientific imperative in social work research. *Social Service Review, 55,* 371–396.

Hersen, M., & Barlow, D. H. (1976). *Single-case experimental designs: Strategies for studying behavior change.* New York, NY: Pergamon Press.

Imre, R. W. (1985). Tacit knowledge in social work research and practice. *Smith College Studies in Social Work, 55*(2), 137–149.

Ivanoff, A., Blythe, B. J., & Briar, S. (1987). The empirical clinical practice debate. *Social Casework, 68*(5), 290–298.

Karvinen-Niinikoski, S. (2009). Promises and pressures of critical reflection for social work coping in change. *European Journal of Social Work, 12*(3), 333–348.

Kirk, S. A., & Reid, W. J. (2002). *Science and social work: A critical appraisal.* New York, NY: Columbia University Press.

Ladson-Billings, G. (2003). It's your world, I'm just trying to explain it: Understanding our epistemological and methodological challenges. *Qualitative Inquiry, 9*(1), 5–12.

Laska, K. M., & Wampold, B. E. (2014). Ten things to remember about common factor theory. *Psychotherapy, 51*(4), 519–524.

Lubove, R. (1965). *The professional altruist: The emergence of social work as a career, 1880–1930.* Cambridge, MA: Harvard University Press.

Martinez-Brawley, E., & Zorita, P. (2007). Tacit and codified knowledge in social work: A critique of standardization in education and practice. *Families in Society: The Journal of Contemporary Social Services, 88*(4), 534–542.

McNamee, S., & Hosking, D. M. (2012). *Research and social change: A relational constructionist perspective.* New York, NY: Routledge.

McNeece, C. A., & Thyer, B. A. (2004). Evidence-based practice and social work. *Journal of Evidence-Based Social Work, 1*(1), 7–25.

Mishler, E. (1979). Meaning in context: Is there any other kind? *Harvard Educational Review, 49*(1), 1–19.

Myers, L. L., & Thyer, B. A. (1997). Should social work clients have the right to effective treatment? *Social Work, 42*(3), 288–298.

Mykhalovskiy, E., Armstrong, P., Armstrong, H., Bourgeault, I., Choiniere, J., Lexchin, J., … White, J. (2008). Qualitative research and the politics of knowledge in an age of evidence: Developing a research-based practice of immanent critique. *Social Science & Medicine, 67,* 195–203.

Oeberst, A., Kimmerle, J., & Cress, U. (2016). What is knowledge? Who creates it? Who possesses it? The need for novel answers to old questions. In U. Cress, J. Moskaliuk, & H. Jeong (Eds.), *Mass collaboration and education* (pp. 105–124). Switzerland: Springer International Publishing.

Okpych, N. J., & Yu, J. L.-H. (2014). A historical analysis of evidence-based practice in social work: The unfinished journey toward an empirically grounded profession. *Social Service Review, 88*(1), 3–58.

Parton, N. (2007). Constructive social work practice in an age of uncertainty. In S. L. Witkin & D. Saleebey (Eds.), *Social work dialogues: Transforming the canon in practice, inquiry and education* (pp. 144–166). Alexandria, VA: Council on Social Work Education.

Parton, N., & Kirk, S. The nature and purposes of social work. In I. Shaw, K. Briar-Lawson, J. Orme & R. Ruckdeschel (Eds.), *The SAGE handbook of social work research* (pp. 23–36). London: Sage.

Polkinghorne, D. E. (1988). *Narrative knowing and the human sciences*. NewYork, NY: SUNY Press.

Reason, P. & Bradbury, H. (Eds.) (2007). *The SAGE handbook of action research: Participative inquiry and practice*. Thousand Oaks, CA: Sage.

Reid, W. J., Kenaley, B. D., & Colvin, J. (2004). Do some interventions work better than others? A review of comparative social work experiments. *Social Work Research, 28*(2), 71–81.

Ruch, G. (2009). Identifying 'the critical' in a relationship-based model of reflection. *European Journal of Social Work, 12*(3), 349–362.

Ryle, G. (1949). *Knowing how and knowing that. In idem. The concept of mind*. London: Hutchison's Universal Library.

Sackett, D. L., Rosenberg, W. M., Gray, J. A., Haynes, R. B., & Richardson, W. S. (1996). Evidence based medicine: What it is and what it isn't. *British Medical Journal, 312*, 71–72.

Sackett, D. L., Straus, S. E., Richardson, W. S., Rosenberg, W., & Haynes, R. B. (2000). *How to practice and teach EBM*. New York, NY: Churchill Livingstone.

Smith, R., & Rennie, D. (2014). Evidence-based medicine – An oral history. *JAMA, 311*(4), 365–367.

Tarlier, D. (2005). Mediating the meaning of evidence through epistemological diversity. *Nursing Inquiry, 12*(2), 126–134.

Tenkasi, R. V., & Hay, G. W. (2004). Actionable knowledge and scholar-practitioners: A process model of theory-practice linkages. *Systemic Practice and Action Research, 17*(3), 177–206.

Thyer, B. A. (1996). Guidelines for applying the empirical clinical practice model to social work. *Journal of Applied Social Sciences, 20*, 121–128.

Wampold, B. E. (2001). *The great psychotherapy debate: Models, methods, and findings*. Mahwah, NJ: Lawrence Erlbaum.

Wampold, B. E. (2005). Do therapies designated as ESTs for specific disorders produce outcomes superior to non-EST therapies? Not a scintilla of evidence to support ESTs as more effective than other treatments. In J. C. Norcross, L. E. Beutler, & R. F. Levant (Eds.), *Evidence-based practices in mental health: Debate and dialogue on the fundamental questions* (pp. 299–308, 317–319). Washington, DC: American Psychological Association.

Webb, I. (2002). *Knowledge management in the KIBS-Client Environment: A case study approach*. PREST, University of Manchester, UK. Downloaded from http://les.man.ac.uk/PREST/

Webb, S. A. (2001). Some considerations on the validity of evidence-based practice in social work. *British Journal of Social Work, 31*, 57–79.

Weisz, J. R., Ng, M. Y., & Bearman, S. K. (2014). Odd couple? Reenvisioning the relation between science and practice in the dissemination implementation era. *Clinical Psychological Science, 2*, 58–74.

Witkin, S. L. (1991). Empirical clinical practice: A critical analysis. *Social Work, 36*(2), 158–163.

Witkin, S. L. (1996). If empirical practice is the answer, then what is the question? *Social Work Research, 20*(2), 69–75.

Witkin, S. L. (1998). The right to effective treatment and the effective treatment of rights: Rhetorical empiricism and the politics of research. *Social Work, 43*(1), 75–80.

Witkin, S. L. (2011). Why do we think practice research is a good idea? Comments and musings inspired by the Salisbury statement. *Social Work and Society, 9*(1), www.socwork.net/sws/article/view/3/14Why

Witkin, S. L. (Ed.). (2014). *Narrating social work through autoethnography.* New York, NY: Columbia University Press.

Witkin, S. L. (2015). Issues in researching professional practice: Deriving knowledge from professional practice. In V. Collington, J. Fook, F. Ross, G. Ruch (Eds.), *Critical reflection: The research way forward.* New York, NY: Routledge.

Witkin, S. L., & Harrison, W.D. (2001). Whose evidence and for what purpose? *Social Work, 46,* 293–296.

Witkin, S. L., & Iversen, R. R. (2012). Contemporary issues in social work. In C. N. Dulmus, & K. M. Sowers (Eds.), *The profession of social work: Guided by history, led by evidence* (Chapter 10). Hoboken, NJ: John Wiley and Sons.

Wyer, P. C., & Silva, S. A. (2009). Where is the wisdom? A conceptual history of evidence-based medicine. *Journal of Evaluation in Clinical Practice, 15,* 891–898.

Zimerman, A. L. (2013). Evidence-based medicine: A short history of a modern medical movement. *Virtual Mentor: American Medical Association Journal of Ethics, 15*(1), 71–76.

Index